The New Death

The New Death

American Modernism and World War I

PEARL JAMES

University of Virginia Press

CHARLOTTESVILLE AND LONDON

University of Virginia Press

Printed in the United States of America on acid-free paper

First published 2013

9 8 7 6 5 4 3 2 1

LIBRARY OF CONGRESS CATALOGING-IN-PUBLICATION DATA

James, Pearl.
  The new death : American modernism and World War I / Pearl James.
    pages cm
  Includes bibliographical references and index.
  ISBN 978-0-8139-3407-5 (cloth : acid-free paper)
  ISBN 978-0-8139-3408-2 (pbk. : acid-free paper)
  ISBN 978-0-8139-3409-9 (e-book)
  1. Modernism (Literature)—United States. 2. World War, 1914–1918—Literature and
the war. 3. Death in literature. 4. Psychic trauma in literature. 5. American literature—
20th century—History and criticism. I. Title.
PS228.M63J36   2013
810.9′112—dc23

                                         2013001156

A book in the American Literatures Initiative (ALI), a collaborative
publishing project of NYU Press, Fordham University Press, Rutgers
University Press, Temple University Press, and the University of Virginia
Press. The Initiative is supported by The Andrew W. Mellon Foundation.
For more information, please visit www.americanliteratures.org.

THE
AMERICAN
LITERATURES
INITIATIVE

In loving memory of
Ruth Short Easton (1920–2005)
and
Robert Sidney Easton, Sr. (1921–2010)

Contents

Illustrations

Acknowledgments

I have had the support and help of many people and institutions during the process of writing this book and am deeply grateful. The origins of this project lie in conversations from very long ago with Kevis Goodman, Maurice Wallace, and Cliff Wulfman. During that same period, Alan Trachtenberg, Michael Trask, Elizabeth Dillon, and Amy Hungerford were important mentors. Vera Kutzinski's friendship, intelligence, good sense, and calm sustained me. Jay Winter's infectious enthusiasm for the history of World War I spurred me to engage new questions. Though the writing I did in those years does not appear much here, the groundwork I did for the book with help from all these and others remains fundamental to it.

Several libraries and museums have allowed me to use their holdings and to reproduce images here. They include the Hoover Institution at Stanford University, the Historial Museum of the Great War (Péronne, Somme), Yale University Manuscripts and Archives Collection, the University of Minnesota, the Amon Carter Museum of American Art (Ft. Worth, Texas), the George Eastman House International Museum of Photography and Film (Rochester, New York), and the Imperial War Museum, London. I am grateful to the John F. Kennedy Presidential Library for allowing me to consult the Hemingway Papers. I also thank the Associated University Presses and the University of Nebraska Press for permitting me to include portions of previously published work.

Many people have read chapters or offered comments on parts of the book. In particular, I am grateful to Patricia Rae and Steven Trout, whose editorial interventions helped me reframe and broaden my arguments about Faulkner and Cather, respectively. Kathy Ashley, Suzanne Churchill, Mitch Breitwieser, Greg Forter, David Lubin, and Keith Gandal all provided insights and encouragements at varying stages.

I have been fortunate to have Michael Trask as my colleague. He has generously shared his time with me and has consistently challenged me to do my best.

The University of Kentucky has provided the material means for me to write this book—generous dispensations, two summer fellowships, travel support, and a room of my own. The College of Arts and Sciences' humane policies allowed me to maintain both my personal and professional commitments simultaneously. I am grateful to Jen Bartlett in the University of Kentucky library for her research help and to Anna Brzyski and Lesley Chapman for their assistance with images. Ellen Rosenman's guidance helped me at pivotal moments. Karen Petrone's passion for World War I is inspiring. She and other fellow travelers in the War and Gender Working Group helped me think about my topic in new ways. Peter Kalliney, Marion Rust, Matthew Giancarlo, Virginia Blum, and Rynetta Davis have been stalwart friends. Jeff Clymer cheerfully read drafts and offered constructive criticism and sound encouragement. I am grateful to all of my colleagues and to the College of Arts and Sciences.

My friends Tony Choi, Brooke Sawyer, and Jonathan Goldman have supported me throughout the process. More recently, Paul A. Guthrie and Martha Murray introduced me to a fellow and long-dead Lexingtonian, Alexander McClintock, whose narrative helped me frame the book's concerns. Sian Hunter gave me excellent advice as I sought a publisher. Cathie Brettschneider and the readers at the University of Virginia Press have been thorough and thoughtful. Their generous comments improved the book.

One of the clichés about war experience is that it exceeds language. Despite my professional suspicion about that frequent claim, I find myself strangely without words when I try to express my gratitude to my family for their love and forbearance. Thank you to Robert, Darlene, and Elissa James, to Steve and Sheila Sachs, and especially to Leon and Chloe Sachs.

Introduction

*Never before in history has death been so prominent a fact. Always before
it has been possible to avoid thinking about it. To-day no one can escape
the constant presence, before his mind, of dissolution. . . . No one can
forget them, no one can get away from them, those boys dead upon the
battle-fields of Europe. . . . There is not one of us who has not thought more
about death within the last four years than in a whole lifetime before.*

—WINIFRED KIRKLAND, *THE NEW DEATH*

In 1918, the popular religious writer Winifred Kirkland described a
change in American life: people were preoccupied with death as never
before. The war raging in Europe, she claimed, made death "new." So
many men were dying; so many of them were the "shining best" of their
generation. All Americans felt the loss, from the "humblest" to the "most
intellectual." What strikes her, though, is not primarily the numbers of
dead. Instead, it is *how* people are dying and that, once dead, they often
remain unburied. She writes not just of death but of "dissolution": the
grotesque physical breakdown of the dead body over time. She dwells on
death's physical texture and its duration. "The boys upon the battlefields
have seen the forms of their comrades rot before their eyes for months.
They write of the stench of putrefaction, of its colors and shapes." The war,
she insists, has put death's sheer physical horror on display in an entirely
unprecedented way; people feel compelled to talk and think about death
in detail and at length, to dwell publicly on what "used by general consent to be shoved out of sight." "From countless sources, familiar to every
reader, comes testimony" of death. According to Kirkland, the ubiquity
of dead bodies among these reports makes it possible to infer their presence, even in accounts by soldiers who try not to mention them. Indeed,
she explains, some survivors "preserve a reticence that is even more evidence of their tortured senses." Confrontations with death are so pervasive in the literature of the time that readers can recognize its intensity
precisely, if paradoxically, by a tell-tale silence. Thoughts of death are "by
their very intensity . . . new"; "one may well term this naked intimacy
with facts formerly avoided, the New Death."[1]

If Kirkland overstates the impact of World War I's killing fields on Americans, subsequent commentators have almost universally done the opposite by understating it. The present work, taking Kirkland's largely forgotten treatise on the American experience of death during World War I as its namesake, tests her proposition and finds her preoccupation with death to be typical of her time, rather than that of an outlier. It seeks to recover a moment when the war was recent and its pains were fresh and, in so doing, to reembed American novels of the postwar period within a context of pervasive death and unfinished mourning. *The New Death: American Modernism and World War I* interprets not only the words but the silences of its chosen texts. It identifies modern, mechanized, mass death as one of the signal preoccupations and structuring contexts of canonical American modernist writing—and this, despite the relative brevity of U.S. involvement in the conflict and its geographic distance from the war theaters. In so doing, it seeks to complicate Paul Fussell's influential Anglo-centered literary history of the war, *The Great War and Modern Memory*, and its assertion that "the year 1928, a decade after the war," produced "the first of the war memoirs setting themselves the task of remembering 'the truth about the war.'"[2] In contrast, *The New Death* posits that writers had been telling American readers "the truth about the war," specifically about its unspeakable horrors (here euphemized by Fussell as "truth"), almost since the beginning of the war. Years before the emergence of canonical literature of postwar "disillusion," audiences read popular literature of *dissolution*. When the war ended, the specter of mass death haunted survivors. Novelists responded by writing about male injury, death, and disappearance, even in texts where the war seems peripheral.

A work such as Alexander McClintock's *Best O' Luck* (1917) exemplifies the literature of dissolution that informed Americans. *Best O' Luck*, a first-person account of war experience on the Western Front, has been largely forgotten today. However it sold well and went into multiple editions in 1917 and is in many ways typical of a large corpus of popular wartime writing that, I suggest, forms a crucial context for the modernists we still read today.[3] It was one of many memoirs that depicted the war zone in realistic detail and that conveyed the realities of New Death to faraway readers.[4] McClintock's account offers a typical portrait of New Death, detailing the scenes that readers such as Winifred Kirkland internalized. He describes his own near-death experience as well as his work near the front, which includes handling corpses, attending funerals, and seeing a soldier there one minute and the next blown to bits.

The vision his text creates is one I want my reader to have in mind, for I argue that it is a vision that externally structures the postwar writing under consideration here. It is a vision that later writers conjure up with a bare allusion or truncated reference. Accounts such as McClintock's conveyed a textual record of the war that passed into popular imagination and that established the familiar, even clichéd images and tropes of the war which later writers, as we shall see, would evoke and assume.

Before the United States declared war, McClintock served under Canadian command on the Western Front, where he was wounded and decorated with a Distinguished Conduct Medal. After being discharged, he returned to the United States, reenlisted with the American Expeditionary Force, and addressed himself (both in public speeches and in his printed narrative) to Americans about what to "prepare for, personally and individually" as they headed for war.[5] As he had, his intended readers would face "the imminent prospect of sudden death," and he warns them with examples of men "changed . . . utterly" by "the prospect of sudden death and the presence of death and suffering around" them (18). This looming and unpredictable danger structures his entire account.

McClintock's narrative follows what was, I posit, already in 1917 a well-worn track from the humorous enlistment anecdote, through the hijinks and boredom of the military training camp, across the submarined waters of the Atlantic, up through the French countryside with masses of men and supplies, into a series of brutal and climactic episodes in the trenches, where he receives a "clean" (meaning "not fatal") wound and is sent back to a hospital (153).[6] This narrative arc emphasizes survival. Still, encounters with death dominate the account. Its tidy combat plot, which organizes dozens of narratives, provides a coherent frame for narrating the unpredictable, often traumatic, encounters with death that punctuate accounts of the war and that provide their raison d'être. In McClintock's narrative, as in many other soldiers' narratives, death makes both scheduled and surprise appearances. We expect death in the combat section, when the protagonist arrives at the front, witnesses death repeatedly, and then either dies, gets relieved, or is wounded. The front is the much-anticipated danger zone, where a majority of deaths occur and where dead bodies remain. But death also functions as a variable whose unpredictable temporality creates instability. It occurs when it is not expected; it is recalled after the fact and feared constantly in advance. Anticipation of death in such texts operates as what Paul Saint-Amour describes as "a preposterous traumatic symptom," one that happens in advance. The constant vigilance, the need to prepare for death,

Saint-Amour explains, amplifies the trauma of battle "insofar as those undergoing the trauma [have] to confront not the question 'What is this?' but the more horrifying question 'Is *this* the real thing, then, which I have dreaded all along? Is this *really* it?'"[7] Death is both predictable and sure, and unpredictable and random. Death pervades McClintock's account, from the beginning, when he first meets the "pal" whose death he announces will come, until the end, when he reminds his reader why he has been describing the "tough," "bloody," and "sorrowful" war: because Americans are headed right into it (170). In other words, McClintock invited American readers to imagine the Western Front in vivid detail and as if they themselves would soon witness its horrors. His account—again, typical for a whole genre—brings a vision of New Death before Americans. This vision is one that modernist writers, a few years later, draw on as part of an assumed understanding of what it was like to live through, and to read about, the war.

McClintock sees several men die before he gets to the front. But once there, death becomes all pervasive. It is a place "dreadful *beyond words*. The stench of the dead was sickening. In many places arms and legs of dead men stuck out of the trench walls" (112–13). Surrounded by dead bodies, McClintock himself has a near-death experience: "At last we reached the proper position, and fifteen minutes after we got there a whiz-bang buried me completely. They had to dig me out. A few minutes later another high-explosive shell fell in a trench section where three of our men were stationed. All we could find after it exploded were one arm and one leg which we buried" (113). In this place, bodies are peculiarly vulnerable. The dead and the living mingle in obscene intimacy. They occupy the same holes, are buried and unburied together. Samuel Hynes describes an aesthetic of "battlefield gothic," an aesthetic that amplifies its nineteenth-century antecedent by being real.[8] Here, the terror of being buried alive familiar from Poe and other gothic writers functions as a mere prelude to a whole new terror: total disappearance. Three men's bodies are vaporized except for two dismembered parts, which might have belonged to one or another of them. This threat seems worse than death alone. Physical damage on this scale threatens our ability to find, name, bury, and mourn the dead. Though it really happened, then, it pushes the boundaries of what realism, even a gothic realism, can describe. Were any of the three, as McClintock had been just moments before, hidden in the muck? Were they waiting to be unburied? Or were they completely gone? When three men go missing, the retrieval of one arm and one leg signals the absence of tangible evidence as much as it signals presence. One arm and one leg leave as many questions unanswered as answered. McClintock can only assume they are dead but cannot point to where they lie. For some writers, if not McClintock, this sort of experience made writing in any realistic mode both impossible and, as Evelyn Cobley asserts, immoral.[9] Recalling popular writers such as McClintock, in other words, helps contextualize why other, canonical writers would write in more allusive, cryptic, or symbolic styles and, indeed, why some of them would reject traditional realism for more modernist aesthetics.

In McClintock's narrative, every small action becomes fraught with the potential for horror. Far worse than the noise, the wet, the irregular and inadequate resupply, the lack of sand bags and shelter, what McClintock finds "most awful" is "that the soil . . . was filled with freshly-buried men": "If we undertook to cut a trench or enlarge a funk hole, our spades struck into human flesh, and the explosion of a big shell along our line sent decomposed and dismembered and sickening mementoes of an earlier fight showering amongst us. We lived in the muck and stench of 'glorious' war; those of us who lived" (114–15). What beggars description here is death's precise location. Unidentified dead bodies, broken into parts and mere matter, have become maddeningly ubiquitous; they pervade the entire landscape, both at its surface and below, in its textures, smells, sounds, and sights. As so many writers do, McClintock signals that in such a place, language itself is inadequate; speaking from where reality is "*beyond words*" (emphasis in the original), language starts to break apart. Sometimes, irony surfaces as a sign of the rupture: one way of saying what this place *is* is to use irony to say what it is not: "glorious." Elsewhere, McClintock complains, "In none of the stories I've read, have I ever seen trench fighting, as it was then carried on in Belgium, adequately described" (47). Many writers and witnesses insist on the fundamental inadequacy of language. What matters here is not whether war really is unspeakable but that unspeakability itself becomes a trope for talking about war.[10] McClintock repeatedly finds himself challenging the traditional decorum that has "grown up in long years of peace and traditional decency" (37), not because he is a literary modernist but because his experience, he says, requires it. Modern war has antiquated traditional norms of propriety. As we shall see, this issue is one that Ernest Hemingway raises directly and that informs *The New Death* as a whole.

For anyone who took up the challenge of writing about the war, how to write about modern war without doing verbal and psychic violence either to the reader or to the men who were their subject matter was a problem.

In many instances, indirection offered a partial solution. McClintock's narrative draws attention to the problem both when he talks about death and when he deals comically with more banal matters. For instance, he offers a roundabout and euphemistic description of how soldiers survived a chlorine gas attack by virtue of the fact that "certain emanations from the body throw off the ammonia fumes" (38) that neutralize chlorine gas: in other words, men urinated onto their handkerchiefs. His self-reflective circumlocution draws the reader's attention to the preposterousness of trying to speak of modern war within the bounds of traditional language and while respecting cultural prudery about men's bodies. Relating conditions at the front requires writers to push right up to and, if possible, beyond the norms of what one can say directly in print.

The dividing line between experience at the front and the innocence on the home front to which McClintock refers was, and is, often gendered. Men die and fight; women read and write. As is usually the case, the binary opposition valorizes one of its terms over the other. Words come all too easily for women, particularly those who create and consume propaganda, while men are silenced either by death, trauma, inhibition, or censorship. According to Sandra Gilbert and Susan Gubar's *No Man's Land*, the war's wages seemed inequitable: men seemed to suffer and pay costs, women seemed to profit.[11] Yet as pervasive as this equation may have seemed, it does not hold true in McClintock's account, where death transgresses even this boundary. It comes even to women, whose femininity offers little protection in modern war. When McClintock is ordered to clean out a German dugout, he finds "two dead nurses, one standing with her arm 'round a post, just as she had stood when gas or concussion killed her" (115). Despite all he has already been through, this is too much. "The task of cleaning up was too dreadful for us. We just tossed in four or five fumite bombs and beat it out of there. A few hours later we went into the seared and empty cavern" and set up the battalion headquarters (115–16). Burying dead women is something McClintock cannot or will not do; he prefers to immolate them. For all his contact with corpses, dead female bodies cross a line; their unexpected gender makes them "too dreadful." Dead bodies are everywhere, but not like this. These nurses should not be there, looking so innocent and lifelike in this place of enmity and death. His refusal might be understood as an attempt to preserve boundaries, to "avoid" unseemly "intimacies" with death. But his account also suggests just how impossible that was. This episode hints at what, I argue, is gender's paradigmatic function in accounts of New Death, in which its supposed stability frequently reverses, and female bodies signify the most abject wounds and deaths in wartime. Images of women function as a governing, organizing paradox in many wartime and postwar narratives. On the one hand, women seem immune to and ignorant of war's realities; at the same time, those realities seem to find clearest expression when they are imagined as happening to women. McClintock's discovery of nurses in the middle of a bombed-out shell hole is at once surprising (what are women doing at the front?) and utterly in keeping with New Death's chaotic and transgendering ubiquity.

McClintock's account also offers insight into what New Death did to mourning practices. As we will see, the war disrupted people's ability to prepare for, witness, and ritualize death according to customs of deathbed attendance, funerals, and burials. Soldiers died at a distance. They often died instantly. Others died all too slowly, but out of reach and alone. Many were simply gone. According to John Keegan, "at the war's end, the remains of nearly half of those lost remained lost in actuality," leaving families in doubt.[12] Later in the century, writing in part as a response to modern war, psychologists would give this doubt a name: "ambiguous loss." Pauline Boss describes it as "the most distressful of all losses."[13] In order to mourn, people need to confront evidence and name the person or relationship that has ended with death. Without confirmation, mourners often miss "the symbolic rituals that ordinarily support a clear loss—such as a funeral after a death in the family."[14] During World War I, ambiguous loss occurred on a mass scale, though no psychologist had conferred the term on it.

In McClintock's account, he struggles to frame and articulate the problem. But he only does so in a roundabout way, by insisting on the singularity of an event that would have been quite common in peacetime:

> I witnessed a scene which—with some others—I shall never forget.
> An old chaplain of the Canadian forces came to our trench section seeking the grave of his son, which had been marked for him
> on a rude map by an officer who had seen the young man's burial.
> We managed to find the spot, and, at the old chaplain's request,
> we exhumed the body. Some of us suggested to him that he give us
> the identification marks and retire out of range of the shells which
> were bursting all around us. We argued that it was unwise for him
> to remain unnecessarily in danger, but what we really intended was
> that he should be saved the horror of seeing the pitiful thing which
> our spades were about to uncover.
> "I shall remain," was all he said. "He was my boy."

It proved we had found the right body. One of our men tried to clear the features with his handkerchief, but ended by spreading the handkerchief over his face. The old chaplain stood beside the body and removed his trench helmet, baring his gray locks to the drizzle of rain that was falling. Then, while we stood by with bowed heads, his voice rose amid the noise of bursting shells, repeating the burial service of the Church of England. I have never been so impressed by anything in my life as by that scene.

The dead man was a young captain. He had been married to a lady of Baltimore, just before the outbreak of the war. (116–17)

Some might assume that what so "impresse[s]" McClintock here is the father's intrepidity, his willingness to brave the danger of shell fire in order to find, exhume, and rebury his son. Certainly, its setting makes an otherwise traditional ritual "new." The danger underscores the father's deep need to find his son, to see his body, and to ritualize his death. The singularity of this episode, the fact that McClintock was never more "impressed by anything in [his] life as this scene," also suggests, I would argue, just how much the war disrupted mourning. It transformed the simplest funeral into a remarkable event, a superlative oddity. In this context, the funeral's transformation of the dead body from a "pitiful thing" into a tangible link to a life that has ended, a son and husband mourned by father and wife, is almost miraculous. For the war often made such moments impossible. The norm was loss without ritual or good-bye, as it is when McClintock's commander dies. All he can say is, "I never saw him again" (139).

Alexander McClintock committed suicide in 1918, and his narrative, like Kirkland's treatise, has been mostly forgotten. I recover it as an example of one of the many texts that brought Americans into "naked intimacy" with New Death. It epitomizes a whole genre of writing popular during and immediately following the war but largely unread since. It addresses itself to the young American men who planned on going to war and who imagined it from afar.

Texts such as McClintock's articulated for Americans what it felt like to do what historian Drew Gilpin Faust has called "the work of death": to anticipate death, inflict it, experience it, imagine it, clean up after it, and work to assimilate the losses and fears it left behind.[15] During the war, Americans and other combatant nations undertook this work on a mass scale. Yet its particulars were hard to talk about then and have been largely obscured or forgotten in the intervening century. Horrific realities evoked the desire to look away from the carnage and the need to sanctify the dead. Mourning rituals seemed both necessary and inadequate without a body to bury; notions of heroic masculinity seemed both essential and far-fetched when male bodies became sites of industrial-scale damage. What governments left uncensored conflicted with civilian codes of decorum. As prominent and inescapable as it was, the war's death was sanitized and denied. It was there and not there, central but often invisible.

Iterations of this cultural paradox inform and shape the canonical modernist narratives I examine in *New Death*. Though we know these texts much better than we know McClintock's narrative, we may not understand them as intimately as we think. These narratives all enact the difficulty of doing the "work of death." By historicizing these texts and analyzing how they refer to and narrate death, I uncover how modernist novels reveal, refigure, omit, and aestheticize the violent death of young men in the aftermath of World War I.

This introduction provides a historical and theoretical context for the ensuing chapters. I cite and extend arguments for thinking of the United States' experience of the war as deeper and more traumatic than has been acknowledged generally. I situate this oversight within a larger, international aporia identified by cultural historians of the war, an aporia that opens around and that has obscured the pain, suffering, and often-blocked need to mourn that the war left in its wake. The difficulty of mourning the losses incurred during the war stems from overlapping circumstances: the collision between modern warfare and the cultural tradition of sanctifying male death as "sacrifice"; the technologies of violence that obliterated bodies; the fact that mourning rituals themselves had been disrupted by cultural modernization; and, for Americans, the distance involved in fighting a war an ocean away. Compounding all these was the popular sense that, though the United States had helped win the war, it had lost the peace. These (and other) factors made it difficult to take stock of the war's damage and to mourn.

With that context in mind, this introduction offers a new vantage on the ongoing analysis of American modernism as a literature of melancholia, or failed mourning. While influential critics in the field of American modernism, notably Seth Moglen and Greg Forter, have interpreted the works of Willa Cather, F. Scott Fitzgerald, Ernest Hemingway, and William Faulkner in terms of melancholia and loss, World War I has been until now largely absent from the discussion. The war, I argue, shapes the thematic and formal ways that these writers represent damage, loss, and wounded masculinity in their texts. New Death was a problem that these writers in particular responded to by writing melancholically about damaged men and mechanized violence and by narrating traumatic plots, where violence happens, seemingly without effect, only to return in moments of uncanny repetition. Violence reappears, often in sanitized forms or on the bodies of women rather than men. "American modernism is famously a literature of loss," as Moglen says, and considering the specific losses inflicted during the war gives us a better understanding of why they were so hard to represent directly, and to grieve.[16]

For a long time, historians have reasoned that the United States' late entry into the war and its relatively small numbers of casualties minimized World War I's impact on it. This has become axiomatic. When one compares American losses in World War I to either the American Civil War on a chronological axis or to contemporary European losses on a geographic axis, the American death toll in World War I seems slight. Thus, the war was not traumatic for Americans. This line of reasoning has limited our understanding of American culture of the 1910s and '20s.

Recent scholarship on the American experience of World War I has begun to counter that narrative and to foreground the war's importance to American culture in economic, military, institutional, and civic terms.[17] Such arguments inform recent reevaluations of American writing of the era, which also center on the war in new ways.[18] As such arguments have proliferated, historians and critics have begun to explore the extent to which the war was traumatic for Americans. Once upon a time, that went almost without saying. In Alfred Kazin's 1942 study *On Native Grounds*, for instance, he asserts that a generation of American writers felt the war's damage:

> Writers like Fitzgerald, Hemingway, and Dos Passos were significantly the evangels of what had been most tragically felt in the American war experience. They were "the sad young men," the very disillusioned and brilliant young men, "the beautiful and the damned," and counterparts of all those other sad and brilliant young men in Europe, Aldous Huxley and Louis Aragon, Ernst Toller and Wilfred Owen, who wrote out of the bitterness of a shattered Europe and the palpable demoralization of Western society. . . . The war had dislodged them from their homes and the old

restraints, given them an unexpected and disillusioning education, and left them entirely rootless.[19]

Kazin's assertion seemed straightforward at the time. But the interpretive field of American modernism has changed considerably in the intervening decades, and the war's relevance to American writers is now a point of dispute. Kenneth Lynn, for instance, argues that the war's impact on even Ernest Hemingway has been grossly overstated, both by Hemingway himself and by his contemporaries and early critics (notably Malcolm Cowley).[20]

The New Death argues not simply for a return to, but for a reconsideration of, the assumptions that undergird early accounts of American writing after the war. Kazin's quote in the preceding paragraph insists on a particularly masculine experience of loss, but in what looks like, retrospectively, rather cryptic terms. He asserts the war's importance in two main ways: by connecting American writers to European writers of the same generation and by referring to the war's meaning in title phrases from F. Scott Fitzgerald (*The Beautiful and Damned* [1922], *All the Sad Young Men* [1926]). Instead of discussing the war in detail, Kazin glosses it as what Fitzgerald's works refer to. Yet neither the novel nor the collection of short stories to which Kazin alludes contains anything explicitly about World War I. When it comes to the war, Kazin suggests, Fitzgerald's own words say it best; but when we turn to Fitzgerald's words, we find little or nothing about the war. Given the shadowy nature of Kazin's claim, then, later critics have been right to interrogate more rigorously the war's importance to American writers. However, instead of dismissing such claims altogether, I suggest we read them and the terms in which they are made as symptomatic of a larger difficulty that its contemporaries had when it came to enumerating the war's damages. Modernists and their critics often refer to the war in a language of key words (such as "disillusionment" and "rootlessness") that deserve, rather than advance, analysis. They often refer to the war, I would suggest, through imprecise evocation. Both canonical modernist literature and its contemporary criticism tend to allude to, sometimes to mystify, historical sources of pain and loss. In order to develop an understanding of the issue that is adequate to our own historical and critical remove requires us to reinterpret the shared understandings, mutually instantiated implications, and clichés of an earlier generation.

For Keith Gandal, the "Lost Generation" should be renamed the "Lost Out" generation. World War I was traumatic for male American modernist writers, he argues, but not, as one might expect, because of trench warfare. In fact, the army rejected Hemingway and Faulkner and passed over Fitzgerald for promotion. Therefore, Gandal reasons, the U.S. military pronounced their masculinity inadequate; these writers did not suffer "war wounds" but "mobilization wounds."[21] These instances of rejection undoubtedly did inform these authors' perception of the war's legacy and the ways it had it wounded others individually and collectively. Gandal's account licenses my argument in *The New Death* by putting war trauma at the center of American modernism. However, our accounts differ considerably. Gandal highlights authors' biographical experiences with the army and the wounds it inflicted, and especially how those wounds shaped their subsequent representations of ethnicity and cross-ethnic romance. In contrast, *The New Death* considers a cultural preoccupation with how modern warfare changed the experience and meaning of male *death*.

We have yet to develop a full account of how the war's New Death was registered and felt in the United States. From the war's outbreak in 1914, Americans perceived and described some of its most fearful aspects. It terrorized Americans from afar and in advance. Lewis Mumford described the "collective psychosis" that gripped Americans in a time that was "masquerading as peacetime" but that was "equally a state of war: the passive war of propaganda, war-indoctrination, war-rehearsal."[22] From the moment the war began, the United States was the target of mass amounts of propaganda, some of it quite graphic. As I have shown in previous work, visual propaganda circulated to an unprecedented extent and in unprecedented ways in the United States: posters were routinely hung in cities and shops but also in workplaces, libraries, classrooms, banks, grain markets, and homes.[23] According to Walton Rawls, America produced more war posters than all the other belligerent nations combined.[24] In one of them, Joseph Pennell depicts New York Harbor in flames, under aerial bombardment by Germany (see figure 1). As this popular poster shows, Americans imagined the war happening on their own soil. Indeed, Pennell's original caption for the image was "Buy Liberty Bonds Or You Will See This."[25] Such a vision was not as far-fetched as it might now seem. Americans did experience war-related violence. Pennell's illustration is instructive: though he himself described his lithograph as a product of his own imagination, New York Harbor had been the site of an enormous munitions explosion perpetrated by German-paid saboteurs in 1916.[26] The damage symbolized in Pennell's poster was not only symbolic. Though not as deadly as the infamous 1917 explosion of an ammunition-laden ship in Halifax Harbor, the explosion in New York underscored the fact that political "neutrality" offered little protection from the risks involved in building and shipping war materials. From this perspective, the period of United States' neutrality looks decidedly less benign.

When the United States entered the war in 1917, American attention to the war became even more intense. Four million men were drafted and two million sent overseas to fight. In 1918, just as large numbers of troops were sent abroad, the Spanish flu epidemic broke out and killed hundreds of thousands of Americans. As Carol Byerly has shown, the flu was linked in the popular mind to the war, both insofar as it was (falsely) rumored to have been intentionally unleashed on America by a German U-boat, and because it (truly) killed American soldiers with particular ferocity. American training camps were hard hit. Having been selected by the military as the fittest of American men, thousands of newly trained soldiers died helplessly as they drowned in their own blood.[27] As Katherine Ann Porter's character in "Pale Horse, Pale Rider" puts it, "The men are dying like flies" out at the training camp, prompting another to ask, "Did you ever see so many funerals, ever?"[28] Byerly explains that "the crowded and chaotic living conditions" of mass warfare, in which new recruits continually replaced the wounded and the dead, thus "continuously bringing the virus into contact with new hosts—young, healthy soldiers—in which it could reproduce," led to the 1918's peculiarly virulent strain of the flu.[29] It was a defining factor in the U.S. war effort, and ultimately more American soldiers died—abjectly, ingloriously—of the flu than did in combat.[30]

Among the American troops who made it overseas, many never returned. Indeed, as Steven Trout reminds us, "American soldiers died at a faster rate during the final summer and fall of World War I than during almost any other period of American military history." During this period, a "sudden avalanche of death and suffering" bore down on "Americans at home."[31] Despite both the large scale of death and suffering and the fact that America had helped win the war, the war's meaning was ambiguous and contested. Trout enumerates several factors that split Americans' understandings of what the war meant: "racial injustice" within the armed forces; the "violent . . . impact on domestic policies; the dubious performance of the AEF in combat; the lack of shared experience among veterans"; "the military consequences of the Spanish flu"; but, above all, "the human cost of the conflict: 125,500 Americans killed; 205,690 wounded—and the absence of a clear-cut answer to the question, *why*?"[32]

THAT LIBERTY SHALL NOT
PERISH FROM THE EARTH
BUY LIBERTY BONDS
FOURTH   LIBERTY   LOAN

FIGURE 1. "That Liberty Shall Not Perish From the Earth" / Fourth Liberty Loan, Joseph Pennell, color lithograph, 22 × 33 inches, 1918. (Hoover Institution Archives, Stanford University)

Perhaps because Americans were so divided on this question, the war's costs were in fact hard to reckon. In accounts of American modernism, this problem has largely faded from view. Instead, the war's cultural impact has been measured much more frequently in relation to British, German, French, and other national literatures. Paul Fussell's *The Great War and Modern Memory* still exerts a strong influence on the field, even as Modris Eksteins's *Rites of Spring* and, particularly, Jay Winter's *Sites of Memory, Sites of Mourning* have called attention to its limitations and expanded the canon of relevant texts. Fussell drew what has become the standard line of connection between the war's devastation and modernism's irony and disillusion, and much of his insight remains invaluable. Irony, he posited, served to make the war's horror intelligible. Drawing ironic boundaries between prewar innocence and postwar disillusion, between "us" and "them," between front and home front, for instance, were habits of mind that allowed Britons to make sense of the catastrophic changes wrought by war experience. Fussell's attention to irony and postwar disillusionment, however, has been faulted for being too selective. Winter emphasizes, in contrast, the vitality and utility of more traditional modes of representation after the war. He, like Eksteins, considers both an international and much wider range of texts and cultural producers in his search to understand how people represented, mourned, and memorialized the damages of the war. Among them, Winter finds many cultural forms utterly lacking in irony, including the postwar fascination with spiritualism. If the war contributed to modernism, he argues, it also deepened people's need for more traditional art and writing.[33]

Eksteins's and Winters's research, like that done by Vincent Sherry, Margot Norris, and others, underscores the need to continue to tease out and further explore the complicated but profound relationship between cultural modernism and the war.[34] As we shift from Fussell's archive and his insistence on irony to American writing about the war, we particularly need strategies for interpreting what Kirkland described as meaningful silence, the "reticence" that signifies "tortured senses." We have to read what is *not* said. In many texts, writers convey the horror of war death through the trope of unspeakability, of experience outstripping language, or Kirkland's "reticence"; this trope, in particular, requires careful glossing from a later historical remove. Its once-obvious referent has been overlooked by generations of scholars who have assumed that World War I meant little to Americans and for their writing. Silence, I posit, implies different things in different historical moments and contexts. For instance, as Alan Sinfield has shown, in the wake of Oscar Wilde's highly publicized trial for the crime of a "love that dare[d] not speak its name," silence, circumlocution, and omission became a code for oblique references to love between men.[35] In some instances, omission continued to function in that way during the modernist 1920s.[36] But during and after the war, as people read accounts such as McClintock's, silence, unspeakability, and pained allusion became codes for traumatic war experience.

Parsing the silences left behind by war experience is a difficult task for a variety of reasons. Several commentators have warned that when war enters the written record, it is sanitized. Killing, dying, and bodily suffering are all minimized. Bertrand Russell tracked one instance of sanitization in the cultural valorization of men's willingness to "die for their country." He pointed out that war is not just dying but killing. Yet we are reluctant to celebrate men's willingness to "kill for their country." Horace's "old lie," from this perspective, is double: not only is dying not beautiful, but going to war requires soldiers both to die and *to kill*.[37] Elaine Scarry's account of sanitization is more sweeping. She reads Russell's distinction as just so many words and argues that killing and dying *alike* tend to disappear. She focuses on the broad category of injury, relentlessly trying to make this often-invisible experience and its consequences more salient. "Injury," she insists, is not ancillary or incidental to war; it "is war's product and its cost, it is the goal toward which all activity is directed and the road to the goal." Despite this centrality, injury often disappears from accounts and descriptions and discussions of war. It "may be disowned in endless ways," often through metaphor, redescription, and omission.[38] Historians specifically concerned with World War I have corroborated the accuracy of Scarry's philosophical analysis in relation to the historiography of World War I. So, for instance, echoing Russell, cultural historian Joanna Bourke contends that although "the characteristic act of men at war is not dying [but] killing," "the lengths some commentators will go to deny the centrality of killing in modern battle" is "striking."[39] Stéphane Audoin-Rouzeau and Annette Becker concur that "why we accept the violence of warfare has remained a taboo subject"; we continue to think of soldiers as victims of war rather than as its willing agents. They complain that though "everyone knows war is violence," we tend to sanitize it in "unacceptable" ways.[40] For them, part of the problem is the way we talk about death. We know it happens and use various terms "to assess the glaring demographic factor of mass death, but it has not really been analyzed using the yardstick of deep pain."[41] They posit that "the history of warfare—particularly academic and scholarly history, but also traditional military history—is all too often disembodied."[42]

In response, Bourke, Audoin-Rouzeau and Becker, and others have developed historical accounts that focus particularly on the body. *The New Death* not only draws on these and other accounts but aims to enrich them and the understandings they offer. By foregrounding how narratives represent the experience of injury, dying, witnessing, and surviving death and by paying particular attention to the silences that surround such experiences, this book looks at how literary texts alternately sanitize death and make it apparent.

One reason death haunts its survivors yet can seem unspeakable stems from shock. Death in war differs from death in peacetime. According to Samuel Hynes, death in wartime "isn't what you expected, . . . it's uglier, more grotesque, less human."[43] Several factors worked to make death unexpected and grotesque during World War I. Men were dying in unprecedented numbers—millions. The age of death disrupted expectations. Populations in the industrialized world were living longer lives, enjoying lower infant-mortality rates, and developing life narratives in which death was increasingly the plight of the aged. The war reversed that by sending millions of young, healthy, able-bodied men to die in the prime of their lives. Death seemed new in other ways, as well. New technologies of war changed its aspects. Chemical warfare, long-range and high-volume artillery, and military aeronautics changed the face of battle and the look and feel of soldiers' deaths. As Bourke puts it,

> Death was obscene: . . . Men were roasted alive. Death descended from the skies and disappeared without being sighted by those who survived. It was like black magic: bodies continued walking after decapitation; shells burst and bodies simply vanished. Men's bodies "shattered": their jaws dropped out and poured "so much blood." Aeroplane propellers sliced men into pieces. In death, white soldiers turned blackish and black Senegalese soldiers turned whitish. Bodies lay forever unburied, eaten by the dogs, birds, and rats.[44]

Americans read about such obscene death repeatedly and in great detail. McClintock's is only one of many memoirs by Americans serving in the war zones that circulated and informed the public about what it was like to anticipate death by bombardment, to suffer the effects of poison gas, to be buried alive, and for bodies to be obliterated without a trace. Narratives also reported that death was often drawn out. Men were sometimes saved only to die later, in a slower and more painful fashion. Survival itself was experienced by some soldiers as a trauma to be endured—going to a hospital offers relief in some accounts but elsewhere means being victimized by overeager surgeons. For those who did die at the front, they often remained unburied or were buried once but unburied later. Dead bodies of men and animals were ubiquitous and often left unburied together.

These and other wartime conditions made it nigh impossible to rit-ualize death in customary ways. Grief could not run in its time-worn channels, and while in some quarters it flooded uncontrollably, elsewhere it was blocked, channeled underground, or diverted. Traditions of mourning seemed inadequate in the context of modern war. Audoin-Rouzeau and Becker describe postwar mourning as "complicated, sometimes impossible, always protracted." Even after the war was over, they argue, "the survivors were by and large not allowed genuinely to mourn; it was one of the hidden objectives of the post-war commemorations to forbid protracted mourning, which was seen as a betrayal of the men who had sacrificed themselves on the battlefields. These were impossible bereavements to come to terms with."[45] Other historians attribute greater satisfaction to survivors, at least with some of the postwar commemorations, such as the overwhelming British response to the interment of an Unknown Soldier in Westminster Abbey.[46] But the popularity of that commemoration is, after all, predicated on the failure of more individual rituals. It was meaningful to bury an unidentified body precisely because so many masses of people needed a stand-in for their own missing dead. Allyson Booth argues that some modernist writing emerges directly out of the split between the corpse-filled world at the front and the eerie "corpselessness" of the (British) home front. Narratives had to help fill the gaps of awareness created by missing dead.[47]

"Corpselessness," I would argue, meant something different in the United States and evoked different responses from writers. As we shall see, the problem of mourning without a body is the central issue of William Faulkner's postwar novel *Sartoris*. Without a body, it is difficult for survivors to believe that the dead are really dead; they have no visual or physical evidence with which to confront the reality of loss. In Faulkner's account, this enables survivors to nurse fantasies that the dead still live. Worse, it inspires homicidal and suicidal actions, in which survivors try to re-create the scene of death and gain the satisfaction of a corpse with which to verify their feelings of anger and loss. A more vivid depiction of frustrated mourning in the wake of World War I can hardly be imagined. Indeed, Faulkner's decision to depict a lost aviator may have stemmed directly from his own (limited) experience in the Royal Air Force in Canada, but in so doing, he seems to have intuited the symbolic value of lost aviators, who become, in later decades, the textbook examples of what psychologists describe as objects of "ambiguous loss," or loss without confirmation.[48]

The wartime debate over how to mourn for dead soldiers and how to treat their remains was anguished even when bodies were not lost. The war coincided with and accelerated a slow change, already under way during the early decades of the twentieth century, in funerary, mourning, and burial practices. As James Farrell has shown, even before the war, no one ritual was in universal use; families had no singular way to signify their loss, its meaning, and their own stature to their larger community. Some families kept their dying and dead at home until burial; others used hospitals and professional funerary services. No one had arrived at the level of commercialized ostentation that Jessica Mitford would deplore in the 1960s as the "American Way of Death," but the modernization and professionalization of the funerary industries had begun, and both costs and trappings had begun to change. Farrell recounts the various changes to custom, designed to "reduce . . . the consciousness of individual death" and to eliminate its "'grewsomeness' [sic]."[49] Throughout the end of the nineteenth century and the beginning of the twentieth, he shows, death was increasingly cordoned off from daily life. Cemeteries were no longer adjacent to churches in the centers of towns; instead they occupied large parklike spaces in suburbs or outside cities. New aesthetics in cemetery planning aimed to create a sense of beauty by "eliminating suggestions of death" or at least making it anonymous. They did so by "leveling the traditional grave mounds, eliminating or limiting gravestones, and reducing inscriptions on gravestones or monuments." Such changes contributed to what Farrell calls the "dying of death"—the end to its significance in modern American life.[50] He points also to the fact that calling an undertaker to tend to a loved one's dead body became increasingly common. Undertakers professionalized (becoming "funeral directors") and became increasingly respectable. Embalming gradually gained more acceptance. Funerals increasingly took place outside the home, in professional funeral "parlors" (though the word itself attempts to replicate the home environment it hoped to replace). Together these changes made it increasingly possible for people to limit their contact with the process of death, and many did.

As a result, as Farrell concludes, "the slaughter in the trenches" of World War I "stunned some people who were accustomed to evading the reality of death."[51] He corroborates Winifred Kirkland's sense that during the war, death seemed shockingly new and physically appalling. From a later historical perspective, this seems obvious. Samuel Hynes posits that one reason death has such an important place in soldier's tales from the twentieth century is because, by then, "most young men . . . reach adulthood without ever having confronted death face-to-face, or not until the morticians have turned it into unreality."[52] But less obvious is that death in World War I would have stunned others for the opposite reason—for those who still practiced traditional funerals at home and who wanted family buried nearby, death in an anonymous no-man's-land where bodies could not be tended was also horrifying. In other words, although a variety of funerary practices were in use at the time, the war's violence and distance disrupted all of them. As Americans sent their own men to fight, they had to reconsider the physical and emotional tasks associated with burying the dead. No solution, old or new, seemed adequate to the problems posed by modern, mass, mechanized, and global war.

Americans had to take up issues of death and burial they had not dealt with on a mass scale since the Civil War. That earlier war offered a powerful, if complicated, example of how Americans responded to mass death. According to Lisa Budreau, the precedent of that earlier war was clear: "By the close of the Civil War in 1865, Americans expected national cemeteries for those who chose not to bring their dead home; they also anticipated an unrestrained right to erect monuments on former battlefields." They were likely to hold "their government and military leaders responsible for the care of their deceased," including the use of "modern funereal procedures and advanced search and identification methods."[53] These expectations reflected both the successes and failures of mourning the Civil War dead, which was itself an extremely complex process—one that is still not, Drew Gilpin Faust argues, "adequately understood or recognized."[54] In response to this aporia in historical understanding, she has developed a more sustained account of what she calls "the work of death" done by Americans in the Civil War, which encompasses

> the duties of soldiers to fight, kill, and die, but at the same time invoking battle's consequences: its slaughter, suffering, and devastation. "Work" in this usage incorporated both effort and impact—and the important connection between the two. Death in war does not simply happen; it requires action and agents. It must, first of all, be inflicted; and several million soldiers of the 1860s dedicated themselves to that purpose. But death also usually requires

participation and response; it must be experienced and handled. It is work to die, to know how to approach and endure life's last moments. . . . It is work to deal with the dead as well, to remove them in the literal sense of disposing of their bodies, and it is also work to remove them in a more figurative sense. The bereaved struggle to separate themselves from the dead through ritual and mourning. Families and communities must repair the rent in the domestic and social fabric, and societies, nations, and cultures must work to understand and explain unfathomable loss.[55]

As Faust explains, during the Civil War, Americans developed traditions—albeit imperfect ones—for doing the "work of death" on a mass scale. Soldiers often acted as proxies for family members as witnesses to a loved one's "good death." They transcribed the dying person's last words and often wrote long letters containing accounts of the moment of death. They also provided information about the location of burial in order to enable loved ones to find their dead. These measures were, themselves, stopgap adaptations to the national holocaust, which "violat[ed] . . . prevailing assumptions about life's proper end—about who should die, when and where, and under what circumstances."[56] In the nineteenth century, people were expected to die at home and to foresee, accept, and even superintend their own death. Families gathered around their dying members and listened for last words and looked for evidence of the dying person's preparedness. A "good death" was a death that was expected and accepted, and it signified a peaceful transition to the next world. Circumstances of the Civil War sorely strained such expectations. Strangers often provided what a family would have under more normal circumstances. Walt Whitman famously nursed hundreds of wounded and dying soldiers and, crucially, wrote letters to their families. Faust recovers just how laborious and time-consuming it was for Americans to do this work of death. They did it imperfectly, and over decades. Searching for the missing dead and gathering their bodies into national cemeteries, for instance, was a costly and lengthy endeavor.

By 1917, of course, a detailed memory of this work had largely faded, leaving behind the expectations Budreau describes—that the government would care for its wounded and gather, identify, and properly bury its dead. But it was more difficult than ever to meet those expectations during World War I. For one thing, notions of what constituted both a "good death" and a decent burial had become less clear. For another, war was being waged differently and at a much greater distance. As

Hemingway's *A Farewell to Arms* famously declares, traditional languages of commemoration seemed to fail, leaving soldiers such as Frederic Henry with "nothing to say"; he thinks about, but never writes, a letter home to his dead friend's family.[57]

For Americans, distance exacerbated the difficulties associated with burial and memorialization. As Budreau shows, the debate over where to inter dead American soldiers was fierce, and families were agonized by the decision-making process. Cost was an issue, logistics another; politics, as always, complicated matters. In the end, the government gave families a choice about whether to leave their sons buried abroad in national cemeteries, to have them buried in Arlington Cemetery, or to have them brought home for burial by the family. "The anxious uncertainty" of this process, according to Budreau, precipitated "a heartbreaking period for all concerned."[58] Families wrote to the War Department asking, "Are the bodies of the soldiers who die now embalmed?" "What kind of casket has been used for burial?" "Will it be possible to allow relatives to have caskets, containing bodies returned to this country, opened for inspection?" "Can a tentative date for starting removal of bodies to this country be given?"[59] Major General John F. O'Ryan, one of the officials charged with developing a policy that would govern these and other matters, "acknowledge[d] privately that in many cases, there was 'very little to ship back in the way of remains as many bodies were blown into fragments.'"[60] Families were polled, and a majority wanted their dead brought home. But "the agonizing wait for the body's return could take years."[61] Budreau chronicles the material difficulties of exhuming bodies (or body parts), identifying them, enclosing them in coffins, and getting them each to their destination, all on a mass scale. For families who chose not to have their dead shipped home, "the decision to leave their deceased overseas came at an equally high price. There would be no funeral service, no headstone at a local cemetery, nothing left to venerate, and no closure so necessary in the grieving process."[62]

American modernist writing repeatedly portrays the "work of death" as unfinished, unsatisfactory business. As Budreau's study demonstrates, it was. The process of returning bodies, memorializing the dead, organizing and making pilgrimages to European cemeteries went on for years. It did not end on "the eleventh hour of the eleventh day of the eleventh month" of 1918, despite the incantatory hope of an ending that this phrase conveys. Throughout the 1920s, when the novels under consideration here were being written and read, bodies continued to be brought home, and Congress continued to wrangle over appropriations for consolatory measures such as the "Gold Star Mothers" pilgrimages. According to Steven Trout, "the war dead remained omnipresent in American interwar culture"; the 1920s in particular was a time, he insists, of "frenetic commemoration and simultaneous reappraisal."[63] The work of death continued, particularly for the veterans who had been closest to the experience of war. Their struggles (with morphine addiction, suicide, unemployment, shell-shock, reintegration into society, crime, and so on) were items of daily news and made the returning soldier himself a figure for the war's lack of closure. The war was over, but its effects were still being felt. Not only were its damages not yet repaired or accepted; they had not even yet been fully enumerated. Enumerating them was difficult, sometimes taboo, since that task required frankness about trauma, the male body, dissolution, and death.

The New Death traces, in particular, how cultural norms of masculinity complicate the work of death in narrative. In the novels under consideration here, codes of masculinity limit the means male characters have to express themselves. Hemingway and Faulkner both depict men who either refuse or seem unable to tell their war stories. As aware, or even as critical, as writers may have been of such limitations, the drafts of their novels reveal the extent to which they, too, hesitated to breach traditional decorum when it came to depicting male wounds and trauma. Hemingway, Fitzgerald, and Faulkner all struggled, as we shall see, to depict wounded bodies and psyches in ways that satisfied their editors' dual, essentially paradoxical, demands for realism and marketability. This pressure may account for the fact that in *A Farewell to Arms* and in *The Great Gatsby*, female bodies suffer more elaborately than male ones. Portrayal of an abject male body—a corpse or a body with an open, bleeding wound—goes against ingrained cultural norms. Elizabeth Grosz traces this taboo across Western tradition, arguing that aspects of "corporeality" that are "uncontrollable, excessive, expansive, disruptive, irrational," including wounds, have been "attributed to women" and female experience; in contrast, male bodies are rarely depicted in such terms and thus come to seem "clean and proper."[64] In the specific historical context under consideration here, suppurating, bleeding, oozing, and filthy male bodies were a kind of open secret. In Britain, for instance, photographs of soldiers' corpses were forbidden by law, and access to the front by newsmen and photographers was restricted. But despite the regulations, "photographs of dead soldiers were widely circulated."[65] As I will show, even in the state-authorized British propaganda film *The Battle of the Somme* (released in Britain and the United States in 1916), male wounds and death appear repeatedly and in gruesome detail. Writing about the war after the fact, writers no longer faced military censors. But they still had to contend with notions of decorum and sensibility—their readers' and their own.

As Greg Forter has shown, the works of Fitzgerald, Cather, Hemingway, and Faulkner—the very writers under consideration here—betray a deep and complex ambivalence toward their culture's norms of masculinity. For him, canonical American modernism is a literature that "respond[s]" in "a melancholic manner" to the loss of a form of "white manhood that had been dominant in the years prior to 1880" but that was imperiled by economic changes. These modernist writers evince a "melancholic grief" for a complex masculinity that combined aggression and competition with a "'feminine' capacity for sympathetic identification," creativity, and "sensuous responsiveness."[66] Perhaps because of the unequal burden men bore during the war directly as a result of their manliness, the war only exacerbated this ambivalence. This ambivalence helps explain why these writers shared, in Seth Moglen's terms, an "underlying conviction that things of ultimate value to them had been imperiled or destroyed in their own generation"; they experienced a "collective" crisis and "sense of loss" that they ultimately found difficult to mourn. Though Moglen traces the loss at their center to "broader and more systemic social causes," particularly to "the destructive processes of monopoly capitalism," he notices that the war is often one explanation "hovering in the background" for this sense of loss.[67] The difficulties of mourning in the wake of war, elaborated earlier, may help us further understand why canonical modernism both "astutely record[s]" and "mystifies" or "naturalizes" recent historical injuries to men. Moglen's paradox speaks directly to the problem of protesting New Death: to do so is tantamount to calling soldiers' deaths meaningless. As Moglen has shown, enumerating the sources and causes of damage is a demanding and difficult process. And the generation of men who fought the war, Forter makes clear, had reasons to be ambivalent about the regime of masculinity that they had inherited. The perplexities identified by Moglen and Forter help frame, I would argue, the difficulties postwar writers faced as they attempted to put the war's meanings for men into narrative.

In this context, American writers used, sometimes invented, various rhetorical and narratological means to represent the unspeakable aspects of the war, particularly what it did to and looked like on male flesh. They developed their own aesthetics of withholding, delaying, and omitting information to represent the so-called "unspeakable" horrors of war. Omission became, in fact, an authorial mantra both for Cather and for Hemingway. Hemingway claimed that "if a writer of prose knows enough about what he is writing about he may omit things that he knows and the reader, if the writer is writing truly enough, will have a feeling for those things as strongly as though the writer had stated them. The dignity of the movement of an iceberg is due to only one-eighth of it being above water. A writer who omits things because he does not know them only makes hollow places in his writing."[68] He reiterated this when George Plimpton interviewed him for the *Paris Review*, and it has come to be known as his "iceberg principle."[69] Willa Cather proceeded from a similar principle, the "thing not named," that writing was best when it evoked things without making them explicit.[70] For Cather, this offered a way of evoking the reader's feelings and imagination. Through omission, modernists adapted realist fiction to a new historical reality in which what was most important was often unsayable or physically lost. They created narrators whose voices register psychological damage. Frederic Henry's affect is remarkably flat; Nick Carraway's perspective continuously wavers. Although much has been written about these narrators, we gain new insight into them once we consider, as I do here, that both of them are war veterans.

In the wake of war, then, writers used representational modes such as (but not only) tropes of omission, implication, and inference; gendered metaphors; unreliable narrators; and disjointed, jarring, narrative structures in order to evoke without naming the obscene realities and fantasies that shape the lives of their characters. By focusing on particular and highly suggestive examples in detail, *The New Death* develops an account of some ways in which injury is disguised, evoked, sanitized, and regendered in modernist writing. It pays close attention to the ways in which its chosen texts delineate the taboos about representing male wounds and death. It identifies some of these taboos by looking at the revisions that editors requested and that authors did or did not make in response. For instance, in *The Great Gatsby*, as we shall see in chapter 2, Fitzgerald defended his explicit depiction of Myrtle Wilson's torn breast. His debate with his editor over this detail reveals how closely his imagery skirted the boundary of acceptable violence. The detail was not just acceptable, Fitzgerald argued, but necessary. Meanwhile he eliminated other references to World War I. I interpret these various textual changes as steps in an elaborate dance between the author and his reader around and through the topic of war and the death it made new. As authors explored in their fiction the new world that the war had made, they encountered the resistance that, in turn, spurred their own modernist innovations in storytelling.

Modernist writers provide narrative maps of traumatic experience's strange effects on identity, speech, memory, and action. Their narratives anticipate the theorization of trauma by the likes of Dominic LaCapra, Shoshana Felman, and Cathy Caruth. Trauma theory has more often been invoked to explain the textual aesthetics not of World War I but of World War II. But as we shall see, in narratives written after World War I, traumatic experience often impinges on characters' speech and point of view and novels' plots. Nick Carraway, for one, cannot remember parts of his past. Though reminders of the war are, for him, everywhere, they often go without elaboration. The traumatic path surfaces, as Caruth suggests it will in *Unclaimed Experience*, not as story but as repeated action.[71] In losing Gatsby, Nick repeats one of the central experiences of war—losing a comrade. By repeating, he comes to possess knowledge about himself that had before been inarticulate. Rather than using contemporary trauma theory to interpret these narratives, however, I draw out the ways in which they engage with and diverge from their contemporaries' ideas about trauma and rituals of mourning.

With this overarching interpretive context in mind, the chapters turn to individual textualizations of New Death. Chapter 1 interprets the deceptive representation of male injury and death in Willa Cather's Pulitzer Prize–winning war novel *One of Ours* (1922). Long faulted by readers (Ernest Hemingway, most infamously) for sanitizing the war, this novel climaxes when its main character dies a "clean death" atop a parapet on the Western Front. I analyze this novel and its reception and find both to be more complicated responses to death than has been reckoned. The depiction of a worthwhile "clean death" certainly exemplifies the valorization of sacrifice so common during and after the war among mourners who needed to justify their losses. Cather's novel is not simply celebratory or hagiographic, however. The war's ugly damage is there in disguise. The novel splits the war's violence into different locales and blames it on diverse actors. Long before Cather's protagonist dies a "clean death," he suffers shameful and painful injuries at the hands of his wife and family. What damages him, then, is not the big guns but the upheaval of gender roles the war brings about. Cather links her protagonist's gender trouble to the war—not directly but by connecting its modernity to his wife (who drives cars, acts as a nurse, and conserves food). This subtle connection went largely undetected by Cather's contemporary audience, who were blinkered by their own gendered notions of war writing.

Chapter 2 considers a novel that is usually considered to have little or nothing to do with World War I but that is, I argue, centrally preoccupied with New Death. Fitzgerald's *Great Gatsby* is, as I have already suggested, Nick Carraway's attempt to assimilate the death of a fellow veteran, Jay Gatsby. Carraway's narration should be read as that of a shell-shocked soldier whose access to the past is imperfect. Witnessing Gatsby's death, burying him, setting the record straight, defending his reputation, all make Nick's account one that resembles (and may be a substitute for) a war story. But Nick's tale of losing Gatsby is far from idiosyncratic. It betrays the same ambivalence Americans felt about returning soldiers and the killing they endured, inflicted, and represented. Gatsby's murder and the need to justify it offer a belated analogy for coming to terms with the war. The novel signals that the work of burying and mourning the dead goes on long after the war is over.

Chapter 3 analyses the presentation of death in what is probably the most famous American novel about World War I, Ernest Hemingway's *A Farewell to Arms*. I take issue with the novel's self-proclaimed frankness about the war's "obscene" violence. Although Frederic Henry is wounded himself, although he kills and sees other men wounded and killed, the novel's central and climactic instance of violence is feminized. Catherine's Caesarean section leaves Frederic feeling alone and betrayed, but he remains a survivor. The female body becomes the site of the novel's most damaging, wasteful, and shameful wound.[72] Catherine's death suggests both the incompetence of authorities and the needlessness (or obscenity) of death—hallmarks of World War I stories. The dead female body also becomes the central object of the male narrator's depiction. Witnessing Catherine's death *is* Frederic's war story. This analogy displaces the war's violence elsewhere and translates it into a set of ideologically inflected and gendered figures. In the result, Hemingway's fiction sanitizes the violence of the war and recuperates a version of the heroic masculinity used in wartime propaganda that his narrator claims to reject.

Chapter 4 considers William Faulkner's *Sartoris*, a narrative about the difficulty of mourning a body that has been lost in the fighting and is therefore unavailable for interment. Such a loss was a frequent occurrence for families during World War I. Without the body, in Faulkner's novel, it is hard to speak of the loss and to do "the work of death." The missing body becomes a hole in the social fabric and an impalpable stumbling block to conversation and storytelling. This particular problem led Faulkner to invent several of the modernist strategies for which he is now recognized, particularly omission, delay, and the shuffle between different flawed and proto-stream-of-consciousness narratives. Faulkner's modernism emerges, I argue, from an attempt to represent the unspeakable, hidden horrors of death in the recent war.

The conclusion draws a connection from the canonical modernist American representations of New Death and another literature of violence: the popular genre of crime fiction and, in particular, to its "everyman," the soldier-turned-gangster. New Death's violence, we shall see, breaches the most entrenched canonical boundaries.

1 / "Clean" Wounds and Modern Women: World War I in *One of Ours*

*Woman, German woman or American woman, or every other sort of
woman, in the last war, was something frightening.*

*The very women who are most busy saving the bodies of men ... : these
women-doctors, these nurses, these educationalists, these public-spirited
women, these female saviours: they are all, from the inside, sending out
waves of destructive malevolence which eat out the inner life of a man, like
a cancer.*

        —D. H. LAWRENCE, *STUDIES IN CLASSIC AMERICAN LITERATURE*

In the epigraph, D. H. Lawrence relocates the spectacle of New Death
from a war between nations to a war between the sexes. He describes
the war as an occasion on which women exerted a "destructive malevolence" toward men, rather than as a conflict during which armies of
men wounded and killed each other. In this vision, male bodies suffer
not from wounds but from illness caused by a monstrously strong New
Woman.[1] Lawrence effectively sanitizes the effects of war first by leaving the soldier's wounds unspecified, then by directing his reader's gaze
away from the soldier to the active nurse, and finally by using illness as
a metaphor for wounds. Referring to the war allows Lawrence to evoke
righteous anger about what soldiers suffered and then to direct it at an
imaginary female perpetrator.

D. H. Lawrence's misogyny will come as no surprise. Indeed, this
kind of postwar male modernism led Sandra Gilbert and Susan Gubar
to posit sweeping differences between male and female modernisms and
how they relate to World War I.[2] But this chapter will trace a misogyny
similar to Lawrence's to a more surprising source: the woman writer
Willa Cather. This is surprising because, as Marilee Lindemann argues,
elsewhere Cather "responded directly and resistantly to the all-male
pantheon ... erected by her acquaintance D. H. Lawrence in his controversial *Studies in Classic American Literature*."[3] Arguing that Lawrence's
and Cather's works exhibit a similar misogyny goes against the grain
of Cather criticism.[4] Yet the ways in which her war novel *One of Ours*
(1922) subtly relocates the violence of World War I and its effects on male

bodies justifies the comparison. Her protagonist, Claude Wheeler, suffers wounds, illness, and indignities at home (and implicitly at the hands of his wife, Enid). Then he goes to war, where he sustains, in contrast, "three clean bullet holes" that kill him but mark him as a hero.[5] In McClintock's account of life at the front, "clean" wounds were those that sent a man home and did not kill him.[6] Cather's portrayal of a polluted domestic life allows her to sanitize, to make "clean," the deadly wounds of war. By focusing her reader's attention on a narrative conflict between the sexes, Cather, like Lawrence, refigures the dangers men face and what it means for them to be hurt and killed in war. Cather's novel ultimately blames the damage men suffer on female monstrosity—a monstrosity expressed, for her as for Lawrence, by female action and independence called up by the war effort.

Before turning to *One of Ours*, I want to distinguish the logic of the *post*war misogyny at the heart of Lawrence's remarks and Cather's novel from a different, war*time* (but enduring) misogynistic trope that conflates femininity with the home front. The culture of World War I, as Paul Fussell has famously insisted, was pervaded by "gross dichotomizing," by a habit of thought that separated "us" from "them." Though this "gross physical polarization" may have emerged from "the trench predicament," he suggests, it also became a way of articulating the soldier's feeling of separation not only from his invisible male enemy but from his distant support at home.[7] As Gilbert and Gubar have argued, the entire domestic world became conflated with the women whom soldiers left behind; this female, leisured home front became the object of their resentment. Henri Barbusse's *Under Fire* (1917) contains paradigmatic accounts of women enjoying life while men suffer in the trenches. The experience of going on leave in Paris reveals the "great truth" to Barbusse's squad of soldiers: "a Difference . . . becomes evident between human beings, a Difference *far deeper than that of nations* and with defensive trenches more impregnable; the clean-cut and truly unpardonable division that there is in a country's inhabitants between those who gain and those who grieve, those who are required to sacrifice all, *all*, to give their numbers and strength and suffering to the last limit, [and] those upon whom the others walk and advance, smile and succeed." The binary opposition of the trench is reversed and comes to separate men of both armies from the "women and children" back at home.[8] Soldiers suffer and sacrifice everything; women consume and profit.

In popular imagery, the United States' neutrality landed Americans on the wrong side of the divide between "those who sacrifice" and those who "gain": images of America as both an effeminate consumer and an overfed war profiteer implicated the entire nation, regardless of gender. If France was split in two—into soldiers (men) and civilians (not-men)—the entire population of the United States was frequently figured as a feminine figure. For instance, in James Montgomery Flagg's poster "Wake Up America!," America is personified as a sleeping woman, whose leisure signals both vulnerability and youthful, feminine carelessness.[9] After the United States' declaration of war in April 1917, the trope was redeployed within America, as it had been in other combatant nations, to figure a difference between soldiers (as men) and civilians (as women). Many illustrations, posters, and printed texts depict a world in which men suffer and fight while women stay home and profit from the wartime economy. According to this logic, women deserve scorn because they feed like vampires off the blood sacrifices of male war victims.

This imagery differs from the misogyny Lawrence and Cather direct at women, however. In their accounts, women are monstrous not because they stay home and live in ignorance of the war but precisely because they successfully join the war effort. In other words, misogyny originally directed at women and justified in terms of women's difference from men and their distance from the war gets refocused, with even greater animus, around the specter of woman as essentially similar to men. In both cases, the struggle between the sexes stands in for the war itself. Both cases suggest an attempt to imagine that men's real enemies are women. Placing the blame on women serves as one of the many ways in which the central fact of war, "injury," and specifically men's *consent* to injure each other and to sustain injury threatens, "disappear[s] from view," as Elaine Scarry suggests it often does.[10] Refiguring the perpetrators and the victims allows for a redescription and a sanitization of war.

Since the publication of *One of Ours* in 1922, its reception has turned on the questions of whether it accurately depicts the war and, by extension, whether women can write about soldiers' experiences. The novel won both popular and critical success, receiving the Pulitzer Prize in 1923. Many readers—several of them self-identified veterans—praised its accuracy as a picture of American war experience. But other critics condemned the novel because it offered a heroic version of the war, and some did so in terms that cast aspersion on Cather as a woman writer. H. L. Mencken's review did so in a rather subtle way by comparing *One of Ours* to its detriment with John Dos Passos's "bold realism" in *Three Soldiers* (1921):

> What spoils [Cather's] story is simply that a year or so ago a young soldier named John Dos Passos printed a novel called *Three Soldiers*. Until *Three Soldiers* is forgotten and fancy achieves its inevitable victory over fact, no war story can be written in the United States without challenging comparison with it. . . . At one blast it disposed of oceans of romance and blather. It changed the whole tone of American opinion about the war; it even changed the recollections of actual veterans of the war. They saw, no doubt, substantially what Dos Passos saw, but it took his bold realism to disentangle their recollection from the prevailing buncombe and sentimentality. . . . The war [Miss Cather] depicts has its thrills and even its touches of plausibility, but at bottom it is fought out, not in France, but on a Hollywood movie-lot.[11]

The opposition Mencken sets up between the "young soldier's" view of the war and that offered by "Miss Cather" hinges on the authors' gender and the access to war that gender supposedly provided. He offers this critique in literary terms but edges it with gender-biased belittling: a "blast" of "bold realism" versus "fancy," "oceans of romance and blather," "buncombe and sentimentality." In a letter Ernest Hemingway wrote to Edmund Wilson, he made a similar criticism in much harsher terms. He echoed the idea that Cather's battle scenes came out of Hollywood. In a phrase that has become notorious among critics, he complained that Cather copied—"Catherized"—the battle scenes from D. W. Griffith films. "Poor woman she has to get her war experience somewhere."[12] His withering attack faults Cather as a woman who dared to write about male experience.

The identity politics that characterize these early criticisms long continued to define the parameters of discussions of *One of Ours*. In Stanley Cooperman's 1967 *World War I and the American Novel*, his analysis of *One of Ours* and the war fiction of Edith Wharton justifies his conclusion that women cannot represent war. Both authors earn Cooperman's disapproval for "sentimentality and intrusive rhetoric"—for being too propagandistic and for offering a romantic view of the war.[13] He reiterates Mencken's and Hemingway's criticisms and declares that as a woman, Cather "knew very little about the war she was describing."[14] Collectively, such criticism reads the novel as a continuation of, rather than a reflection on, wartime propaganda. Women writers are pictured as beating the drums of war enthusiasm despite the fact that (or precisely because) they cannot fight themselves. From this perspective, the idealism of *One of Ours*'s protagonist, his sense of mission, and his heroic action in battle all sound not just preposterous but politically reprehensible. During the war, positive portrayals of the fight to "save democracy" helped support the war. The fact that Cather was writing after the war, when those dangers had passed, earned her no clemency.

Scholars have continued to disagree about the novel's attitude toward the war.[15] In 1975, David Stouck challenged the prevailing understanding that it celebrated war when he described the ironic separation between the protagonist's point of view and the novel's, between the heroic sentiment of a soldier-character and the detached perspective of his author-creator. Several subsequent critics have continued to drive a wedge between the novel's portrayal of its protagonist's "clean" wounds and its larger account of the war. As scholars have learned more about Cather's research for the book, particularly her use of letters written by her cousin G. P. Cather, it has become increasingly apparent that Cather based Claude's experience of the war on real-life models. His idealism, it seems, was real enough. Most recently, Steven Trout's *Memorial Fictions* makes an authoritative case for reading the novel as "a war memorial in prose," a text that "both employs and deconstructs patterns of meaning used by countless Americans in the 1920s to *remember* the war and to make sense of" its human costs.[16] For Trout, Cather both captures and questions American languages of commemoration. He argues that she "weaves" the "then-popular discourse of military remembrance and mourning" into "its modernist and ultimately cryptic rendering of war."[17] She evokes popular accounts of combat (including the iconic heroism of the "Lost Battalion") but, according to Trout, does so while remaining skeptical about the heroism those accounts celebrate. Crucial for my purposes here, she portrays New Death in all its gruesome detail, but she also depicts her protagonist's immunity to it. Despite his proximity to dead bodies and his awareness of the costs of war, he embraces it as a heroic opportunity. Indeed, Claude dreads death and putrefaction before he goes to war; once there, the ideas no longer threaten him. War itself paradoxically acts as the "clever shift" he has hoped for all along to "save himself from dissolution" (43). Through Claude, Cather honors the notions of heroic sacrifice that were so necessary to people still mourning the losses of the war. But through other characters and the novel's mobile narrator, she also documents the growing skepticism toward Claude's heroic vision.

The interpretation I advance here assigns slightly less agency to Cather as an author. Despite her text's decidedly ambiguous treatment of some languages of commemoration, its narrative logic scapegoats women for damages sustained by men in the war. On the other hand, I think her ambivalence toward certain aspects of the war drives most of the novel's misogynistic energy. As I will argue in relation to *A Farewell to Arms* as well, we cannot isolate this novel's treatment of the war from its treatment of heterosexual romance. The two halves of the novel are profoundly imbricated in ways most readers tend to ignore. Rather than depicting the war as traumatic for men, *One of Ours* traces its modern wounds to women—particularly to Claude's wife, Enid—and then jettisons them from the novel. Marilee Lindemann notes that both war and misogyny play a role in the recuperation of Claude's masculinity.[18] What has not been appreciated, though, is the relationship between the war, particularly its modernity, and Enid's "unnatural" femininity. Cather characterizes Enid through a series of tropes that pervaded representations of women's roles in the war: practicing home economy, nursing, and driving. Through these tropes, Enid comes to stand for a paradigmatic New Woman, who emerged from the war stronger than ever and whose new independence seemed profoundly threatening. She takes the fall for the damage the war does to men. In other words, Cather's novel develops two accounts of the war: one in her description of the trenches and another in a gendered metaphor far from the sounds of the guns. Read this way, Cather's war novel shares something of the cultural logic I will delineate in Hemingway's *A Farewell to Arms*. Both novels use gendered metaphors to make the war's damages felt.

"What's Wrong with That Boy?": Claude's Wounded Masculinity

One of Ours is a masculine coming-of-age story. Masculine achievement poses a problem for the protagonist, Claude Wheeler, who grows up in Nebraska feeling unfulfilled and tormented by vague desires. He articulates those desires to himself in capacious, empty terms: he desires a more "splendid" and meaningful "life" (46). He makes various attempts at self-realization, through education, work, marriage—all with frustrating results. The war provides the solution to Claude's problem. It provides him with a goal, a purpose, even a crusade. As a soldier, his discontents and fears disappear. The war's solution becomes ultimate when Claude dies a glorious battlefield death before he has to reckon with the disturbing news that his friend and comrade has been "blown to pieces" (367). Cather ends the novel on a further ironic note: Claude's mother concludes that death saved him from the otherwise inevitable loss of his naïve illusions.

Unlike most criticism of the novel, this chapter argues that its depiction of war begins back in its Nebraska section, in what Sinclair Lewis dubbed "the Enid problem." The novel's real interest, he argued in his review, was the problem posed by Claude's wife, who refuses to consummate their marriage: "Here is young Claude Wheeler, for all his indecisiveness a person of fine perceptions, valiant desires, and a thoroughly normal body, married to an evangelical prig who very much knows what she doesn't want."[19] Having created this interesting conflict, Lewis argues, Cather did not know how to finish her story. She "throws it away" by arbitrarily sending Claude off to war; "she might as well have pushed him down a well."[20] In lamenting the novel's turn to the war, Lewis underestimates the pathos that it was still capable of evoking in many readers (as many reviews attest). He also oversimplifies the novel's central problem, which centers not just in Enid but in Claude. In pronouncing that Claude has a "thoroughly normal body," Lewis ignores his dread of sexual encounters with women, his "sharp disgust for sensuality," and his peculiar vulnerability to fear, humiliation, and violent injury (Cather, *One of Ours*, 56). The "Enid problem" makes these other problems easy for Lewis—and many readers—to forget. Enid's refusal to consummate their marriage takes the focus away from Claude's ambivalent masculinity and leaves the reader to assume, as Lewis does, that Claude has a "normal" body, with normative desires. But before Enid refuses him, Claude seems less normal, even "queer," as his friend Ernest puts it (138). In Lewis's reading of the novel, he accepts and reiterates its scapegoat structure, remaining blind to the ideological work done by Cather's pejorative picture of the war era's New Woman.

Cather invites this reading by making Enid extremely unsympathetic. She portrays Enid's refusal of Claude on their wedding night in a way that forbids sympathy: Enid locks him out of their stateroom on the train with a complaint so trivial it cuts: "Claude, would you mind getting a berth somewhere out in the car tonight? . . . I think the dressing on the chicken salad must have been too rich" (195). The next morning, after Claude's humiliation has been compounded by a "long, dirty, uncomfortable ride," Enid greets him with a "fresh smiling face" and the (cruelly?) ironic observation that "[she] never lose[s] things on the train" (198)—including her virginity. Enid's portrayal plays a crucial role in the novel's economy of sympathy. As if in accord with a law of constants that governs the distribution of the reader's finite amount of sympathy, Cather demonizes Enid so that the reader will begin to favor Claude. The explicitness of the "Enid problem" compensates for and adumbrates the "thing not named" in *One of Ours*: Claude's "problem."[21]

This more latent conflict remains cloaked in obscurity. Claude is simply, as his mother describes it, "on the wrong side" of his differences with and from the men around him (53). The vagueness of this phrase reflects not only a mother's desire to shield a beloved son but the imprecision that characterizes this conflict within the text at large. Cather equivocates about whether Claude's differences reflect his inadequacies or those of his society. Claude's "case," as Timothy R. Cramer has observed, recalls Cather's earlier story "Paul's Case," in which the protagonist's unnamed difficulties haunt him and the text that bears his name.[22] The apparent inadequacies of both these male characters reflect the changing notions of manhood during this period and the generalized "crisis of masculinity" that those changes engendered. Recent scholars (including Anthony Rotundo, Michael Kimmel, Gail Bederman, and Greg Forter) have all worked to specify the origins of this cultural shift and to detail its various consequences in actual life and in the symbolic realm.[23] Cather's text works, in precisely the opposite way, to hide and generalize masculinity's discontents. Vague descriptions of Claude's "problem" pervade the first section of the novel: he harbors unreasonable fears; his attempts to be valiant fail; he is easy to manipulate; and he pleases himself best by "impos[ing] physical tests and penances upon himself" (29). Cather's portrait emerges: weak, at the mercy of his emotions, and vulnerable to others' manipulations, Claude develops masochistic tendencies. Claude's masochism shapes the reader's response; his impatience with himself exhausts our patience in turn, which is worn thin by the repetitious, and repetitiously superficial, accounts of what is "wrong" with him (53).

Claude's problem provokes continual speculation:

Claude knew, and everybody else knew, seemingly, that there was something wrong with him. . . . Mr. Wheeler was afraid he was one of those visionary fellows who make unnecessary difficulties for themselves and other people. Mrs. Wheeler thought the trouble with her son was that he had not yet found his Saviour. Bayliss was convinced that his brother was a moral rebel, that behind his reticence and his guarded manner he concealed the most dangerous opinions. . . . Claude was aware that his energy, instead of accomplishing something, was spent in resisting unalterable

conditions, and in unavailing efforts to subdue his own nature.
When he thought he had at last got himself in hand, a moment
would undo the work of days; in a flash he would be transformed
from a wooden post into a living boy. He would spring to his
feet . . . because the old belief flashed up in him with an intense
kind of hope, an intense kind of pain,—the conviction that there
was something splendid about life, if he could but find it! (103)

Here Cather introduces a series of codes to describe what is "queer
about that boy," each inflected by a different ideological perspective and
anxiety: his father fears he is a "visionary fellow" (a Greenwich Village
"artistic" type); his mother fears he is a sinner; his brother fears he is a
secretive radical. The characters who attempt to name what is "wrong"
with Claude fall short—a warning for later generations of readers and
critics. For although Cather's lack of specificity invites interpretation,
it also defies it.[24] That said, a certain gender trouble seems undeniable:
Claude fails to express a maleness that is often assumed to be natural
and struggles with "his own nature." Not surprisingly, recent critics have
read Claude's problem as that other unnameable, the love that dare not
speak its name. Echoing Cather's own account of her aesthetic practice
of withholding information in "The Novel Démeublé," Timothy Cramer
glosses Claude's mysterious problem as a counterpart of her lesbianism:
"the thing not named in Cather's life, of course, is her homosexuality,
and its presence is divined throughout much of her work."[25] According
to this line of thinking, the war provides a solution to Claude's crisis by
giving him a chance to work and live not just in a homosocial relationship to other men but in an explicitly homosexual one. Once in France,
Claude meets David Gerhardt, and their relationship eventually inspires
confidence in Claude.[26] But reading their relationship as "openly gay,"
as Cramer does, overstates matters. Army life does consolidate Claude's
masculinity, but the malaise it cures seems to stem from broader problems than Cramer considers.

Cather's depiction of Claude's problem evokes a widely perceived
crisis in American masculinity. For decades, people had worried that
American men were losing ground, becoming weak and feminine.
Urbanization and a culture of consumption both seemed to limit men's
physical activity and threatened to make them "soft." Teddy Roosevelt
famously called American men to a more "strenuous life," urging outdoor adventure and scouting. Many trends (such as body building) and
institutions (including elite male boarding schools) evoked this crisis

to create demand. Relevant to the argument here, expanded rights for women seemed like incursions into male domains of power. During the war, popular imagery figured joining the military as an "opportunity" for men, even though registration for the draft was, after all, mandatory. However, worries about masculinity did not disappear with the war. On the contrary, as we shall see in the next chapter, the experience of "shell-shock" exposed even greater vulnerability. We can hear an articulation of the fear that men's nerves made them weak in a 1919 article in which "American Nervousness," an ephemeral neurosis, is described as sapping American manhood. "Our whole continent has been growing nervous. Everywhere we have had a steady increase in all forces making for neuroticism," Frederick E. Pierce worried in the *North American Review*.[27] According to Pierce, modern life was corroding the virile traditions of American life. In Cather's various allusions to Claude's "nerves," she inscribes this perceived cultural crisis on her character's body. Claude recalls his life before the war as a "nervous tension" (*One of Ours*, 332). He worries that his name makes him a "sissie."[28] Cather figures what's "wrong" with Claude through a series of sexually- and gender-coded keywords, including "nervous" and "queer," that, as Marilee Lindemann puts it, "snap, crackle, and pop" with the tensions of "acute anxiety and ideological work."[29]

Claude's problem thus surfaces as an overdetermined resistance to, or failure to meet, a variety of social expectations that he faces as a man. In some moments, for instance, Claude's inadequacy surfaces as a lack of vocation. He chafes at the question of money and profession: "I don't believe I can ever settle down to anything," he tells a friend; he feels "a childish contempt for money-values"—a phrase that traces his failure to come of age to his attitudes toward modern, consumer society (52, 101). This failure to fit in to existing economic structures seems odd in a novel about a western farmer. Claude's economic and social standing locate him within a producer class of yeoman farmers rarely associated with effeminacy or "nervousness." Claude will inherit a farm; he is neither at leisure nor alienated from his labor (as are his father's hired men). Instead, the strength he exerts with his male body on what will be his own land would seem to offer a solid material basis on which to build a coherent identity. But it does not because, in Cather's novel, the West—so long imagined as an escape from the degenerate, modern world—has been infiltrated by both industrial machinery and what Anthony Giddens describes as "disembedding mechanisms," or new technologies that reorganize space and time and uproot individuals from their cultural and vocational traditions.[30] Claude, unlike most of his community, responds to these changes with hostility. "With prosperity came a kind of callousness," he muses; "the people themselves had changed" (101, 102). Cather figures this callousness as a new consumerism enabled, and symbolized, by the automobile: "The orchards . . . were now left to die out of neglect. It was less trouble to run into town in an automobile and buy fruit than it was to raise it" (102).

In this instance, Claude's reflections resonate with more narrative authority and eloquence than is usual. His thoughts in this passage might easily have been lifted from one of Cather's other novels or essays.[31] Visions of the lost Eden of a fruit orchard appear throughout her fiction; she repeatedly figures encroaching modernity as an assault on such a pastoral setting. This signature trope appears most memorably in *O Pioneers!* (1913) when an orchard provides the setting for the novel's climactic murder scene. In *One of Ours*, it is embedded in a lost past, when Claude recalls his father's murder of a cherry tree: "The beautiful, round-topped cherry tree, full of green leaves and red fruit,—his father had sawed it through! It lay on the ground beside its bleeding stump" (27). Claude identifies the "bleeding stump" of the cherry tree with himself and his future. The scene and its memory leave Claude feeling angry and paralyzed; his father's power to cut down the fruitful tree turns the pastoral landscape of childhood into a site of Oedipal castration.

With the vision of the murdered cherry tree, Cather portrays the advent of modernity as a brutally inflicted wound to a male body. The details of Claude's castration anxiety seem inspired not by Freud but by American myth, in which cherry trees have an archetypal significance in the relationship between fathers and sons. In the tale of George Washington and his father's cherry tree, the father's law stands for right, honesty, and forbearance. Young George breaks that law by cutting the tree down. But when questioned, he finds that he "cannot tell a lie." Thus, in breaking the father's law, he learns to respect and abide by it. Once chastened, George Washington grows to embody and enforce the law himself, taking his place in a patriarchal line and ultimately becoming the "father" of the nation. By reversing this myth, Cather suggests the nation's modern degeneration. In the Wheeler family, Mr. Wheeler does not teach Claude respect for the past, since he chops down the tree he himself had cultivated for years; nor does he teach Claude to respect the future, since the tree will never bear fruit again. Mr. Wheeler commits an act of violence that disrupts the passage of just rule from one generation of American men to the next. In Claude's fall from innocence, the father's will seems capricious, unpredictable, impossible to learn, and despicable to imitate, leaving the son ambivalent about becoming a man in his own right. Not wanting to be like his father, Claude is bereft of male models to emulate. This episode constitutes the novel's primal scene—the original, mythic conflict that structures Claude's problem and its narration in the novel. The whole novel seems to be an attempt to reverse this action. Or, to put this another way, it foreshadows without naming where Claude's fate will lead. This evocative account of patriarchal brutality resonates, however faintly, with the trope of filicide used by the likes of Wilfred Owen to condemn the war as one in which fathers callously slew their sons.[32]

This primal scene deidealizes the West as a masculine space free both of women and of domestic entanglement. The Wheeler farm is no longer virgin land; it has been claimed and violated in a scene of implicitly sexual violence. Modernity's arrival is signaled as a brutal wound. The adventure of settlement over, the only masculine way to engage in the frontier is to fight to preserve it—to fight a battle that has already been lost. Claude witnesses the scene of pastoral trauma and becomes a figure of melancholic nostalgia. Several episodes hint at the potential eruption of trauma on the farm: Claude's obsession with dying and decay (43); the hired man's ("Jerry"—slang for German soldier) cruelty to animals, which is so bad that Claude thinks of it even to himself in vague terms— "he had seen things happen in the barn that he positively couldn't tell his father" (41); dead steers, dead chickens, and suffocated pigs. All of these provoke profound anxiety from Claude and seem to play on the foreboding that is, for him, both memory and anticipation.

Like both Claude's trepidation and his sensitivity to death, his nostalgia separates him from other men: Mr. Wheeler speculates in land and chops down the tree; Bayliss wants to tear down the oldest home in town, built (complete with the traditionally masculine retreat, the billiard room) by two "carousing" "boys" back when the town was "still a tough little frontier settlement" (109); and Ralph buys an endless series of modern "labour-saving devices" that are too difficult to use (19). In contrast, Claude shares his mother's attitude toward the past. When their neighbor Mr. Royce converts his mill to electric power, he thinks, "There's just one fellow in the county will be sorry to see the old wheel go, and that's Claude Wheeler" (148). Seen from this perspective, Claude's gender "problem" stems from his location in time. The frontier used to be a space where "carousing" "boys" could be men. It was a site of adventure, beauty, and drama: rugged Nature *made* men. All that has passed Claude by. Machines and the matrix of consumer culture that accompany them have made western life too easy, too mundane, not "splendid." His quest in "a modern wasteland" against "the foes of materialism" (though difficult, as Rosowski notes) does not seem to be enough to bring Claude's masculinity into being.[33] Encroaching modernity makes Claude's masculinity seem vulnerable, anachronistic, and effeminate.

Cather crystallizes the threat modernity poses to Claude's masculinity in the scene of an accident, which connects mechanical violence to the male body with a debilitating dependence on women. This scene, described by a neighbor, acts as a lynchpin for the novel's ideological conflicts:

> "Have you heard Claude Wheeler got hurt the day before yesterday? . . . It was the queerest thing I ever saw. He was out with the team of mules and a heavy plough, working the road in that deep cut between their place and mine. The gasoline motor-truck came along, making more noise than usual, maybe. But those mules know a motor truck, and what they did was pure cussedness. They begun to rear and plunge in that deep cut. I was working my corn over in the field and shouted to the gasoline man to stop, but he didn't hear me. Claude jumped for the critters' heads and got 'em by the bits, but by that time he was all tangled up in the lines. . . . They carried him right along, swinging in the air, and finally ran him into the barb-wire fence and cut his face and neck up." (137–38)

Modernity has invaded the family farm: Claude works in a "deep cut" that evokes both a primordial wound and the land's division into pieces of private property. The pastoral labor of man and beast has been transformed as modern machinery, in the form of a motor truck, brings terrible consequences. Cather's "picture making" of Claude's accident evokes archetypal expressions of masculine anxiety about dependence, lack of agency, and the entanglements of fate that seem to deprive men of their power and autonomy.[34] "It was the queerest thing I ever saw": it resembles a fantasy in which all man's traditional subjects rise up against Claude—the machine, the earth, the beasts of burden, and even inanimate tools (plough and wire) conspire against their master and inventor. Yet this scene pictures modernity's wound in terms that are both primordial and historically particular: the image of a man tangled in barbed wire and the anachronistic use of animals amid machines does allude to the closing and domestication of the American frontier but also to the apocalyptic landscape of no-man's-land on the Western Front.

Having emphasized the fragility of male bodies in an industrial-ized world, Cather goes on to suggest that the traditional masculine response—stoicism, or attempts at heroic denial of bodily suffering—further endangers them. Claude attempts to deny his wound, resuming his work the day after his accident and so becoming seriously ill. There is no particular glory to be gained by working in the hot sun the day after his accident, but Claude does it anyway, acting out a masochistic martyr fantasy and displaying his ability to endure physical trials. Cather sug-gests that, in the absence of meaningful opportunities to demonstrate heroism, the performance of masculinity has degenerated into a series of futile and self-destructive gestures. Claude's masculinity emerges in relation to traumatic repetition, as a dynamic in which wounds can only be compensated for by further trials. The male body becomes increas-ingly vulnerable, even as it performs manliness. Here, more than in the novel's ending, Cather signals the tragic futility to which a regime of heroic masculinity leads.

In the scene of Claude's accident and the plot developments that lead from it, Cather explores the war's damage at a distance and in metaphor. This element of the novel anticipates how Cather would represent the war a few years later, in *The Professor's House* (1925). As Cather critics includ-ing Steven Trout have shown, the war is "the thing not named" in that novel, which depicts postwar life in a midwestern college town.[35] In *One of Ours*, too, the war's damage surfaces elsewhere and in disguise, in the relationship between Claude and Enid. At the level of plot, what happens is simple: after being cut by the barbed wire, Claude becomes infected with erysipelas (a bacterial infection that causes the eruption of painful red blisters, especially on the face). He looks like nothing as much as a wounded soldier, wrapped in cotton dressing, confused by morphine, and tossing "restlessly" on his sick bed. "He [is] disgusting to himself; when he touche[s] the welts on his forehead and under his hair, he [feels] unclean and abject" (118). Claude is wounded, he is nursed by Enid, and he falls in love with her. He imagines that marrying her will solve his "problem," as if playing opposite a woman in a marriage plot will bring his manhood to the fore. Claude is disappointed in this hope, since Enid refuses to play the feminine role that he casts her in. This plot develop-ment and the imagery that surrounds it establishes "the New Woman" in the role of, as Lawrence would have it, a "destroyer." It does offer a "solution" of sorts to Claude's "problem," since marrying Enid *does* make him seem "thoroughly normal," as Sinclair Lewis puts it—both to char-acters within the novel and to readers. The spectacle of Claude's male abjection is replaced, as his body heals, by a narrative focus on Enid's "not natural" (131) femininity. As a result, Claude's struggle evokes sympathy; rather than a fool, a misfit, or "queer," he seems more like a victim. After this point in the narrative, Claude's crisis becomes the "Enid problem." Enid's rejection of traditional femininity acts as a magnet, binding Claude's inadequacies to it and liberating him from their taint.

As in other postwar fiction discussed here, an unsympathetic female figure serves to distract the reader from the discomfiting spectacle of male inadequacy and vulnerability. This narrative strategy appeared during and after the war as a way of framing and containing anxiety-provoking evidence that manliness was a rather fragile bulwark against death and danger. For instance, one Red Cross poster pictured a nurse speaking over the body of a wounded soldier, saying "If I fail, he dies" (see figure 2). The scandal at the heart of this image is, of course, the wounded soldier: why were men counted so cheap? Why were male bodies yielded up en masse in a war of attrition? Although the wounded male figure implicitly poses such questions, the motto redirects the viewer's gaze to women and what they can(not) do. The poster gives the responsibility for the soldier's life to the nurse, and the crisis of whether or not the man will live becomes, instead, a crisis over whether or not this woman will act effectively. Putting the problem in these terms, I suggest, transfers an inordinate amount of responsibility for male wounds to women. When read as a larger statement about the war (admittedly beyond what the artists intended), the poster offers a false proposition. In fact, this man's life depends on a great deal more than this woman's success or failure. The artists seem to admit, almost in spite of themselves, the false limitations of their representation—to admit that the nurse is merely an artificial placeholder in a much larger equation, rather than an agent in her own right. By using the same model on both sides of the poster, the artists created a strange impression of stasis and helplessness. The image's inadequate realism makes it seem as if the woman is gazing into a mirror rather than enlisting the help of another.[36] This odd visual repetition adumbrates the poster's intrinsic problem, its fake self-enclosure. Because the problem of male injury has been presented in such narrow terms, nothing like a full solution is possible. So, too, the real problem of male wounds was far more complicated and involved whole societies' consent to a war of attrition. Making women feel responsible for male wounds was one way of manipulating their support for the war. Enlisting them in circumscribed roles of caregiving may have kept some women from inventing other roles to play.

FIGURE 2. "If I Fail, He Dies," S. A. Iciek and A. G. McCoy, black and white lithograph, 28 × 21 inches, circa 1918. (Hoover Institution Archives, Stanford University)

In the tableau of Claude's sickroom, Cather turns her reader's attention away from his abject and wounded male body to the abnormal feminine body that nurses him. At this point, the novel turns toward resolution and does so by demonizing Enid, on the one hand, and celebrating Claude's experience of fighting in World War I, on the other. Cather's novel wishfully splits Claude's problem—modernity—in two. Enid comes to embody the threatening aspects of modernity and machine culture, while the war comes to stand for an ironically antiquated, antimodern crusade carried out in the name of "history." The drive for narrative resolution outweighs the imperatives of realism (and, we might add, feminism).

Claude imagines himself fighting not just the Germans but an attitude toward modernity that exists in the United States as well: "No battlefield or shattered country he had seen was as ugly as this world would be if men like his brother Bayliss controlled it altogether. Until the war broke out, he had supposed that they did control it; his boyhood had been clouded and enervated by that belief. The Prussians had believed that too, apparently. But the event had shown that there were a great many people left who cared about something else" (419). Claude's anachronistic fantasy enables him to filter out awareness not just of the war's ugliness but of its modernity: "The intervals of the distant artillery fire grew shorter, as if the big guns were tuning up, choking to get something out.... The sound of the guns had from the first been pleasant to him, had given him a feeling of confidence and safety; tonight he knew why. What they said was, that men could still die for an idea; and would burn all they had made to keep their dreams. He knew the future of the world was safe" (419). "Safe," the phrase goes, "for democracy." In the way Cather's text echoes Wilson's famous declaration, it registers ideology's power to shape point of view and experience far beyond the limits one might imagine. The sounds of the "big guns" meant something else altogether to most who heard them: not that the "world was safe" but that machines had facilitated a new level of danger. In 1918 (when this scene is set), the German army was using the long-range "Paris Gun" to send an altogether different message to the civilians of France: that *nothing* was "safe"; that the front lines of the battle extended to what seemed like almost infinite distances. The "big guns" metonymically evoke the range of innovative technologies used in World War I—including not just artillery but also submarines, airplanes, chemical weapons, and so on—and so mark the *modernization and mechanization* of war, the very things Claude wants to vanquish. Yet ironically, Claude hears the sounds of bombardment— the voice of mechanized war, pure and untranslated—as evidence that he is winning a war against modernity. In moments such as these, Cather's novel strains against a difficult contradiction.

The war's destructive violence does find its way into the novel— but not where it is most often sought, in the final third, set in France. Instead, the most dystopic elements of the war and its modernity surface and disappear in the Nebraska part of the novel. Enid embodies what is to Claude—and to Cather, I think—the most frightening aspect of the war: its man-eating modernity, its reduction of heroic manliness to the futile gestures that precede mechanized slaughter. And here, Cather's narrative *does* harbor and structure romantic sentiments; Cather, too, is fighting Claude's fight. What is most curious, though, is that her narrative frames the fight against modernity as a war between the sexes, as a fight for sympathy between Claude and the New Woman. *One of Ours* conflates a nostalgia for "natural" preindustrial frontier life with a nostalgia for traditional femininity and a traditionally heterosexual union and division of labor.

The "Enid Problem" Revisited: Enid's Dangerous Femininity

In Book II ("Enid"), Cather's novel turns away from what is "wrong" with Claude to what is "not natural" (131) about Enid's femininity. Enid comes to stand for the war's dystopic aspects through her association with a series of visual and verbal tropes that present women in relation to the war effort. Cather specifically refers to popular media and the powerful ways gender had been displayed in images, including war posters, designed to generate consent for the war. Walton Rawls reports that "America printed more than twenty million copies of perhaps twenty five hundred posters, more posters than all the other belligerents combined." Cather's novel corroborates his claim that "it was on the main streets of Home Front America that these posters did their job so effectively."[37]

In *One of Ours*, Cather alludes to visual propaganda in a variety of ways. Claude's fight against modernity echoes pictures of the American forces as "Pershing's Crusaders," a band of chivalric knights (see figure 11, in chapter 4). Before that, when Claude tells his neighbor Leonard that he plans to enlist, Leonard responds,

> "Better wait a few weeks and I'll go with you. I'm going to try for the Marines. They take my eye."
>
> Claude, standing at the edge of the tank, almost fell backward. "Why, what—what for?"
>
> Leonard looked him over. "Good Lord, Claude, you ain't the only fellow around here that wears pants! What for? Well, I'll tell you what for," he held up three red fingers threateningly, "Belgium, the Lusitania, Edith Cavell. That dirt's got under my skin. I'll get my corn planted, and then Father'll look after Susie till I come back." (236)

Leonard lists the highlights of the Allied propaganda campaign: "Belgium, the Lusitania, Edith Cavell." All three were pictured in propaganda posters that appealed particularly to men by presenting the war as assaults on vulnerable women. Cather draws our attention to visual mediation: the Marines "take [Leonard's] eye"; "he looked Claude over" before suggesting they both "wear[] pants"—a visual trope for manhood; his words are accompanied by a striking physical pose—"he held up three red fingers threateningly." Visual tropes of female vulnerability in need of male defense have reinforced Leonard's sense of his role as a man in the family (he "wears pants") and of his wife's vulnerability ("Father'll look after Susie").

Cather depicts the impact of printed visual propaganda even more explicitly in her characterization of Mahailey, the Wheelers' servant, who takes graphic representations of the war as pictures of reality. Mahailey feels as if she has direct access to the war through these images. Her distance from the war is overcome by the immediacy of the graphic image, and she feels herself to be at war. Though Mahailey is simple-minded, her response to propaganda alerts the reader to the reach of visual propaganda. In this way, Cather provides narrative evidence for what historians would describe as the war's totalization, its militarization and mobilization of civilian life. Even by staying at home and within a traditionally feminine domestic sphere, women such as Mahailey begin to think of themselves as combatants on the home front. Total war was a byproduct not only of an industrialized economy but also of new modes of mass communication, including newspapers, film, and war posters.

Alerted by Cather to the effectiveness of visual propaganda, and the extent to which it reached Americans even in rural areas, I suggest that we attend to the ways in which Enid reflects and condenses images of a certain kind of active and modern femininity that appeared in war posters. Unlike the images of women in need of male defense that seem to motivate Leonard, many posters figured women as contributing to the war effort in a variety of ways: by doing either "women's work" or more masculine kinds of labor on the home front and by working abroad near the front. As I have argued elsewhere, such representations hold out a potential to advance feminist ideals.[38] They suggest the war sparked a reevaluation of the notion of female passivity and fragility and offered a new range of actions to women. But however positive these roles might have seemed to some people, in Cather's novel they become, quite surprisingly, the signs of a dangerous female independence.

Cather's portrayal of Enid, I suggest, emerges directly from a series of tropes that called for women to participate in the war effort. Even when Enid seems reassuringly traditional, as when she sews her trousseau, she evokes the modern femininity pictured in war posters such as W. T. Benda's "You Can Help" (figure 3).[39] Even this modest activity, its legend suggests, can help win the war. Such images left women in the home but placed the home on the front line. In other words, they strike a fragile balance between traditional and new roles for women. Even as they assert women's place in the domestic sphere, these images covertly modernize, nationalize, and professionalize women's roles. Despite their traditional imagery, they contribute to an ultimately radical change in the way "women's work" could be understood. Such images

FIGURE 3. "You Can Help," Wladyslaw Theodore Benda,
black and white lithograph, 20 × 30 inches, circa 1918.
(Archives and Manuscripts Collection, Sterling Memorial
Library, Yale University)

were central to the processes of national incorporation that Claude finds
so alienating and of which Cather's narrative at large seems so disap-
proving. Most negative, in Cather's account, is the extent to which such
images covertly modernize traditional labor. Enid's execution of traditional women's work is problematically but surreptitiously modern.
This makes her faults as a wife hard to see: "She managed a house easily

FIGURE 4. "Help Feed Yourself," anonymous, published by the U.S. Food Administration, Washington, DC, black, white, and red lithograph, 16 × 24 inches. (Hoover Institution Archives, Stanford University)

and systematically. On Monday morning Claude turned on the washing machine before he went to work, and by nine o'clock the clothes were on the line. Enid liked to iron, and Claude had never before in his life worn so many clean shirts, or worn them with such satisfaction. She told him he need not economize in working shirts; it was as easy to iron six as three" (*One of Ours*, 209). Enid's domestic labor is both mechanized and rationalized according to clock time. Moreover, as if benefiting from the workplace-efficiency innovations of Fordism and Taylorism, more work simply makes Enid more efficient: it is "as easy to iron six shirts as three." But although Claude wears his shirts "with satisfaction," Cather portrays that pleasure as a poor substitute for the fulfillment of more primal desires.

The scientific domestic economy that defines Enid's housekeeping and cooking reflects the discourse used to mobilize women on the home front, in their kitchens, parlors, and gardens. One of Enid's most unsympathetic moments emerges directly from wartime educational propaganda aimed at women. The U.S. Food Administration used a series of posters to indoctrinate a primarily female audience into a new science of domestic economy. One poster in this series informs its viewers that unfertilized poultry eggs "last longer" (see figure 4). Enid uses this piece of scientific information in *One of Ours* and separates her hens from the rooster. The neighbors, who prefer to do things the "natural" and "old-fashioned" way, disapprove of Enid's "fanatic" enforcement of sexual discipline and condemn her modern methods (203, 204). Through their remarks, Cather frames an essentially positive and empowering wartime script for women as one that makes them monstrous and unfeminine. Both Enid's scientific farming and her vegetarianism emerge directly from publicity disseminated as part of the war effort, in which "Eat Less Meat" and "Eat Less Wheat" were popular commands. Women were supposed to support the war by disciplining the family's appetite (see figure 5). In *One of Ours*, such traits take on negative connotations as the symptoms of Enid's retreat from sexuality and the body, which leaves Claude feeling sexually frustrated and underfed.

But Cather grounds Enid's lack of sympathy in other, less traditional wartime images of women as well. In addition to collecting money and goods, knitting for soldiers and refugees, and growing and conserving food, women also participated in the war in less "feminine" ways. Not long after the United States declared war in 1917, the navy began enlisting women as a way of coping with an intense demand for personnel.[40] In addition to those who enlisted in the armed forces, many women were

FIGURE 5. "In Her Wheatless Kitchen She Is Doing Her Part to Help Win the War," Howard Chandler Christy, color lithograph, 15 × 30 inches, circa 1918. (Special Collections Rare Books & Manuscripts, University of Minnesota Library)

mobilized by volunteer organizations such as the Red Cross, the Salvation Army, and the YMCA/YWCA. According to historian Susan Zeiger, "women's work at the front was much more than a simple extension of their participation in the civilian labor force. It was also military or quasi-military service and therefore had profound implications for a society grappling with questions about the nature of women and their place in the public life of the nation, in war and peacetime."[41] As women began to work near the front, posters contained images that played with the possibility of women taking traditionally male roles. We catch a glimpse of this in "The Salvation Army Lassie" (figure 6). This poster works to reassure viewers that serving abroad will not require women to sacrifice their femininity. "The Salvation Army Lassie" exemplifies a traditional vision of women serving men. She is in the poster's background, while the male soldier stands in the foreground and speaks for her. Despite the poster's insistence on female subordination, however, it flirts verbally and visually with the similarity between the soldier and the "quasi-military" female volunteer. Its text, "Oh, Boy! *that's* the Girl!," demonstrates the arbitrary signification of words such as "boy" and "girl." They both wear khaki uniforms, steel helmets, and youthful smiles—features which create an impression of sameness and exchangeability. This poster gives visual shape to an actual gender confusion surrounding the mobilization of women in France. The presence of Salvation Army "Lassies" was predicated on male dependence on women and on a notion that women could contribute in a fundamental way to the American Expeditionary Force's (AEF) strength. Male soldiers, it was argued, would naturally be homesick; and American women could comfort them in a way French women, imagined as inherently more sexual, could (or should) not. The Salvation Army, the Red Cross, and the hospitality services of the armed forces took a good deal of care to supervise and desexualize the interactions of American soldiers and their female support corps. The kind of bond that Salvation Army "Lassies" such as this one were supposedly able to offer male soldiers was continually figured as a sibling or maternal one. "American women . . . were expected to provide the troops with a wholesome but winning distraction from French prostitutes or lovers"; American women, by their presence, could comfort soldiers and help them observe the AEF's "policy of sexual continence" against venereal disease.[42] In other words, women working at the front had to walk a thin line between being feminine (comforting) but not too feminine (alluring)—they had to enact their difference from soldiers while still being their "chums." They had to be both domestic and professional.

FIGURE 6. "The Salvation Army Lassie. Oh, Boy! That's the Girl!," anonymous, color lithograph, 30 × 40 inches, 1918. (Hoover Institution Archives, Stanford University)

Such imagery inflects Cather's portrait of Enid's asexuality. Enid refuses her husband as a sexual partner and often thinks of him as a brother or even a son. Cather's portrait recalls the deliberate desexualization of women war workers in France, who "were envoys of the American home front, representatives of the mothers, wives, and sisters left behind," but as such were represented in imagery that emphasized "sentimentality and homey comfort" over sexuality.[43] Policies governing the recruitment of women (in the armed forces and in relief agencies) largely "excluded those with husbands in the war. . . . Organizations were looking for a special type of volunteer" who would not be "preoccupied with finding their loved ones" and who were "independent of familial and marital ties."[44] In direct correlation, Enid describes herself as "not naturally drawn to people" and "free" to move abroad (Cather, *One of Ours*, 131).

The official and conscious intent of assuring sisterly or maternal roles for women was to contain and discipline the threat of female sexuality, particularly the threat of its free expression outside the bounds of marriage. But this campaign to desexualize women's presence had an ironic result in that it gave form and coherence to a new kind of female independence which was equally, or perhaps even more, threatening. Certainly, Enid's lack of sexual desire is her most threatening quality, the one that makes her most unsympathetic to readers and critics—*that* is what exercises Sinclair Lewis in his review. The "Enid problem" is that Claude needs Enid, but Enid does not want Claude: he needs a wife to make him the man of the house; he needs her care and her domestic labor as a grounding contrast to his masculinity. But the very things that make Enid useful and necessary to Claude also make her strangely independent and unnaturally asexual.

Cather's description of this lack of traditional reciprocity evokes the new gender relations established during the war. Claude's need for Enid originally surfaces as a need for nursing. After Claude's accident in the barbed wire, she visits him every day, she brings him flowers—reversing the traditional courtship ritual, as Rosowski notes[45]—and she helps him pass the time while he convalesces. Enid's nursing activity conflates traditional femininity (providing support to men) with New Womanhood (lack of concern for decorum). If this conflation causes confusion to Mrs. Wheeler and to Claude—blinding them to Enid's lack of physical attraction to him, and to her sexual unavailability—this too alludes to a constellation of fascination and anxiety that coalesced around the figure of the nurse during the war. As we will see in chapter 3, the image of the nurse merges both feminine roles (nurturing) and masculine roles (being a new kind of soldier). We can see this in the ethical confusion provoked by the murder of Edith Cavell: was she a civilian (a woman) or a soldier (a man)?[46] In killing her, did the Germans commit an atrocity on an innocent civilian woman or a justifiable act of war on the body of an enemy? As a "quasi-military" person, Cavell's status was a source of disagreement. Total war confused the gendered categories that war had traditionally enforced and made visible. Enid's role in nursing Claude invites us to see her as powerful and to see him, by contrast, as weak and ill, making it easy to read him (as Lewis does) as her victim. Cather makes Enid's nursing duplicitous and anxiety provoking rather than admirable or courageous. In this, Cather's novel resembles largely anxiety-ridden male-authored representations of nurses, rather than female-authored ones. Although she treats nursing rather briefly, her portrait predicts the nurse's popularity as a signal figure in the mediation of postwar gender anxiety. Other texts deflect anxiety about masculinity onto a nurse figure, who heals wounded men only to entrap them in a painful and compromised life. This trope of the dangerous nurse—a version of Lawrence's threatening "woman-saviour"—threads through fiction by male American modernists, including Hemingway and Faulkner, as we shall see in subsequent chapters.

During the war, the profession of female nursing confounded gender difference by merging categories of soldiers and civilians and by reversing its opposite, the other popular plotline in propaganda: women in need of male rescue. Female nursing also raised questions of sexuality and propriety by bringing upper- and middle-class women into unsupervised, physical contact with soldiers. But if the nurse was a locus of anxiety about women's new independence, in the hands of some postwar writers, the sexuality of female nurses also provided the means of restoring gender difference: feminine sexual weakness foils male independence. Cather's narrative does not provide the same comfort. She portrays the nurse as desexualized and, in consequence, dangerous.

Cather figures Enid's monstrously independent femininity most deliberately through another trope: the figure of the woman driver. This, the most explicitly negative sign of Enid's independence, is also the one that ties her most explicitly to the war and to modernity. The figure of Enid at the wheel condenses these various aspects of Cather's narrative. Enid's skill as a driver first appears in a dramatic storm scene. After taking a day trip in the car, Claude and Enid find themselves seventy miles away from home with a storm coming up on the prairie. Claude suggests that they wait until the next day to drive home, but Enid refuses.

This episode allows Cather to showcase Enid's "quiet"—and ominous—"determination": she "[can]not bear to have her plans changed by people or circumstances" (*One of Ours*, 133). She exhibits a fearlessness that embarrasses Claude into acquiescence. But his unmanly caution seems justified when the storm arrives and he loses control of the car. He reiterates his suggestion that they seek shelter until the storm is over. Enid refuses, again, complaining that the nearby farm is "not very clean" and too crowded with children (134)—foreshadowing her "unfeminine" attitude toward domesticity. At that point, Enid herself takes the wheel. She insists that Claude is "nervous" (a watchword for effeminacy and for unmanly response to the pressures of war) and that she has more experience driving:

> [Claude] was chafed by her stubbornness, but he had to admire her resourcefulness in handling the car. At the bottom of one of the worst hills was a new cement culvert, overlaid with liquid mud, where there was nothing for the chains to grip. The car slid to the edge of the culvert and stopped on the very brink. While they were ploughing up the other side of the hill, Enid remarked, "It's a good thing your starter works well; a little jar would have thrown us over." (134)

Although Enid gets them home safely, Claude's manhood sustains some injury. On the very next page, Claude's accident occurs. The danger of injury, once averted, quickly returns, again tied to driving machines. Claude's accident with the truck and the mules in a sense reiterates the symbolic castration of his drive with Enid. His accident, along with his frustrated response to it, triggers his effeminizing illness and leads directly to his need for Enid's nursing—which leads, in turn, to the ultimate castration of their unconsummated marriage. Although Claude keeps Enid's sexual refusal a secret from his family and friends, her driving makes her physical abs(tin)ence visible to everyone: "Having a wife with a car of her own is next to having no wife at all," Leonard exclaims. "How they do like to roll around! I've been mighty careful to see that Susie never learned to drive a car" (202). Enid's driving condenses everything unsympathetic about her: her determination, her inflexibility, her independence from Claude, her flight from domesticity and sexuality.

Embedded in a landscape of treacherous mud, Cather's portrayal of Enid's driving emerges directly from representations of women drivers for the war. Enid's driving establishes the fact that steely nerves and determination reside within an otherwise feminine and supposedly fragile body. Cather's portrayal seems indebted to images of war because it differs from the other dominant trends in the way that women's access to cars was pictured by the automobile industry and in other popular representations.[47] For instance, although most car advertisements before the 1920s picture women as passengers, Cather insists that Enid is the better driver. Contrary to other popular beliefs about how women would experience cars, Enid is not interested in the car as an accessory or as a sign of status or yet as a vehicle for unchaperoned sexual adventure (which is the fantasy implicitly keeping Leonard from letting his wife learn to drive—"How they do like to roll around!"). Electric cars were marketed to women because it was assumed that women would want to drive short distances, that power and speed would be far less important to them than features of comfort and aesthetic appeal, and that they would not be able to handle starting a combustion engine. Enid differs from this imagined woman consumer in all ways: she drives far and fast and has a good deal of technical knowledge. She even appreciates the starter. Cather also underscores that Enid's primary interest in the car is as a vehicle for getting somewhere, rather than as a pretense for being unchaperoned with her beau. The secluded and mobile privacy that the car made possible alarmed parents and others concerned with the morals of American youth; its speed and danger became a symbol, early on, for both sexual desire and female availability.

In all these particulars, Enid's driving resembles the professional attitude of women who served during the war under the auspices of various motor corps. Edward Penfield's "Yes Sir—I Am Here! Recruits Wanted Motor Corps of America" (figure 7), for instance, shows a woman working in uniform as an agent in her own right. Rather than serving male soldiers, who pose in front of her and speak for her, this female figure stands independently. She drives, she answers for herself, she seems serious and professional rather than friendly and hospitable. Women who drove in France worked hard hours on bad roads, they did their own maintenance, and they worked alone close to the front.[48] Posters depicting them feature female figures with ambition, independence, and responsibility—all characteristics of Enid, who has a strong sense of her own personal mission for demanding labor in an international setting.

Penfield's driver has a more obviously "quasi-military status" than does the Salvation Army "Lassie," and her femininity is more ambivalent. The viewer must surmise whether her hair is cropped short or pulled back in her cap. Her Sam Browne belt accentuates both her feminine, narrow

FIGURE 7. "Yes Sir—I Am Here! Recruits Wanted, Motor Corps of America," Edward Penfield, color Lithograph, 27 × 40 inches, 1918. (Special Collections Rare Books & Manuscripts, University of Minnesota Library)

waist *and* the fact that she is serving, like men, at the front (these belts could only be worn abroad).[49] Her sex appeal is similarly ambivalent: it emerges primarily from the challenge provoked by a lack of traditional femininity. It is precisely this kind of challenge that makes Enid such a treacherous figure. Enid's body both draws and resists Claude's sexualizing gaze: "he wonder[s] why she ha[s] no shades of feeling to correspond to her natural grace, . . . to the gentle, almost wistful attitudes of her body" (Cather, *One of Ours*, 211). Though she looks "wistful" to Claude, what she longs for is not the reassuringly "natural" desires he imagines. For, Cather writes, "Everything about a man's embrace was distasteful to Enid. . . . She disliked ardour of any kind" (210). Cather depicts Enid's body—like the female figure in Penfield's poster—as wistfully feminine *but also* efficient, Taylorized, even machinelike. Enid's body works rather than reproduces. Enid has exactly what Claude feels that he lacks as a man: she wholly identifies with a mission larger than herself. Unlike Claude, and in a reversal of traditional gender stereotypes, Enid does not need her purpose in life to be embodied by another person. In contrast to the notion that women develop strong social bonds and define their identity in social terms rather than abstract ones, Cather describes Enid as "not naturally much drawn to people" and "free" from domestic bonds (131). Enid's ministrations to Claude after his accident—ostensibly the sign of female service to men— signify precisely the opposite. She cares for him because his accident gives her an opportunity to enact, in a small way, her professional ambition of becoming a missionary. Missionary work ultimately takes her, as it had her sister Carrie (a name that evokes the dangers of a more sexualized female mobility in early twentieth-century fiction), to China.

What makes Enid so monstrous is her lack of need for a man. She does not need a masculine partner against whom her own femininity can cohere in contrast. Enid never seems as tormented by her lack of traditional femininity as Claude is by his failure to be a "normal" man. Her lack of sexuality aligns her with Claude's castrating father, because she withholds and forbids what Claude imagines he needs to make his manhood real in the world. It would be possible to read this as lesbianism, and yet Cather figures the danger the New Woman poses not as undisciplined desire but as erotophobia.[50] Enid's monstrosity exists not in her appetites but in her lack of them: she is a virgin, a teetotaler, and a vegetarian. Cather pictures her not as overly or voraciously feminine but instead as androgynous and autotelic. Like one of Lawrence's "women saviours," Enid drives herself to save the world. That drive makes her an unfit wife, one who wounds her husband and who is perceived as posing a general threat to men and male homosociality: "Within a few months Enid's car traveled more than two thousand miles for the Prohibitionist cause"—a cause which leaves Claude home alone and alienates him from his male friends (Cather, *One of Ours*, 209).

Having depicted this dangerous New Woman, Cather banishes her from her novel. Enid takes the dangers posed by modernity with her and makes the war "safe." Before Claude goes off to war, Enid goes off to China, and his masculine crisis disappears with her. Once she is gone, machines no longer seem to pose the same threat. Treacherous mud and lacerating barbed wire only seem to threaten Claude when Enid is nearby. In comparison with the "queer," disfiguring, and infection-prone wounds Claude receives at home, Cather describes his war wounds as "clean" (453). Cather depicts death in war, but she takes away its "newness" and its filth.

Indeed, even the automobile—which Cather describes elsewhere as "misshapen and sullen, like an ugly threat in a stream of things that were bright and beautiful and alive"[51]—can be recuperated once Enid is no longer at the wheel. Toward the end of the novel, Cather suggests that the automobile will provide postwar consolation to men: "What Hicks had wanted most in this world was to run a garage and repair shop with his old chum, Dell Able. Beaufort ended all that. He means to conduct a sort of memorial shop, anyhow, with 'Hicks and Able' over the door. He wants to roll up his sleeves and look at the *logical and beautiful inwards of automobiles* for the rest of his life" (*One of Ours*, 456–57, my emphasis). If cars had once been vehicles of castration, Cather associates them here with healing and with male agency ("Able"). Similarly, while Enid's driving isolates Claude, postwar driving will bring men together: "Though Bert lives on the Platte and Hicks on the Big Blue, the automobile roads between these two rivers are excellent" (456).

The negative aspects of modernity disappear with Enid. Interestingly, Cather suspends her portrayal and judgment of the character at that point in the narrative. She never disciplines Enid within the plot itself, which may be why critics such as Lewis felt the need to condemn the character so vociferously. The fact that Enid disappears does not, of course, mitigate the misogyny of Cather's portrait. Instead, Cather's suspension of discipline makes itself felt as the "thing not named" in the text and in turn engenders the tradition of name-calling (Enid is "an evangelical prig who very much knows what she doesn't want") which so many critics have relished.

In an ironic way, then, the novel authorizes the misogyny that has marked its critical reception, in its own time and in later decades. This explains why it has also proven somewhat intractable to feminist reevaluations of Cather and her work. The novel's misogyny disrupts the neatness of Sharon O'Brien's description of Cather's progress as a woman writer. Cather published it years after having, as O'Brien suggests she had, replaced an early identification with men and male authors with a feminine aesthetic.[52] My reading of *One of Ours*, like Greg Forter's of *The Professor's House*, suggests that gender is, in Cather's work, a more ambivalent and complex problem than does O'Brien's—admittedly more appealing—narrative of Cather's feminist awakening.[53] For in *One of Ours*, Cather expresses what seems like an atavistic doubt and dread about femininity. This contributes, I think, to the comparatively little attention the novel has received among Cather scholars. Too "womanly" for some, not "womanly" enough for others, the novel long continued both to provoke and to betray a desire for coherent and predictable differences between masculinity and femininity.

Rather than offering a psychological account of the sexual and gender conflicts that Cather as an individual may have been working out in *One of Ours*, I conclude by considering its use of gender to organize what was an extremely confusing and painful cultural experience. What men did to each other during the war, what havoc men wreaked on male flesh, provoked deep and lasting pain and anxiety. Death seemed new; wounds seemed obscene; male bodies became the public site of abjection and trauma. The need to exorcise or sublimate that vision called forth a variety of responses, few of them logical. The deepest insight of Mencken's review of the novel comes in the form of his admission that people needed help ordering their "memories" of the war in the postwar process of determining what it had meant: "[Dos Passos's novel] changed the whole tone of American opinion about the war; it *even changed the recollections of actual veterans of the war*," he writes.[54] If "actual" witnesses of the war could change their "recollections" of what happened there, then the mutability of visions of more distant observers is hardly surprising. Retrospective fictions about the war, then, were vehicles for the negotiation of unresolved conflict and pain. Telling the story of the war offered individuals and the culture at large ways to debate how to value the violence suffered and inflicted in the name of manhood and the nation and how to judge the nation that had demanded such sacrifice in such terms.

Misogynistic representations of the war testify, then, not simply to cultural (or personal) attitudes about women but to the depth of anger and resentment that followed the experience of war, even among the so-called victors. The need to find a scapegoat overwhelmed many level-headed and well-meaning attempts to account for and remember the war. Coming to terms with the losses it left behind was difficult. The scale of death of World War I provoked a crisis in cultural mourning practices, which in turn triggered a variety of postwar rituals and narratives, both innovative and traditional. Holding women responsible for the war was only one of several responses. The difficulty of telling the story of the war made that story porous: it repeatedly absorbed and was used to formulate other anxieties and conflicts. Cather's war novel encodes a melancholic and nostalgic desire for the past, for a time before the war, and for a time when some people, including Cather and her character Claude, had "hoped extravagantly" to win a fight against the traumatic elements of modernity (*One of Ours*, 459).

2 /   The Story Nick Can't Tell: Trauma in *The Great Gatsby*

"It ripped her open—"
"Don't tell me," he winced, "I saw enough of that in the war."
                    —F. SCOTT FITZGERALD, *THE GREAT GATSBY:*
                              A FACSIMILE OF THE MANUSCRIPT

In F. Scott Fitzgerald's novel *The Great Gatsby* (1925), death happens on the highway, the lawn, and in a swimming pool; it happens to men but most spectacularly to a woman. If the war made death "new," Fitzgerald made it new again by refiguring it within a postwar perspective that sees death in postwar locales. Fitzgerald depicts violence that calls the war to mind instead of writing about the war itself. War stories crop up in the novel, but they are allusive, short, and sometimes—as in the instance in the epigraph—cut off or cut entirely from the finished version, or both. In the epigraph, Gatsby interrupts Nick and refuses to hear the particulars of Myrtle Wilson's bloody death. His refusal provides an apt figure for the novel's narration at large, which turns violent acts into shimmering prose. The novel only hints at the things that make Gatsby wince; it shies away from accounts of what Nick Carraway and Jay Gatsby would have experienced as members of the Third Division and as participants in the Meuse-Argonne Offensive.[1] Instead, what they "saw enough of . . . in the war" resurfaces in the novel as new instances of death, rather than as remembered war stories.[2]

This chapter explores various ways in which *Gatsby* responds to World War I. It begins with an insistence that being a veteran informs Nick's point of view. I trace his pose of "cardinal," almost naïve, honesty and his bond with Gatsby—aspects that many critics have debated in terms of his (un)reliability—to his unelaborated and implicitly traumatic war experience.[3] I then argue that, far more than a mere background shared by Nick and Gatsby, war experience is a historical trauma that the novel repeats through its characters' various plots and in the novel's structure. Fitzgerald refigures both the violence of World War I and the way that its violence had been sanitized, regendered, and disavowed through the novel's climactic car accident and murder-suicide—crimes for which no one is held accountable. Finally, the chapter considers how Nick's false innocence gives way to a more experienced perspective through his survival and narration of these events. It is as if, through his encounters with violent death, he gains a story that approximates war trauma. For Nick, as it must have for legions of Fitzgerald's readers, the unfinished work of coming to terms with the war's New Death impinges on and shapes perception of the postwar present.

In other words, *Gatsby* enacts the postwar problem of narrating—and making literature about—encounters with New Death. This is not how it is usually read. When it was published in 1925, H. L. Mencken hailed it as a story of "modern American life" that had little to do with the recent war in Europe.[4] As recently as 1997, Ronald Berman called World War I "the wrong war" to bear in mind when reading the novel.[5] In arguments that consider history in *Gatsby*, American contexts are what matter.[6] In Seth Moglen's account of American modernism, *Gatsby* responds to the "destructive effects of modern capitalism," the "staggering economic transformation" that produced deep "psychic injuries" and limited the possibilities of both "social solidarity" and personal intimacy.[7] In a related account, Greg Forter traces the effects that that economic transformation had on the sex-gender system in America and posits that *Gatsby* is concerned with the social loss of a masculinity that put "receptivity, lyrical interiority, a belief in the colossal power of desire, the possibility of economic and imaginative self-making" within the male purview.[8] Forter reads *Gatsby* as Fitzgerald's ambivalent and ultimately incomplete attempt to work through the wounds men suffered as new economic forces devalued their affective capacities, interpolated them in industrial and mechanized labor, and required them to become more aggressive and "hard." Forter and Moglen both focus on *Gatsby*'s response to long-term historical changes wrought by modernity. For them, looking to World War I as "the primal trauma of a lost generation" seems inadequate, first because it is a cliché and second because it is, in Moglen's words, "just the tip of the iceberg."[9] In other words, focusing on the war obscures the bulk of historical wounds inflicted by modern capitalism and privileges the importance of male suffering.

The same redefinitions of gender and loss that drive these new accounts of American modernism, however, also compel us to look

THE STORY NICK CAN'T TELL / 65

again and more deeply at its relationship to World War I. Together they describe the longer-term historical and cultural changes within which World War I's specific damages can be reckoned anew. We have not, I argue, looked closely enough at the male violence and injury at the center of the experience of that war. Along with other histories, many of the war's aspects have remained submerged or surfaced only partially and by implication. For instance, critics and literary historians primarily interested in World War I's impact on literature often cite *Gatsby* as evidence, but only in passing. Paul Fussell's *Great War and Modern Memory* provides a typical example: "the literary scene [before the Great War] is hard to imagine. There was no *Waste Land*, with its rats' alleys, dull canals, and dead men who have lost their bones: it would take four years of trench warfare to bring these to consciousness. There was no *Ulysses*, no *Mauberly*, no *Cantos*, no Kafka, no Proust, no Waugh, no Auden, no Huxley, no Cummings, no *Women in Love* or *Lady Chatterley's Lover*. There was no 'Valley of Ashes' in *The Great Gatsby*."[10] *Gatsby* becomes one item in a catalog of "postwar" texts, and Fussell hints that its landscape, in particular, recalls the war. But that is where he leaves it.

This chapter returns to and elaborates on both Fussell's implication and an opinion that was first voiced, but never developed, in early commentary on Fitzgerald. Midcentury appraisals tended to identify Fitzgerald as a matter of course with "the war generation." His contemporary Edmund Wilson grouped Fitzgerald with "the young men" who "have had to derive their chief stimulus from the wars, the society and the commerce of the Age of Confusion itself."[11] But Wilson's generalized account assumes without describing in detail the experience of this generation, and his mention of "the wars" testifies to a denial of the singular importance of World War I. Here, I reassert the war's relevance to Fitzgerald's text and delineate its importance in more specific detail than early commentators did. In particular, I want to suggest, references to war in *Gatsby* should call to mind the death it inflicted, despite—perhaps even because of—the fact that Fitzgerald's contemporaries (including Edmund Wilson) tended to downplay it. New Death, I argue, is the larger context we need to interpret the odd note of appreciation in the novel's self-reflective remark near its conclusion that "the holocaust was complete" (162) and Nick's strange assertion that "Gatsby turned out all right at the end" (2). Yet by and large, Fitzgerald scholars have dismissed his engagement with and experience of World War I. For them, the war was an experience he missed, a cultural watershed he observed inaccurately and from afar.

In a welcome corrective to this view, Keith Gandal has described the importance of the war to Fitzgerald and to *Gatsby*. According to Gandal, the war sets the novel in motion, and Jay Gatsby is a "historically recognizable" and highly specific kind of soldier to come out of the American Expeditionary Force.[12] The U.S. military used new criteria to promote to officer men from poor or ethnic backgrounds whose results on intelligence tests and whose first languages made them potentially effective leaders. Such promotions sometimes—and not incidentally—raised the rank of men of working-class or immigrant backgrounds over those with more traditional claims to high rank. Army mobilization, "with its new and particular methods for selecting officers—which Fitzgerald knew all about, as an officer in training at Camp Taylor and at other camps—meant that a 'nobody' like Gatsby could be chosen for officer training, and specifically promoted to captain, while still at camp, on the basis of his own measurable and observable abilities, in the context of a new meritocratic moment."[13] Gatsby's success in the army would have made him particularly susceptible to its propaganda, Gandal speculates, which explains why he "embodies the virtues that" epitomize the "new man" of the training camps, including chastity (except with Daisy), temperance, and chivalry.[14] The love affair between Gatsby and Daisy has a "specific historical correlative": many immigrant and working-class men who were promoted to officer enjoyed, among other social benefits, access to women (known as "Charity Girls") who, Gandal recounts, "had sex with soldiers for free" before they went to war.[15] Fitzgerald's novel hints at these details, which Gandal shows to be essential to its meaning. But the novel ultimately focuses not on mobilization but on the war's aftermath. It portrays the postwar "backlash by the traditionally, ethnically privileged against a rising, ethnically blind meritocracy": Tom Buchanan asserts his privilege and manly prowess over "Mr. Nobody From Nowhere," Jay (né Gatz) Gatsby.[16]

This chapter corroborates Gandal's insistence on the war's centrality to the novel's characters and plot. But Gandal's interpretation of why Fitzgerald would choose to write about the war in the terms he does varies from my own. For Gandal, what matters most is that the army hurt Fitzgerald by passing him over for promotion. "Gatsby," Gandal insists, "achieves at training camp what Fitzgerald couldn't."[17] So for him, the novel's sense of loss and disillusionment can be read as a transposition of Fitzgerald's own "mobilization wound."[18] That very suggestive argument will undoubtedly shape the dominant critical understanding of the novel. Here, I am less interested in recovering Fitzgerald's own war experience.

Instead, I highlight ways in which his novel textualizes the war as its primal scene: a strong, repressed, and highly visual context against which its plot unfolds and which its plot repeats. In *Gatsby*, I argue, "the war" is both the source and sign of trauma and operates as a postwar shorthand notation not just for "mobilization wounds" but for the violent world of New Death. Fitzgerald represents both the war and death as topics that require similar sanitization and truncation. Even those characters with most direct experience of the war, namely Nick and Gatsby, give us little access to it. References to war remain markedly unelaborated. Indeed, as this chapter's epigraph and its argument as a whole will show in more detail, Fitzgerald's drafts show attempts to eliminate allusions to the war. In a composition notorious for its errata (spelling and factual), the careful attention Fitzgerald paid to details about the war begs analysis. Its meaning is hinted at between the lines, only to resurface in new acts of violence. We should remember that the context of war would have been familiar to Fitzgerald's contemporary audience. Indeed, it might have been too familiar. The novel's indirect references to the war reflect a collective reticence to dwell on its legacy. The novel invokes the war in its ethos rather than its particulars—in the way that its events have been internalized by characters as structures of perception and denial and as horizons of expectation and in the way that its violent events continue to repeat themselves according to an uncanny logic.

Gatsby illustrates the fact that war shapes identity but that "identities and memories are not things we think *about*, but things we think *with*."[19] The novel portrays what it is like to "think *with*" a memory and identity shaped by war. The context of war connotes trauma, which notoriously complicates psychological and narrative access to events and experience. If we *generally* do not think consciously about the influence of identity and memories on our actions, it stands to reason that we *particularly* do not think consciously about the influence of traumatic experience on identities, memories, and actions. According to trauma theorists, we cannot: traumatic experience is, in Cathy Caruth's phrase, "unclaimed experience"—experience we do not possess but are possessed by.[20] This chapter recalls the context of shell-shock and culls late twentieth-century trauma theory for insights in order to identify ways in which *Gatsby* refers, obliquely, to the psychological and cultural damages of war. Recognizing the rhetorical role the war plays in the text will throw *Gatsby*'s violence into new relief, enabling us to resituate it more precisely within its postwar moment.

The Story Nick Can't Tell

At first Krebs, who had been at Belleau Wood, Soissons, the Champagne, St. Mihiel and in the Argonne did not want to talk about the war at all. Later he felt the need to talk but no one wanted to hear about it. His town had heard too many atrocity stories to be thrilled by actualities. Krebs found that to be listened to at all he had to lie, and after he had done this twice he, too, had a reaction against the war and against talking about it.

—ERNEST HEMINGWAY, "SOLDIER'S HOME"

Scholars have written relatively little about war and *Gatsby*, perhaps because its narrator does not talk about it much and denies its importance. "I participated in that delayed Teutonic migration known as the Great War," Nick declares; "I enjoyed the counterraid so thoroughly that I came back restless" (3). Nick compares himself to his great-uncle, a successful wartime entrepreneur: "[he] sent a substitute to the Civil War and started the wholesale hardware business that my father carries on to-day" (3). By becoming a bonds salesman, Nick seeks to imitate this "hard-boiled" great-uncle, who turned national political catastrophe to a profit (3). While much of the nation remembers the Civil War as a ruinous fraternal struggle that brought death, social upheaval, and economic disaster, the Carraways remember it as the beginning of family financial success. To a certain extent, the Carraway experience of the Civil War resembles the United States' participation in World War I: without suffering the same losses as other nations, the United States emerged from the war with an extremely profitable industrial ("hardware") trade. Not participating in the Civil War becomes the founding moment of the Carraway family, and Nick hopes to carry on the tradition. Nick's father elaborates on this theme when he tells Nick that because he has had "advantages," he must reserve judgment (1). He can and should expect to be spared hardship. In the logic of the Carraway "clan," suffering and grief constitute history, and Nick—like his family before him—can expect to be passed by (3). In identifying with his great-uncle, Nick attempts to find a man with a history analogous to his own. But his account of their resemblance and of the family code obscures the fundamental difference between the Carraway memory of the Civil War and his own experience of World War I: unlike his uncle, he has become a participant, although his participation remains strangely unelaborated. He introduces himself as one who hears others' stories, rather than living his own. If his uncle sent a substitute to the Civil War, Nick seems to need a substitute story to tell. Though he does not dodge the war, he dodges its narration.

Nick's brief description of his own experience harbors a hint of negativity: "Instead of being the warm center of the world, the Middle West now seemed like the ragged edge of the universe—so I decided to go East and learn the bond business" (3). Nick's brevity suggests that he is making a condensed reference to a narrative the reader already knows. For *Gatsby*'s contemporary audience, there were two obvious narratives in play here. Nick's journey conjures up, most obviously, the popular wartime song "How 'Ya Gonna Keep 'Em Down on the Farm (After They've Seen Paree)?" Nick, home from the war, is simply bored by small-town life. But there is another narrative in play here, which is articulated most famously in Hemingway's "Soldier's Home." If Nick has seen more than just Paris, as Krebs has, the difficulty of reassimilating himself into a home life and bonds of intimacy may have other, seemingly unspeakable causes—it may be because of things the narrator never reveals because "no one wanted to hear about" them. From this perspective, Nick's claim to have "enjoyed" the war sounds ironic, and his "restlessness" signals a jittery response to trauma and loss rather than merely youthful excitement. This implication was made more explicit in the novel's draft, in which the narrator was named "Dud," as in an unexploded, but still dangerous, shell. Though no such shells dropped in the American Midwest, they have become embedded in Nick's consciousness, and he now experiences even his hometown as a place of lurking threats, better left behind.

Nick's claims to innocence read very differently than Krebs's bitterness. But there are reasons to question Nick's narration. First and foremost, as we shall see, his encounter with Gatsby is actually a *re*encounter. His move east retraces his prior mobilization and demobilization for war. Instead of entering a new world full of new people, he finds people from the past, many of whom also seem to have been uprooted by or during the war. When Nick admonishes Gatsby, "You can't repeat the past," he belies his own trajectory, which carries him back toward reminders of war (110). Critics have drawn attention to Fitzgerald's geographical reversal of the direction of the traditional American adventure narrative (west to east instead of east to west), but this—the most salient aspect of his design—has gone largely unremarked. Instead, critics typically read Nick's movement east within a country-to-city, young-American-man-comes-of-age topos. According to this logic, he leaves his small town to see the world, loses his innocence during the summer of 1922 (in which *Gatsby* takes place), and returns home a chastened but wiser man.[21] But the fact that Nick's loss of innocence would have logically *preceded* his move east goes largely unnoticed, precisely because his ironic tone and his overlaid retrospective frame make it easy to miss. Although Nick's reencounter with Gatsby does change him, the nature of the change has been largely misunderstood. Understanding the change requires tracing its history, particularly its relation to the recent world war.

The ironic tone that Nick uses to give the war an ostensibly banal place in his coming-of-age story requires careful attention. When he says, "I enjoyed the counterraid so thoroughly that I came back restless," he recalls the war in an idiom of ironic negation. Here, irony operates as a literary denial of affect. The trope of irony "creates distance," while sympathy works "to abolish difference."[22] Irony functions as a rhetorical structure that enables a certain content to be named without its proper qualitative, emotional value—irony drains content of affect. Nick's verbal irony operates defensively; it keeps us from reading him as a wounded man—"enjoyed" takes the place of an admission of suffering. His irony illustrates a mechanism Freud describes in his discussion of negation, by which "the content of a repressed image or idea can make its way into consciousness, on condition that it is *negated*."[23] Paul Fussell identifies irony as a central postwar trope and argues that the conventions of situational irony ("ironic action") *enable* recollection of the war by shaping memories and events "into significance."[24] But the conventions of verbal irony so evident in *Gatsby* enable only a very selective kind of recollection, one that denies and distorts affect. Nick's ironic attitude toward the war suggests its *lack* of significance.[25]

Similarly, when Nick calls the war "that delayed Teutonic migration," a phrase which naturalizes the war in terms of race and biology, he downplays its violence. (It is the movement of a "people" rather than a cataclysmic rupture with progress and civilization.) Yet Nick's characterization of the war echoes, as Walter Benn Michaels has shown, the eugenicist Lothrop Stoddard, who described World War I as Europe's civil war, in which white men slaughtered each other and risked "racial suicide."[26] "Teutonic migration" connotes violence in couched terms. Nick also puts the war's popular name in brackets: his "known as" qualifies "the Great War" as a misnomer, an oxymoron, calling attention to one of the text's governing rhetorical tropes.[27] Oxymora link disparate entities and act as condensed paradoxes. Reading *Gatsby* requires unhinging these paradoxes, noticing the gaps they work to close. "The Great War" is, I would argue, the most important of these oxymora—especially as it echoes, with an important substitution, the novel's similarly oxymoronic title: *The Great "Gatsby."* But although Nick draws attention to a certain gap between the signifier "the Great War" and the events it signifies, he does not elaborate, as Hemingway famously does in *A Farewell to Arms* (as we shall see), for instance, when he complains that what "billposters slapped up" does not correspond to actual war experience. Nick's quali-fier remains cryptic and must be read with reference to other parts of the text and its larger historical context.

Gatsby's most important way of telling about the war, I argue, emerges in its substitution of "Gatsby" for "war." Like the other novels investigated in *The New Death*, *Gatsby* conveys the damages of war through an anal-ogy. Specifically, Nick tells about losing Gatsby the man rather than about "the Great War." Gatsby embodies losses that would otherwise be intan-gible. Like "one of those intricate machines that register earthquakes ten thousand miles away," Gatsby enables Nick to register, after the fact and far away, an imperceptible but terrible change (2). Nick shares Gatsby's feeling of having lost something important. When Gatsby describes his love affair with Daisy, he gives voice to an unidentifiable hole in the center of Nick's experience: "Through all he said, even through his appalling sentimental-ity, I was reminded of something—an elusive rhythm, a fragment of lost words, that I had heard somewhere a long time ago. For a moment a phrase tried to take shape in my mouth and my lips parted like a dumb man's, as though there was more struggling upon them than a wisp of startled air. But they made no sound and what I had almost remembered was incom-municable forever" (111). This inability to articulate his own loss defines Nick as a character, and it generates his need for and interest in Gatsby. In this passage, Nick's identification with Gatsby seems predicated on their stories and their losses being similar but not the same. Nick (re)experi-ences loss, but only in a vague way. Through this illustration of Nick's identification and empathy, Fitzgerald suggests that Nick's war experience cannot be explicitly articulated but must be felt, instead, through forms of repetition and reflection.

By emphasizing what Nick cannot remember, I insist that we read *Gatsby*, like the writings of other modernists, not only for what it says but for what it omits. Many modernists sought the means to imply things without saying them directly: Joyce's parallax, Eliot's objective correla-tive, Cather's "thing not named," and Hemingway's "iceberg principle" are all idiomatic expressions for omission.[28] Though Fitzgerald did not name his aesthetic technique, he did hope that he had found a new sto-rytelling method in *Gatsby*. He condenses losses, one within another. This moment epitomizes the novel's larger pattern of intertwined stories of loss that collectively, I argue, stand in for the war's pervasive damage.

Nick's desire to recover echoes of his past's "elusive rhythm" and "lost words" runs like a thread of unconscious intention through his entire relationship with Gatsby. On the surface, the plot takes shape by coincidence and accident. He moves in next door to Gatsby as "a matter of chance" (4). At the same time, Nick has a dim intuition that his actions accord with a plan. He has the pleasurable feeling of following a pattern without knowing why, which yields an unsought confirmation of belonging. When someone asks him for directions, he imagines himself in one of Cooper's American adventures, as "a guide, a pathfinder, an original settler" (4). He fulfills expectations he does not know he has, so that in doing things for the first time, he experiences a paradoxical sensation of destiny, meaning, repetition. Nick explains this odd simultaneity of newness and repetition to himself as a brush with the mythic past rather than with his own traumatic past or the demonic uncanny: "I had the familiar conviction that life was beginning over again with the summer" (4). Scholars tend to gloss this aspect of the novel, along with its final evocation of the Dutch sailors, as Fitzgerald's allusion to American myth. In contrast, it makes sense to read some of the novel's repetitions in more disturbing terms, as instances of what Freud named the uncanny: a "factor of involuntary repetition which surrounds what would otherwise be innocent enough with an uncanny atmosphere" which "forces upon us the idea of something fateful and inescapable when otherwise we should have spoken only of 'chance.'"[29] Nick's innocent—Jordan Baker might say "careless"—encounters with violence, loss, and New Death in this novel seem meaningful and important precisely because he has experienced versions of them already.

Nick's persona as a midwestern naïf offers the reader the impression of a heterodiegetic, reliable narrator. Like critics before me, I find this pretense unconvincing, but for new reasons.[30] Like some other critics, notably Keath Fraser, I argue that Nick is an unwitting homodiegetic narrator who is involved with Gatsby for unspoken, or unspeakable, reasons.[31] Certainly, as Edward Wasiolek asserts, there is "something more than objective approval and reliability . . . at work in the intense and unqualified way in which Nick approves of Gatsby."[32] Rather than reading Nick's excessive response to Gatsby either as homosexual longing (as Fraser does) or as "the sympathy of one homosexual for another" (as Wasiolek puts it), however, I trace it to their shared historical past.[33]

What makes Gatsby so compelling to Nick, in other words, is not "the love that dare not speak its name" but something else unspeakable: the trauma of having killed, having witnessed death, and having survived the war. Such experiences also, in the 1920s, remained secrets between men. As my introduction explained, modern war experience had been pervasively described as having outstripped language. Fitzgerald compounds the unspeakability of war experience by encoding it as not just unspeakable but repressed—a part of experience or imagination that cannot be called to mind. What draws Nick close to Gatsby and thus drives him to narrate the story is what is "almost remembered"—that is, repressed—and "incommunicable forever." Although it is never fully disclosed, its presentation as what is forgotten is, itself, a clue. Fitzgerald repeatedly invites us to read Nick's forgetfulness (both the involuntary kind, described earlier, and the alcoholically self-induced variety) as a— perhaps *the*—trace of his war experience. His memory lapses often surface in conjunction with references to the war. When Nick meets Jordan Baker for the first time, it occurs to him that he has "seen her, or a picture of her, somewhere before" (11). But like Jordan herself, who has "been lying on that sofa for as long as [she] can remember," Nick cannot bring the past to mind (10). Jordan's angular, hard, masculine body, which she emphasizes by throwing back her "shoulders like a young cadet," both triggers and forestalls Nick's memory (11). He seems to remember her body and sees it in familiar, martial imagery. His simile reveals the militaristic shape of his frame of reference. But the comparison distracts him—Nick fails to recall what he knows about her. Armies, soldiers, the war: they are never the objects of contemplation but only what the objects call to mind; they act as indirect signifiers that impede recognition.

In addition to disrupting Nick's memory and chain of thought, references to war often generate a feeling of fright. For instance, Nick personifies the Buchanan lawn as a soldier crossing no-man's-land: "the lawn started at the beach and ran toward the front door for a quarter of a mile, jumping over sundials and brick walks and burning gardens. . . . The front was broken by a line of French windows. . . . Tom Buchanan in riding clothes was standing with his legs apart on the front porch" (6). This use of personification—the lawn runs rather than is run across—evokes but does not name what Nick seemingly expects to see: the running (perhaps *falling*) soldier. The metaphor generates a sense of violence: Nick's vision covertly figures Tom's "cruel body" in a landscape of war (7). Moreover, Tom's riding clothes create a metonymic affinity between him and the British generals of World War I. He shares their dangerous nostalgia for an earlier, aristocratic form of conflict. (This nostalgia explains Tom's declaration, "I've heard of making a garage out of a stable, . . . but I'm the first man who ever made a stable out of a garage" [119].) Historian

A. J. P. Taylor describes the high cost of such nostalgia during the Battle of the Somme:

> On 14 July [1916] some twenty thousand men attacked at 3.25 a.m. after only five minutes' bombardment. The Germans, who had thought their night's rest secure, were caught asleep. Five miles of their second line was [*sic*] overrun. Now came the great set piece of which all British generals dreamt: the cavalry were to go through. Three divisions were in readiness. They took a long time coming, held up in the mud and craters of the battlefield. At seven in the evening, the British infantry saw a sight unique on the Western Front: cavalry riding into action through the waving corn with bugles blowing and lances glittering. The glorious vision crumbled into slaughter as the German machine guns opened fire.[34]

Tom's longing for sport, particularly sports that evoke an aristocratic past, has dangerous analogs in recent history, and Fitzgerald conveys his violence in a postwar idiom that equates chivalric nostalgia with callous and careless murder.[35]

Nick's awareness of the violence signified by Tom's athletic masculinity hovers around the edges of his consciousness, as if he would like to disavow it and its consequences. Although he identifies himself as "restless," he does not compare his restlessness directly to Tom's. As Fitzgerald revised, he eliminated the hint of Nick's aggression: "I enjoyed the raid so enormously thoroughly in fact that I came back with no mind for a colorless future in the middle-west. Wall Street and the bond business seemed to offer a more stimulating field."[36] As he edits his own draft, "raid" becomes "counterraid"—Fitzgerald makes Nick seem less offensive, more defensive. He also cuts Nick's choice of the bond business as a "stimulating field" (*of battle*). In the draft, Nick explicitly identifies himself as a soldier searching to recapture "the stimulus of the war"—a condition he shares with Tom (and even Daisy): "Why they [the Buchanans] came East I don't know perhaps for the same reason I did, searching among unfamiliar surroundings for that vague lost stimulus of the war. . . . And for no particular reason, except perhaps the recurrent fascination of the war, they [had come East]."[37] But in the published version, Nick identifies this structure of feeling—the unfinished preoccupation with war experience and a desire for its return—with Tom Buchanan alone, and he introduces it metaphorically, in terms of sport. According to Nick, Tom seems likely to "drift on forever seeking, a little wistfully, for the dramatic turbulence of some irrecoverable football game"

(6). Both the feeling and the terms of the analogy still recall the war, but more obliquely. Comparisons between sport and soldiering were common during World War I. In the United States, sport was used to advertise the war as an adventure and a way of asserting masculinity.[38] The ideal British officer, as Samuel Hynes describes him, was similarly one who loved polo and fox hunting, for "these activities were more than sports; they were . . . images of war, ways by which horse soldiers kept their skills honed" while they "impatiently awaited" their chance to go to war.[39] Fitzgerald's allusion to sport calls this association to mind: Tom's love of sport suggests his desire for violent conflict. In *Gatsby*'s postwar context, metaphors of sport evoke killing and death without naming them specifically. *Gatsby* and its drafts suggest a process by which awareness of New Death was shuttled to the margins. The final version condenses references to war experience, making them more indirect and allusive.

As a result, measuring the war's meaning is difficult. Characters refer to the war as a commonly experienced event whose meaning is obvious, clichéd, and unnecessary to elaborate. But the anxiety that ebbs around such references suggests that no one wants to recall the details of the war. Instead, those details surface as if by chance. Fitzgerald suggests that both Nick's neighbor and the house next door, "a factual imitation of some Hôtel de Ville in Normandy," have particular resonances for him (5). Gatsby's house—an inexact simulacrum of a shared past in France—provides an uncanny setting for their so-called first meeting. At Gatsby's party, a man speaks to Nick:

> "Your face is familiar," he said politely. "Weren't you in the Third Division during the War?"
>
> "Why, yes. I was in the Ninth Machine-Gun Battalion."
>
> "I was in the Seventh Infantry until June nineteen-eighteen. I knew I'd seen you somewhere before."
>
> We talked for a moment about some wet, grey little villages in France. Evidently he lived in this vicinity for he told me that he had just bought a hydroplane and was going to try it out in the morning. . . .
>
> I turned to my new acquaintance. "This is an unusual party for me. I haven't even seen the host. I live over there—" I waved my hand at the invisible hedge in the distance, "and this man Gatsby sent over his chauffeur with an invitation."
>
> For a moment he looked at me as if he failed to understand.

"I'm Gatsby," he said suddenly.

"What!" I exclaimed. "Oh, I beg your pardon." (47–48)

Fitzgerald catches us up in experiential transposition: the fact that this man before us on the page is Gatsby surprises the reader just as much as it does Nick. Because of that effect, we risk missing both the encounter's uncanny quality and the weight of its allusions to the war. Yet Nick's misrecognition, or lack of memory, verges on the ridiculous. After all, Nick has already seen Gatsby rather closely: "far as I was from him I could have sworn he was trembling," he reports on an earlier occasion (21); Gatsby's invitation mentions having "seen [Nick] several times" (41); and before the party episode, Nick gives an attentive account of his neighbor's activities. Superficially, the misrecognition may corroborate Nick's naïve persona. But this is more than naïveté or awkwardness: Nick's misrecognition attests to the tricks his memory plays on him *and* on the reader. Nick's story is full of strange encounters with a forgotten past that repeatedly unfolds—*as if* but *not* by "chance"—around shared but untold stories of the war.

Indeed, within the frame of Nick's surprise in this moment, the war story itself disappears—along with Gatsby's specificity of detail—into Nick's vague summary, which blurs the past and gives it a generic quality ("some wet grey little villages in France"). The numbers of regiments and dates—specific details Fitzgerald cared enough about to change—place Gatsby and Nick in the Battle of the Meuse-Argonne, some of the "hardest fighting of the war" from an American perspective, as Richard Lehan explains:

> In the first printing of the novel Fitzgerald had Gatsby and Nick in the First, not the Third Division. In subsequent editions their fighting takes place in the Third Division, but what unit Gatsby served in after June 1918 is left unstated, although clearly he fought in the Argonne.
>
> . . . [One battle was] launched on 26 September and [became] known as the Battle of the Meuse-Argonne; it involved the Americans in the hardest fighting of the war, which is probably why Fitzgerald used it in his novel. . . . The only way to reconcile the facts of the novel with the facts of history is to assume that Gatsby fought with the Third Division at the Battle of the Marne until June and then with the First Division at Argonne from September to November 1918. The Meuse-Argonne campaign was the last great battle in the American effort. More than a million Americans

were involved, many seeing action for the first time, and it involved their bloodiest fighting. In 1926 the War Department released the most accurate battle figures—26,277 Americans dead and 95,786 wounded.[40]

Gatsby and Nick's exchange places them squarely within a context of death and wounding, of violence, of trauma.[41] That context is both historical and literary, since the Meuse-Argonne had been (barely) fictionalized by one of its survivors in a novel that Fitzgerald knew intimately and that had a wide popularity with readers, Thomas Boyd's *Through the Wheat* (1923). That context makes both the rumor that Gatsby may have "killed a man once" (44) and Nick's naïve thrill to that rumor absurd: *of course* Gatsby has killed a man (at least) once, and Nick (above all) should be "hard-boiled" enough to know what that means. Yet the weight of such knowledge seems strangely absent. Fitzgerald waits for five more chapters before the two men resume the interrupted conversation about the war, and even then it is ventriloquized and euphemized: "He [Gatsby] did extraordinarily well in the war" (150). Again in that later instance, Fitzgerald relies on the reader to supply her own knowledge of the context if its details are to have meaning; the violence that Nick and Gatsby must have encountered in 1918 remains a matter of inference. Fitzgerald hints at it through symptoms: "restlessness," forgetfulness, and the fascination with speeding machines such as the hydroplane and Gatsby's "splendid car" (69).

The crucial fact that Nick and Gatsby's acquaintance dates to France disappears as Nick brings his story back to the narrative present. The topic of war disappears as Nick looks at Gatsby's smile and experiences not sadness, loss, or terror but what feels instead like an adoring (almost maternal) gaze: "He smiled understandingly—much more than understandingly. It was one of those rare smiles with a quality of eternal reassurance in it, that you may come across four or five times in life. It . . . concentrated on *you* with an irresistible prejudice in your favor. It understood you just so far as you wanted to be understood, believed in you as you would like to believe in yourself and assured you that it had precisely the impression of you that, at your best, you hoped to convey" (48, emphasis in the original). This magical intimacy supersedes Nick's misrecognition. Nick suggests that the rarity of Gatsby's smile has made him unforgettable—*so* unforgettable, in fact, that we almost forget that Nick has already forgotten him a first time. Nick meets someone he already knows for the first time, and it brings him back to himself—it gives him the uncanny feeling of newness and repetition we have begun to expect from him. Once again, however, something goes missing in the connection between the two men. The reduction of Gatsby to his smile ("It was one of those rare smiles. . . . It concentrated on *you*") makes Nick's partner in this intimate moment merely an "it," while he becomes a "*you*" instead of an "I." Just as Nick draws close to his desired encounter with the past, and seems capable of grasping the past in the present, its details swim away. The gaze ends: "Precisely at that point it vanished—and I was looking at an elegant young rough-neck" (48). Gatsby's oxymoronic class position "just miss[es] being absurd," and Nick's identification breaks off (48).

Whether this rupture of identification comes from Nick (and his oscillating projection of recovery and loss) or from Gatsby (whose paradoxical identity makes him an unstable screen for projection) or is due to mutually repressed memories of the war is, I think, an unresolvable question. This very lack of resolution creates a tension that drives the plot forward: what kind of man is Gatsby? Nick's need for an internally coherent image of Gatsby takes shape in the mind of the reader and generates one of the novel's primary sources of suspense. From the novel's very first pages, Fitzgerald uses this tension to foreshadow and move the plot forward. Describing Gatsby's house, Nick refers to their future intimacy: "It was Gatsby's mansion. Or, rather, as I didn't know Mr. Gatsby it was a mansion inhabited by a gentleman of that name" (5). Nick alludes to the fact that as Mr. Gatsby becomes just plain Gatsby, familiarity will take the place of—even disqualify—his pretensions to gentility. He promises that the mystery of Gatsby will be resolved. Michael Holquist connects this tension and its resolution in *Gatsby* to psychological stereotyping, which he defines as "an event . . . that has three steps: the subject seeks to finalize the other in a fixed identity; events dramatize to the subject that the other may elude or exceed such an identity; but 'finally' the subject finds a way to stitch both lack and stereotype into a unified perception that governs his actions with regard to the other."[42] The means by which Nick can "finally" unify his perception of Gatsby is, as we shall see, death. But while Holquist (via Bakhtin) argues that this stereotyping process is the "normal function of perception," and therefore a universal cognitive structure, Fitzgerald's text does not go so far. For Nick, as I have been suggesting, does not represent universal subjectivity encountering *lack* but instead a specifically postwar and traumatized subjectivity encountering *loss*.[43] Coming across reminders of the war—particularly this man marked by the same history—threatens to return Nick to a traumatic past. Losing Gatsby offers Nick a chance to put his forgotten past to rest. But how do we know Nick's past is traumatic? Why, that is, should we understand his experience as one shaped by historical loss rather than existential lack?

Nick and the Figure of the Shell-Shocked Soldier

Fitzgerald alludes to Nick's losses both directly ("what I had almost remembered was incommunicable forever") and by framing the narrative within the aftermath of World War I. By making Nick a war veteran, Fitzgerald connects Nick's forgetfulness and "restlessness" to an anxiety-provoking figure in the postwar culture: the shell-shocked soldier.[44] Certainly, Nick is less debilitated than other shell-shocked characters such as Virginia Woolf's Septimus Smith and Faulkner's Bayard Sartoris (as a later chapter shows). But "shell-shock" was a complicated and elusive diagnosis, even in the medical community—recognized in some countries but not in others, treated and theorized differently for officers and infantrymen.[45] Its specific causes and its cure eluded definition. The term itself was disavowed by military psychiatrists in 1918 but had taken root in the popular imagination, where it remained.[46] In a 1921 *Atlantic Monthly* essay, an anonymous colonel in the American Expeditionary Force offered a description of what it was like to be "shell-shocked—and after": "it is indescribable"; "weeks intervening . . . are a blank—I simply remember nothing at all." This veteran reports that he "shrank from meeting [his] friends—and the girl [he left behind]"—which sounds a lot like Nick Carraway. He continues, "I was only bored" by people and things that "normally" would have been interesting; "I could not keep my mind on my work, I thought of other things, fumbled with my papers, dreamed and took walks during office hours. . . . I would go to sleep at my desk": at work, "I was practically useless." This too resembles Nick's restlessness, his tendency to doze at work, and his lackluster career. Perhaps most disturbing is the colonel's loneliness and the way he "shak[es] with an intangible fear of a thing not understood." This veteran's account typifies what had become recognizable as paradigmatic symptoms: difficulty readjusting to civilian life, isolation, gaps in his memory, fear, and shame.[47]

We know that Fitzgerald was familiar with popular notions of shell-shock; his character Gordon Sterrett suffers from a fairly obvious case of it. "May Day" (1920) describes Sterrett's nervousness, sleeplessness, and desperation. His desperate plea for help meets with callous rejection by those who never went to war, which leads, in the story's final paragraph, to his suicide. Later, in *Tender Is the Night*, Fitzgerald extends the diagnosis to people without direct military experience when Dick Diver only half ironically diagnoses himself with "non-combatant shell-shock."[48] But even without these examples, Fitzgerald's awareness of the problem is incontrovertible: it was too big a problem for him *not* to know about it. Over eighty thousand soldiers suffered from shell-shock during the war.[49] But it troubled the entire culture. Shell-shock became a nexus for several postwar controversies including veterans' pensions and medical practice and theory. Fitzgerald evokes both a real-life condition and an emerging literary type: shell-shocked men appear frequently in literature as subjects of confusion and tragedy.[50] Crucially, the word "shell-shock" never appears in *Gatsby*. Nick's narrative cannot be reduced to a diagnosis. Without being too literal-minded about his condition, however, "shell-shock" provides an important context for his characterization.

The cultural anxieties around shell-shock can be traced to a few central issues. First of all, as Elaine Showalter has argued, the condition disrupted cultural assumptions about the gender of madness. It demonstrated that men—even the *manliest* of men—were just as vulnerable as women to hysterical symptoms. But since it attacked soldiers, it could not be attributed to an effeminized way of life. Second, shell-shock signaled the war's continued presence long after the Armistice. To be sure, as Ben Shephard explains, the "symptoms of shell-shock genuinely took everyone by surprise" when they appeared in large numbers during the war. But even after the surprise had been assimilated and initial explanations had been postulated, "most doctors expected the end of the war to bring an end to the war neuroses."[51] If shell-shock was, essentially, a result of fear and an unconscious way for even brave, dutiful soldiers to escape the battlefield, as the prevailing psychological explanations would have it, then its source would disappear with the war, and so, the assumption went, would the condition. But it did not. The incidence of war neuroses increased after the war. Showalter estimates that over one hundred thousand servicemen applied "for pensions for shell-shock-related disorders between 1919 and 1929"; Shephard reports that by 1940, the U.S. government "had spent almost a billion dollars on the psychiatric problems of veterans."[52] This raises a further issue: cost. Men damaged by "shell-shock" were imagined as unemployable pariahs: broken men who could no longer function in the traditional role of breadwinner or cope with the demands of a competitive, capitalist society. In these ways, shell-shock further disrupted deeply held assumptions about masculinity. Men were not immune to psychological disturbance, nor were they able to put those disturbances aside once their cause (the war) was no longer present. This context frames Nick's ambivalent masculinity, which the text establishes through comparison with the more manly Tom Buchanan and through Nick's half-hearted pursuit of both women and money.

Just as shell-shock disrupted cultural understandings of masculinity, so too it challenged notions of an illness's (or a wound's) chronological course. Even during the war, it was associated with memory loss and regression (as it is, for instance, in Rebecca West's popular *The Return of the Soldier* [1918]). Freud linked it to another kind of memory disturbance. In "Beyond the Pleasure Principle," which appeared in English just as Fitzgerald was writing *Gatsby*, Freud described shell-shock as a "traumatic neurosis" in which patients "suffer mainly from reminiscences."[53] He was concerned with what they remembered unconsciously. Freud postulates that an initial shocking event breaches a patient's sensory "protective shield" and compromises his ability to admit experience in such a way that it can be available to consciousness. The shock of the event enters the memory but bypasses the cathecting processes that would normally bind it, connect it to other consciously held thoughts, and make it available for conscious recollection. Because of this, traumatic events initiate a condition that becomes manifest not only in a debilitating "subjective ailment" but more particularly in a profound disturbance of memory: a compulsion to repeat and relive an event in the present rather than to remember it as something that happened in the past. That is, despite the unpleasant and disturbing nature of the original event, the subject repeatedly returns to it in dreams and in various forms of action. This, Freud insists, "astonishes people far too little." It certainly astonishes him: it so controverts his theory of human motivation, identified as a search for pleasure, that it forces him to revise his theory of the drives and to go (as his title announces) *beyond* the pleasure principle. Freud writes,

A condition has long been known and described which occurs after severe mechanical concussions, railway disasters and other accidents involving a risk to life; it has been given the name of "traumatic neurosis." The terrible war which has just ended gave rise to a great number of illnesses of this kind, but it at least put an end to the temptation to attribute the cause of the disorder to organic lesions of the nervous system brought about by mechanical force. . . .

In the case of the ordinary traumatic neuroses two characteristics emerge prominently: first, that the chief weight in their causation seems to rest upon the factor of surprise, or fright; and secondly, that a wound or injury inflicted simultaneously works as a rule *against* the development of a neurosis. . . . "Fright" . . . is the name we give to the state a person gets into when he has run into danger without being prepared for it. . . . Dreams occurring in traumatic neuroses have the characteristic of repeatedly bringing the patient back into the situation of his accident, a situation from which he wakes up in another fright. . . .

I am not aware, however, that patients suffering from traumatic neurosis are much occupied in their waking lives with memories of their accident. Perhaps they are more concerned with *not* thinking of it.[54]

Like the soldiers Freud describes, Nick struggles and fails to remember his past; he shows many signs of suffering from a memory he cannot consciously recall. His experience is not wholly forgotten—on the contrary, it continues to make its presence felt in surprising ways. As research on post-traumatic stress disorder (the contemporary name for a condition similar in its symptoms and etiology) shows, connection between the traumatic past and the present takes oddly discontinuous forms compared to the presence of the past in other, nontraumatic forms of memory and custom. Memories of a traumatic past "are apparently contradictory. On the one hand, traumatized people remember too much; on the other hand, they remember too little. . . . The memories intrude when they are not wanted, in the form of nightmares, flashbacks, and behavioral re-enactments. Yet the memories may not be accessible when they are wanted. Major parts of the story may be missing, and sometimes an entire event or series of events may be lost."[55] Though Fitzgerald did not have access to our current theoretical and clinical analyses of trauma, his text is thoroughly engaged with the iterations of war trauma as they appeared in the World War I period. Nick, in both his denial (his "*not* thinking" of the war) and his intermittent feeling of fright, illustrates a particular kind of postwar subjectivity. Fitzgerald not only shows his reader that "major parts of" Nick's "story" are "missing" and that "an entire event or series of events" are "lost" and will remain untold—he says so directly ("what I had almost remembered was incommunicable forever"). To read *Gatsby*, we need to take into account the parts of the story that Nick cannot remember and to understand these omissions as conventional signs of traumatic suffering.

Nick has come home from the war, as Freud would describe other trauma victims, "*apparently* uninjured."[56] But like the colonel who described the condition in the *Atlantic Monthly*, Nick exhibits many of the symptoms—boredom at work, restlessness, a need to flee his home and girlfriend, strange gaps in memory, the conviction that his own experience is "incommunicable"—that were, in the early 1920s, the telltales of shell-shock.

Unreal City: Images of Death and the Displaced Residues of War

Having a better sense of the associations that Nick's status as a potentially shell-shocked veteran would have conjured up for *Gatsby*'s contemporary audience enables us to see how Fitzgerald uses Nick's point of view to bring the war's more insidious and long-term effects into focus. Nick's point of view reveals war's residues: not the battle but the morning after; not official remembrances but unwilling, unauthorized reenactments.

Perhaps because Nick has seen more death than he could assimilate, his story manifests a certain preoccupation with death. It surfaces sometimes through visual symbolization (the Buchanan lawn) and in what Nick notices. For instance, when he and Gatsby drive into New York, Nick looks on as a "dead man pass[es them] in a hearse heaped with blooms" and imagines them taking part in the "somber holiday" of the funeral (68–69). Just a few pages later, Meyer Wolfsheim takes both Nick's and Gatsby's familiarity with violence and loss for granted. He has seen death in all its ugly, intimate details ("I can't forget so long as I live the night they shot Rosy Rosenthal there," Wolfsheim broods [70]) and assumes that they have, too. But although Nick has fought a war, he seems strangely naïve as he hears Wolfsheim's stories of violent death. When Wolfsheim praises Gatsby's war record, the conversation takes a surprising turn:

> "I made the pleasure of [Gatsby's] acquaintance just after the war. . . ." He paused. "I see you're looking at my cuff buttons."
>
> I hadn't been looking at them, but I did now. They were composed of oddly familiar pieces of ivory.
>
> "Finest specimens of human molars," he informed me.
>
> "Well!" I inspected them. "That's a very interesting idea." (72)

Leaving aside the unanswerable question (*was* Nick looking at the cuff links?), we can note that this awkward moment repeats the steps of his conversation with Gatsby at the party: reference to war, misrecognition, revelation, and Nick's concluding stock phrase. Instead of a memory or an affective response, Nick voices only noncommittal surprise ("What! . . . I beg your pardon," "Well! . . . That's a very interesting idea"). In this moment, Fitzgerald again pairs Nick's distraction and almost unbeliev-able naïveté with a reference to the war, this time adding the relics of a corpse. Collecting body parts as souvenirs is relatively rare but not unheard-of in accounts of World War I.[57] "All American soldiers became compulsive collectors of artifacts" and, in doing so, "incorporated parts of the combatant's identity into their own personas."[58] War souvenirs are tangible reminders of killing, though their violent origin is usually implied rather than explained. Such is the case here, since Wolfsheim identifies the objects as human body parts but does not explain how he came to be wearing them.[59] Wolfsheim, haunted by memories of the vio-lent past, wears physical reminders of it. His molar cuff links fetishize traumatic death: "horror . . . has set up a memorial to itself in the cre-ation of this substitute."[60] Wolfsheim verbally disavows death: he refuses to come to Gatsby's funeral and tells Nick, "Let us learn to show our friendship for a man when he is alive and not after he is dead. . . . After that, my own rule is to let everything alone" (172). Rather than bury-ing his dead, Wolfsheim keeps bits of them around and melancholically recalls their deaths. Perhaps the cuff links strike Nick as "an interesting idea" because he has seen oddly dismembered body parts before. But unlike Wolfsheim, who names his ghosts and verbalizes his violent past, Nick's preoccupation with death is not localized in a particular object or given a particular name until Gatsby dies.

In contrast to Wolfsheim's, then, Nick's preoccupation with death and dead bodies seems unanchored and vague. Yet the recent war struc-tures Nick's (and hence the reader's) sight. Fitzgerald takes Joseph Con-rad's injunction to the modern writer "to make you hear, to make you feel . . . before all, to make you *see*" things and applies it to war experi-ence.[61] Vague references to the war pervade Nick's visual imagery, for example, in the "indiscernible barbed wire" he imagines between Gatsby and East Egg (148) or, more spectacularly, in the Valley of Ashes. While many critics have noticed that *Gatsby*'s Valley of Ashes, like T. S. Eliot's landscape in "The Waste Land," evokes the battlefields of World War I, none have gone far enough in reckoning the imagery's closeness to no-man's-land. To be sure, *Gatsby*'s Valley of Ashes is not strictly or only a reference to the Western Front. In the Cambridge University Press edition of the novel, Matthew Bruccoli provides a photograph of the ash dump that Fitzgerald would have seen between Long Island and New York City in the early 1920s.[62] Inscribed on that literal place, the Valley of Ashes more broadly encapsulates dehumanization under industrialization and emergent machine culture and offers a dystopic version of "the machine in the garden," as Leo Marx suggested long ago.[63] But such a landscape had a universally ominous relevance in the 1920s precisely because of the well-documented and publicized destruction of France and Belgium during the war—destruction the Fitzgeralds saw for themselves when they traveled through Europe and to the former battlefields in the 1920s. So although Fitzgerald's "ash-grey" men are not specifically doughboys, they do look like them as they "move dimly and already crumbling through the powdery air" like an army of dead, ghostly soldiers stirring about in lime (23). The Valley of Ashes resembles no-man's-land as Samuel Hynes describes it: "the strange landscape that is not a landscape but the annihilation of what *landscape* means," the place in which "everything natural has been defaced and destroyed."[64] That, of course, is a place Nick has been. Through these examples, Fitzgerald shows us what it is like to see the world through a lens shaped by war experience.[65]

Death surfaces intermittently, in moments that are by turn gratuitous, hallucinatory, and realistic. At the Buchanans', Nick watches Jordan and Tom going into the house "as if to a vigil beside a perfectly tangible body" (16). In the draft, when Nick ("Dud" at this point in Fitzgerald's composition) makes idle conversation to cover an awkward moment, he seizes on the subject of death:

"Did you two have a little heart-to-heart on the verandah?" inquired Tom, looking pointedly at his wife.

. . . I changed the subject by telling informing him that an old friend of ours was recently dead. As it turns out that was an unfortunate move because Daisy had to sit there on the piano stool while we had performed an autopsy on him the deceased.

"You don't mean to tell me he's *dead*!" repeated Tom for the third time.

"Certainly not," Daisy answered for me, "Dud just made it up to give you a thrill."

Men like to say things over and over like that, they resent a wife's ability of immediately accepting an outrageous fact. We both told stories of our last meeting with the corpse and then we eulogized him and then qualified the eulogy a bit and then lowered him back into his grave, while Daisy yawned.

~~"You sure he's absolutely dead?" she said finally.~~[66]

Here, death's temporality is confused: Nick and Tom retrospectively apply the news of the friend's death and imagine him as a "corpse" when they last met. Fitzgerald emphasizes the dead person's body ("we had performed an autopsy," "our last meeting with the corpse"), almost as if it were a physical object being moved about the room ("we . . . lowered [the corpse] back into his grave"). And yet his death remains unreal. Tom, Nick, and Daisy long for evidence—a real corpse—to corroborate their loss. Although Fitzgerald cut this passage, the need for physical evidence remains in the novel. Nick's similes and trains of thought betray his desire for a corpse to make the death that hovers around the edges of his consciousness "perfectly tangible." Death has happened, but survivors struggle to realize it.

Rather than tracing Nick's death imagery directly to his past and his experience in the war, Fitzgerald instead uses such moments to foreshadow the future: they generate an expectation of violence that finds fulfillment in the novel's violent plot and particularly in Gatsby's death. Or, put another way, Gatsby's murder may be a meaningful story for Nick to tell insofar as it evokes his own traumatic past.

Trauma's Return: Narrating *Gatsby*'s "Holocaust"

World War I is relevant in understanding not only *Gatsby*'s narrator and his point of view but also its plot, which serves as an analogy for the war in multiple ways. At one level, the analogy is literal: the climactic car accident and Myrtle's disfigured corpse serve as reminders of mechanized warfare. Fitzgerald originally considered making this explicit, as this chapter's epigraph shows. When Nick tells Gatsby about Myrtle's body, Gatsby interrupts him:

"It ripped her open—"
"Don't tell me." He winced, "I saw enough of that in the war."
~~A wave of nausea rushed over him and he leaned sideways against a tree. "Well,—she stepped on it. I tried to make her stop but she couldn't, and didn't until she I pulled on the emergency brake. Then she fell over into collapsed into my arms. So I went on."~~[67]

Even in this more explicit comparison, the violence of warfare is alluded to as an unspeakable topic. It surfaces only in comparison to a displaced and feminized form of violence, in which a woman driver does damage to a female body. As vague as Gatsby's conflation is ("I saw enough of *that* in the war"), it makes their similarity apparent.

But as Fitzgerald revised, he made the analogy between war and the car accident less explicit. Perhaps he imagined that his audience, like Gatsby, might not want to be reminded of it. In the final version of the novel, Fitzgerald refigures content as form. He censors the war as a subject of recollection and makes its presence felt as point of view, as if the legacy of war can be measured more, as we have seen, in *how* one tells stories rather than in *which* stories one tells. But Fitzgerald also uses the formal device of repetition and structures the novel's temporality in ways that evoke the war's traumatic structure of feeling. *Gatsby*'s repetitive structure offers an implicit record of war which Fitzgerald—and at least some of his contemporaries—understood, even if they did not name, as characteristically posttraumatic. Repetitions structure all the relationships and events of the novel, including Nick's relationship to Gatsby and to Jordan, Gatsby's relationship to Daisy, Daisy's relationship to Tom, and Tom's relationship with Myrtle Wilson. These relationships hinge on repetitive willingness to injure or to be injured and seem founded on traumatic fixations rather than mutual recognition.

As injuries compound and take increasingly violent form, two questions emerge. The first involves the question of consent and complicity: who is to blame for the three deaths, the novel's "holocaust"? The dilemma of complicity provides one of the most subtle aspects of the novel's commentary on the war. *Gatsby*'s dual scene of violence and death is simultaneously accidental and intended. Human hostility is mystified in that it seems to unfold through coincidence and by proxy rather than through wittingly executed individual action. Despite the fact that violence has been done, it is hard to find anyone to blame. This, I suggest, is analogous to the way human actors mystified the question of responsibility for the war. Historical and personal war narratives emphasize the roles played by coincidence and inanimate technology precisely in order *not* to take account of the human willingness to destroy and to be destroyed that is at the center of the war.[68] As cultural historians have argued, "Why and how millions of Europeans and Westerners acquiesced in the war of 1914–1918 has remained buried. Why we accept the violence of warfare has remained a taboo subject."[69] *Gatsby* resembles the ways in which writing about the war mystifies killing through its dominant trope of "careless driving."

The second question to emerge from the wreckage of *Gatsby*'s plot involves mourning and specifically how Nick responds to and makes meaning of Gatsby's death. His failed mourning process has been central, as we shall see, to both critical explorations of the melancholic character of both *Gatsby* and canonical modernism more generally. Nick's melancholic response to losing Gatsby provides a paradigmatic example of Moglen's "melancholic modernism."[70] We can further that discussion by situating Nick's attempt to mourn Gatsby within the very specific context of World War I's New Death. As Nick tells the story of Gatsby's death and burial, he changes as a narrator, and his voice gains an increased sense of mastery. He enacts a series of traditional rituals as if to assimilate his loss. These rituals correspond to what was impossible for many bereaved families, friends, and comrades during the war. Nick's actions after Gatsby's death read like one man's attempt to compensate for the unassimilated deaths that tormented survivors of the war.

Careless Driving

In Fitzgerald's work, car accidents repeatedly figure traumatic experience and his protagonists' vulnerability to disaster. In *This Side of Paradise*, Amory Blaine predicts but misses the accident that kills one of his role models, Dick Humbird, and spends the rest of the novel trying and mostly failing to imitate the manly performance that Humbird vacates so abruptly. Humbird's death is traumatic because he dies without being ready; he fails to have a "Good Death." During the nineteenth century, as Drew Gilpin Faust has shown, Americans tended to dying people at home and watched over them for signs of spiritual readiness to die. They looked for evidence that the dying had settled their accounts with God, particularly in the "last words" spoken by the dying.[71] Fitzgerald depicts the negative consequences of what happens when the dying and the mourners do not share a "Good Death": Humbird's death is unexpected and (by Amory, at least) unwitnessed; his body is horrible to see; his reputation is insecure, and consequently his ghost haunts Amory. The abruptness of Dick Humbird's car accident epitomizes the horrors of unprepared, traumatic death.[72]

Fitzgerald returns to this figure in *Tender Is the Night*. There, a dangerous car accident signals a different kind of failure for another character (also named Dick). Dick Diver's lack of judgment in all things regarding Nicole (faults that have traumatic precedents in the case of her father) are distilled in the moment that he allows her to grab the wheel and steer the Diver family over a cliff. Later, in Fitzgerald's screenplay for *Three Comrades* (Remarque's novel about three damaged veterans trying and failing to remake life in postwar Germany), Fitzgerald uses the car accident repeatedly to signal the recurrence of trauma and disaster in their lives. But car accidents are most important in *Gatsby*, where they resonate across the text as a series of events that are simultaneously connected (and therefore predictable) and abruptly unexpected. This paradoxical quality of meaningful randomness constitutes an element of modernism in the aesthetic organization of Fitzgerald's plot.

Fitzgerald's car accidents modernize the nineteenth-century image for mechanical trauma, that of the train accident. "Railway spine" (the mysterious injury apparently suffered by those who walked away from train crashes only to complain later of nervous problems) was, like "shell-shock," produced by modern technology acting on the body in ways that were difficult to explain. Like victims of "shell-shock," sufferers of "railway spine" were suspected of malingering. Their injuries were located in an unknown nervous zone, somewhere between the mind and the body.

Freud used the figure of the train-accident survivor repeatedly to illustrate his observations about trauma, particularly the split between the event and its effects. In an almost verbatim repetition of "Beyond the Pleasure Principle," he returns to the accident motif in "Moses and Monotheism" (1939):

> It may happen that a man who has experienced some frightful accident—a railway collision, for instance—leaves the scene of the event apparently uninjured. In the course of the next few weeks, however, he develops a number of severe physical and motor symptoms which can only be traced to his shock, the concussion or whatever else it was. He now has a "traumatic neurosis." It is a quite unintelligible—that is to say, a new—fact. The time that has passed between the accident and the first appearance of the symptoms is described as the "incubation period," in a clear allusion to the pathology of infectious diseases, . . . the characteristic that might be described as "latency."[73]

Trauma's first symptom is forgetfulness and denial, or even relief. Other effects of the accident appear later, after an appearance of having escaped unharmed. This latency period, which opens between the infliction of the wound and the appearance of its effects, distinguishes the temporality of trauma from strictly rational notions of time. Traumatic temporality splits the fundamental unit of historical measurement, the event, into separate parts, since a person who gets away from an accident "apparently uninjured" may think that *nothing* has happened to him, only to discover later that *something* did happen. Recognizing this precipitates questions about the human ability to narrate both collective and personal history when trauma is a factor.[74] The messiness that this delay introduces to rational discourse is one factor that has provoked widespread resistance to trauma theory. But Fitzgerald's narrative observes and unfolds according to just such a temporality.

Traumatic temporality emerges particularly in and through the novel's various accidents. Nick dodges a detailed discussion of the war with Gatsby at the party, but he does not get away without having to confront the subject of violence more directly:

> Fifty feet from the door a dozen headlights illuminated a bizarre and tumultuous scene. In the ditch beside the road, right side up but violently shorn of one wheel, rested a new coupé which had left Gatsby's drive not two minutes before. The sharp jut of a wall accounted for the detachment of the wheel which was now getting considerable attention from half a dozen curious chauffeurs. However, as they had left their cars blocking the road a harsh discordant din from those in the rear had been audible for some time and added to the already violent confusion of the scene. (53)

Faced with the scene's violence, Nick's temporality dilates. Although the car left "not two minutes" ago, a line of others has already formed, and their protest has been audible "for some time." In the very midst of violent activity, the car "rested." Nick has difficulty interpreting what he sees. His run-on sentences yearn to determine cause and effect (the wall "account[s] for" the detached wheel; "as" the chauffeurs have stopped to look, the scene's confusion consequently grows). But his anxious attempt to narrate the scene leaves its most pressing questions unasked—how did the car get in the ditch? is anyone injured or dead? The accident precipitates a crisis for which Nick lacks just the right tone. Alliterative description gives way to irony, and the scene unfolds as a farce. Perhaps afraid of what he might witness, Nick puns. Irony, the trope of emotional detachment, once again asserts itself as a defense. One silly gag gives way to another. The man who emerges from the car—the "late" (recent, not dead) patron of Gatsby's library—begins what sounds like an explanation: "I know very little about driving—next to nothing. . . . I wasn't even trying" (54). But as the passenger, his explanations are non sequiturs. And the driver? His brush with death generates a series of puns on death: after a "ghostly pause," "a pale dangling individual," "an apparition" emerges, "part by part" from the car—also not at all dead, or even dismembered (54). Although Nick's diction anticipates a dead or broken body, he sees instead a living person who denies death with drunken, deadpan humor ("Did we run outa gas?") and a disfigured car, a "coupé" (cut) with its wheel "amputated." "Amputated" implies a limb, conveying the trace of an anthropomorphic wound. Thus, the car stands in the place of an injured human body, and it both draws the human gaze and also confuses it: no one knows what the accident means. As the passenger remarks, "it happened, and that's all I know" (54). No one can explain how the event itself came to pass or what it means.

Being attentive to the peculiarities of Nick's perspective might lead us to speculate that the broken machine, the artificially illuminated nighttime sky, the noise, the confusion, and the recently elided war story collectively trigger a memory of the war. World War I, the first fully mechanized war—the war that saw the first use of the tank and the airplane and the first extensive use of the submarine—left an abundance of evidence of how machines intensified human destructive capability. Its survivors often did not, or could not, say what had happened to them. The war left an abundance of bodies with amputated limbs.[75] Many observers were left wondering why the war had been fought. But Fitzgerald does not invite these speculations explicitly. Instead, the origins of Nick's fright are left unspecified. Simply, the accident arouses his expectation but fails to fulfill it: no one is dead.

The crisis provoked by the accident's shock yields to disappointment. Nick does not see what he expects, nor can he assign any intention or meaning to it. This disappointment, in turn, yields to relief—even pleasure. Violent death has been, for the moment, warded off. Thus, if the accident initially has the air of an afterthought, it ultimately bestows a sense of completion on the party. This effect is enhanced as Gatsby, striking his already characteristic pose, his "formal gesture of farewell," restores order (55). Like an orchestral conductor, he raises his arm and transposes the "discordant din" into the recognizable strains of crescendo. Seeing this, Nick attributes the accident to the heterogeneity of Gatsby's party as a place where one can expect the unexpected and Trimalchio oversees it all, where "Tostoff" (tossed-off) improvisation is nevertheless part of a crafted aesthetic (50). Just as Gatsby replaces a guest's damaged dress, here his gesture of farewell reassures Nick that the accident did not, as it were, tear the fabric of the evening. And yet as Nick leaves the accident behind, he throws an Orpheus-like look over his shoulder—a look that suggests it still haunts him. Nick's retrospective glance signals a remainder of loss, which often functions in traumatic narratives as a premonition that an encounter with death, though postponed, will return.[76]

Nick's experience of this accident and his backward glance toward it both adumbrate a crucial aspect of his larger story, in which he continually takes leave of something only to (re)experience it in a new form. Events that are difficult to assimilate return in a different form after a latency period. He leaves the Midwest and then the East; he leaves his (rumored) fiancée and then Jordan; he looks away when Tom breaks Myrtle's nose but later sees her body ripped open on the highway; he leaves the Buchanans and Gatsby and then retells their story. Although Nick turns away from this accident, its threat returns (50).

Just a few paragraphs later, Nick returns to the subjects of driving and injury. The chapter ends with another near miss and a conversation:

> It was on that same house party that [Jordan and I] had a curious conversation about driving a car. It started because she passed so close to some workmen that our fender flicked a button on one man's coat.
>
> "You're a rotten driver," I protested. "Either you ought to be more careful or you oughtn't to drive at all."
>
> "I am careful."
>
> "No, you're not."
>
> "Well, other people are," she said lightly.
>
> "What's that got to do with it?"
>
> "They'll keep out of my way," she insisted. "It takes two to make an accident."
>
> "Suppose you met somebody just as careless as yourself."
>
> "I hope I never will," she answered. "I hate careless people. That's why I like you."
>
> Her grey sun-strained eyes stared straight ahead, but she had deliberately shifted our relations, and for a moment I thought I loved her. But I am slow thinking and full of interior rules that act as brakes on my desires, and I knew that first I had to get myself definitely out of that tangle back home. (58)

This accident repeats the first in some crucial ways: again, Nick feels fright; again, no one is hurt. Jordan turns Nick's anxiety toward herself, and fear becomes desire: Jordan reconstrues his fears about her driving as a trope about their relationship. She makes the car a metaphoric vehicle—not a literal object but one that symbolizes human affairs. One kind of physical encounter (flicking a man's coat with the car) gets reimagined as another kind of (potentially) physical encounter: while noticing Jordan's driving, Nick imagines himself as a car, with convictions that "act as *brakes* on [his] desires." It is not that the car itself becomes erotic but rather that the exhilaration and danger of driving provide an idiom for articulating romantic interpersonal relations.

Just as Jordan "shifts" the meaning of her careless driving to another kind of question, Fitzgerald shifts from one source of textual suspense to another through these repeated car accidents. He evokes a desire in the reader for something to happen. When Jordan and Nick have their "conversation about driving a car" just pages after the car crashes into the ditch, the car accident becomes a motif that Fitzgerald, via Jordan, invites us to read as symbolic. This motif connects a submerged chain of references (Nick's encounters with death) with others closer to the narrative's surface (summer romances). As car accidents take their place in a narrative pattern, they provide the potential for narrative meaning and pleasure.

Gatsby illustrates what Peter Brooks identifies as a commonality between the traumatic compulsion to repeat and the meaning-making that narrative makes possible:

> An event gains meaning by its repetition. . . . Repetition creates a *return* in the text, a doubling back. We cannot say whether this return is a return *to* or a return *of*: for instance a return to origins or a return of the repressed. Repetition through this ambiguity appears to suspend temporal process, or rather, to subject it to an indeterminate shuttling or oscillation that binds different moments together as a middle that might turn forward or back.[77]

Brooks asserts that although this perpetual repetition in texts interrupts movement forward, it is—both in analytic work and in literary form—the stuff from which interpretation emerges: "Repetition in all its literary manifestations may in fact work as a 'binding,' a binding of textual energies that allows them to be mastered by putting them into serviceable form, usable 'bundles,' within the energetic economy of the narrative."[78] In *Gatsby*, Fitzgerald "binds" the violence of war to the car accidents in *Gatsby*'s plot. With the succession of accidents and the use of driving as a trope, Fitzgerald binds violence and romance and binds the violence that pervades Nick's and the novel's vision with the latent violence in the Gatsby-Buchanan plot.

As collisions occur, Fitzgerald makes automobile accidents (and exchanges) the visible nexuses of the novel's crossed lines of desire.[79] Nick becomes involved with others who, it seems, have and repeat their own traumatic pasts. By surviving and narrating their collective traumatic reenactments, Nick's "lost fragment of words" gathers significance and begins to find an echo in stories about others and what they, in turn, have lost.

Gatsby's "Colossal Accident" and the Compulsion to Repeat

Fitzgerald's repeated use of the term and figure of the "accident" suggests that Gatsby and Daisy are, like Nick, reenacting rather than remembering their histories. Just as Nick goes east and moves in next door to a (fake) French Hôtel de Ville, Gatsby has returned to the woman he won, and lost, during the war. As Gatsby repeats his past—his courtship of Daisy—he loses her again. In repeating his loss, he finds himself able to tell Nick his story, which Nick then tells to the reader. The war figures in Gatsby's story, as it does in Nick's, in seemingly coincidental but crucial ways. By giving him a chance to woo Daisy, the war acts as a trigger incident for the events (*fabula*) of his plot. He meets her while in training, when his uniform gives him temporary class mobility. This "colossal accident" brings them together only to separate them (149). Gatsby and Daisy lose each other, and that loss becomes constitutive of Gatsby's desire.

In trying to recover Daisy, Gatsby is not motivated only by social ambition.[80] His desire for Daisy goes beyond her status—it goes "beyond her, beyond everything" (*The Great Gatsby*, 95). Despite this language of excess and overdetermination, however, it is perhaps most important that Daisy stands for life before the war, life before the war made it "confused and disordered" (110). Gatsby's desire for Daisy is, fundamentally, a desire to return to prewar innocence. When he gets back from Europe, Gatsby returns to Louisville even though Daisy has already left. That is where he first assumes what Nick describes as a (not unlike his own, Orpheus-like) posture of outstretched arms, a gesture that is eminently melancholic, expressing both desire and farewell. On a train leaving Louisville, "he stretched out his hand desperately as if to snatch only a wisp of air, to save a fragment of the spot that she had made lovely for him. But it was all going by too fast . . . and he knew he had lost that part of it, the freshest and the best, forever" (153). This scene locates Gatsby's hallmark gesture and his propensity for speeding vehicles (trains, cars, hydroplanes) in the context of his departure from the place where he wooed Daisy and the place where he had trained, but not yet fought, as a soldier.

Gatsby's attempt to "snatch only a wisp of air" echoes Nick's "*fragment* of *lost* words," that "phrase" that struggles to take shape as more "than a *wisp of* startled *air*" discussed earlier (my emphasis). The echo underscores the fact that Gatsby's loss, too, has a certain vagueness. "It" goes by too fast; he has lost "that part of it"—Daisy has the power to evoke "it," but "it" is not her. In other words, Gatsby constructs Daisy as his surrogate in the way that Nick constructs him as one. This explains in part his disappointment when "Daisy tumbled short of his dreams—not through her own fault, but because of the colossal vitality of his illusion"—*and* his loss (95). Later, when Nick listens to Gatsby's story, he surmises that Gatsby "wanted to recover something, some idea of himself perhaps, that had gone into loving Daisy. His life had been confused and disordered since then, but if he could once return to a certain starting place and go over it all slowly, he could find out what that thing was. . . ." (110; ellipsis in the original). I suggest that the "starting place" Gatsby seeks is, not incidentally, the moment before he went to war.

Gatsby's desire to recover Daisy coincides with a desire to return to a time before the war, which is alluded to but not explicitly described as a time of loss and trauma. The intervening time is figured as a kind of latency period. *What* Gatsby has lost only to lose again in the course of the novel has been described most frequently as "the American dream." Gatsby's dream has provoked commentary because it is both elusive and allusive, resonating with several moments and motifs in American history. Gatsby's loss of Dan Cody, for instance, famously evokes the close of the "wild" American West. But Gatsby's experience also traces the experience of the generation of American men who fought in World War I. Many who, like Gatsby, "did extraordinarily well in the war" paradoxically suffered as a result. Many were wounded or traumatized. Even those who were not often faced economic displacement. As men went to the war, jobs that had traditionally belonged to white male citizens were opened to new communities of workers including immigrants, women, and African Americans.[81] Gatsby epitomizes the simultaneous vulnerability and potential danger of the returned veteran. When he returned from Europe, he could not find work until he turned to Meyer Wolfsheim. He then becomes an outlaw in the very country he had fought for and killed to protect. Gatsby's experience as a World War I veteran returning home to be dogged by rumors that he might have "killed a man" offers a paradigmatic story that is told and retold in novels, stories, films, and histories of the interwar period in the United States. But although this trajectory into crime is often explained as a result of shifts in the economy and the distribution of jobs, it also betrays an anxiety about the difficulty of reassimilating trained killers into civilian life. Indeed, as I argue in the conclusion, the economic damage and consequent turn to violent crime, epitomized by the figure of the "Hero for Sale," became a, if not *the*, pervasive narrative about what the war had meant for, and done to, the "typical" American man. As Keith Gandal puts it, *Gatsby* can be read as "an extended, agonized missive to the U.S. military by Fitzgerald on the subject of *The Great War* . . . : 'yes, you have helped win the conflict by creating officers and 'new men' like Gatsby, but look too at what you have thereby let loose in our post-war world.'"[82] Gatsby's desire to return to time before the war bespeaks a collective nostalgia for a "simpler" time—a time before mobilization for and participation in "the business" of war, namely, killing. *Gatsby* condenses this anxiety about violence in the nostalgia of romance: Gatsby hopes to regain the various things he has lost in going away by rekindling his relationship with Daisy.

Instead of recovering love, however, Gatsby's journey is a return to violence. Fitzgerald's language establishes a chain of association between "the colossal accident" of meeting Daisy and the novel's own plot. Gatsby's first "colossal accident" leads him to commit what he describes as a crime: he takes Daisy "unscrupulously" when he has "no real right to touch her hand" (149). Gatsby—by the "accident" of war—has the opportunity to take, and does. Fitzgerald's turn of phrase produces a bizarre sense of scale: in World War I, and in the world of *Gatsby*, many events might without exaggeration be called (and were called) "*colossal accidents*." In comparison, a poor young man's romance with a debutant pales—or rather darkens—in comparison. Despite the accidental quality of Gatsby's initial crime, he is ultimately punished for a more deadly one—the accident that kills Myrtle. In that "accident," the class boundaries disrupted by the war are emphatically reasserted. Neither Gatsby not Myrtle lives to climb the social ladder. The various dreams of classless romances—the individual incarnations of the Progressive myth of a classless American society promulgated during the war—come to a brutal end.

"That's What I Get for Marrying a Brute of a Man": Daisy's Repetition Compulsion

If the war damages and displaces Nick and Gatsby, Tom does something similar to Daisy. In the manuscript, Fitzgerald asserts this analogy more brutally. When Daisy tells Nick ("Dud") about giving birth to her daughter, she figures herself in a landscape of war:

"Listen, Dud," she ~~interrupted suddenly~~ broke out suddenly, ~~"Did you ever hear what I said when my child was born?"~~

"No Daisy."

"Well, she was less than an hour old and Tom was God knows where. I woke up out of the ether with an utterly abandoned feeling as if I'd ~~just been raped by a company of soldiers and left out on a plain in a field to die. I asked the nurse if it was a boy or a girl, and she said, 'You have a beautiful little girl.' I can hear her now just as plainly as if she was on this porch: 'You have a beautiful little girl,' she said, and so I turned my head away and swore and wept—and finally I cried right out in a loud voice: 'Well, if she's a girl all I can say hope is I hope that she's beautiful and a fool—that's the best thing a I girl can be in this world, a beautiful little fool."~~[83]

Daisy's comparison of herself to a woman raped by soldiers connects the trauma that men experience and inflict during war to that experienced by women. Daisy seems to cast herself in the role of "Poor Little Belgium" brutalized by the "brutal Boche invader." Fitzgerald amends this passage to reveal less of Daisy's loss in the final version:

> "Well, she was less than an hour old and Tom was God knows where. I woke up out of the ether with an utterly abandoned feeling and asked the nurse right away if it was a boy or a girl. She told me it was a girl, and so I turned my head away and wept. 'All right,' I said, 'I'm glad it's a girl. And I hope she'll be a fool—that's the best thing a girl can be in this world, a beautiful little fool.'" (16–17)

In the revised version, Fitzgerald distills Daisy's despair into her use of the word "fool," which is a loaded word for the Buchanans, as we learn in the confrontation scene at the Plaza Hotel, when Tom uses it several times to gloss over his repeated betrayals—"sometimes [Daisy] gets foolish ideas in her head"; "Once in a while I go off on a spree and make a fool of myself" (131). Another sign of Daisy's hurt is her tendency to verbally repeat herself, which was recognized as a symptom associated with traumatic fixation. Refiguring Cather's aesthetics of omission, the origins of Daisy's loss are "not named" but are felt, instead, through condensed word choice and tendency to verbally repeat. Indeed, Daisy says most things twice: "You ought to see the baby. . . . You ought to see her" (9–10); "Do you always watch for the longest day of the year and then miss it? I always watch for the longest day of the year and then miss it" (11); "It's about the butler's nose. Do you want to hear about the butler's nose?" (13); "You remind me of a—a rose, an absolute rose. . . . Doesn't he? . . . An absolute rose?" (14); "I hope she'll be a fool, . . . a beautiful little fool" (17). Daisy's seemingly traumatic discovery of herself as a "fool" can be traced, in turn, to something this passage only alludes to: the fact that Tom is "God knows where": utter abandonment.

If God does not know, Dr. T. J. Eckleberg might: Tom is undoubtedly with a mistress. By the time Nick hears Daisy's story, he has already been told that "Tom's got some woman in New York" (15). But this conversation suggests what Jordan will later confirm: the affair with Myrtle is only one in a series of betrayals. Jordan describes the Buchanan marriage in its early days:

> "She used to sit on the sand with his head in her lap . . . looking at him with unfathomable delight. It was touching to see them together—it made you laugh in a hushed, fascinated way. That was in August. A week after I left Santa Barbara Tom ran into a wagon on the Ventura road one night and ripped a wheel off his car. The girl who was with him got into the papers too because her arm was broken—she was one of the chambermaids in the Santa Barbara Hotel." (77)

This car accident breaks the respectful hush around their marriage and catapults the Buchanans "into the papers." The shock of the accident figures Jordan's sudden disillusionment with their marriage, which stands in for Daisy's. Just as Nick's irony distances him (and us) from the war, Jordan's brevity refuses to dwell on Daisy's wound. Jordan vividly depicts Daisy's "unfathomable delight" in the marriage, but when it comes to damage, she becomes evasive. The accident is shocking: it must shatter Daisy's belief in Tom as a faithful husband, just as it shocks Nick and the reader into the realization that Tom has had other affairs—Myrtle is only his latest "working girl."[84] But that shock is elided and muted in the way that the story is told, and despite the literal rupture of this accident, Tom and Daisy go on—the cycle simply repeats itself. The shattered dream of "happily ever after" is not replaced by the kind of plot Nick expects, in which Daisy would "rush out of the house, child in arms" (19). Instead the dream of love yields to a pattern of traumatic repetition.

Through this repetition, the Buchanans' pattern of loss and injury becomes strangely pleasurable. Everyone knows his or her part. Instead of confronting Tom directly about his infidelity, Daisy settles into the role of the repeatedly harmed wife. Her accusation that he has hurt her finger has all the elements of a set piece:

We all looked—the knuckle was black and blue.

"You did it, Tom," she said accusingly. "I know you didn't mean to, but you *did* do it. That's what I get for marrying a brute of a man, a great, big, hulking physical specimen of a—"

"I hate that word hulking," objected Tom crossly, "even in kidding."

"Hulking," insisted Daisy. (12)

Once again, Fitzgerald submerges the harm done within a frame of accident, making it difficult to adjudicate the meaning of, and the responsibility for, damage. At the same time, however, Fitzgerald links an inconsequential injury with a chain of other, more serious ones. Daisy's finger recalls in miniature the chambermaid's broken arm; Daisy's perseveration (here in her repetition of "hulking") prefigures Tom's assault on Myrtle after she repeats the word he forbids her to use ("Daisy!" [37]); and so on.

Another important and missing part of the Buchanans' story takes place in Chicago. Not surprisingly, Nick has no access to it. Like his own movements, he thinks of theirs as accidental: "Why they came East I don't know. They had spent a year in France for no particular reason, and then drifted here and there *unrestfully*" (6, my emphasis). But Daisy alludes to an ominous reason for their move: "Do you know why we left Chicago? I'm surprised that they didn't treat you to the story of that little spree" (131). Given the "little spree" to New York and back, we might wonder if there is an ironic truth in Nick's hyperbolic compliment to Daisy that since they have left Chicago, "the whole town is desolate. All the cars have the left rear wheel painted black as a mourning wreath, and there's a persistent wail all night along the north shore" (9). When the Buchanans do leave death in their wake, the untold story of "that little spree" in Chicago takes on new possibilities as a violent episode which the characters cannot afford to discuss and which the novel represses in one form only to reproduce in another.

But as Fitzgerald creates a pattern of accidents, their meanings begin to change. Each one evokes the other. Tom's accidents (one in which he "ripped a wheel off his car") recall the car with the "amputated" wheel after Gatsby's party. The missing wheels, the wheels turned mourning wreaths, the broken arm, the hurt finger, the broken nose: these details begin to accumulate and describe a pattern of injury. Premonitory of the accident that kills Myrtle Wilson, the August accident in Santa Barbara got into "the papers" and became a spectacle. So although Tom's accident gets brief treatment, its meaning for Nick and the reader is rich. It greatly increases a tension in the plot (what will happen to the Buchanan marriage?) that leads directly to the climactic accident and the novel's resolution.

As "accidents" accumulate, Fitzgerald undermines their status as unintended events. Their perverse logic makes them another one of the text's oxymora: accidents, by definition, happen unintentionally, and yet in *Gatsby*, they become the traces of an unmistakable order. The text continually draws attention to this aesthetic, as in Nick and Jordan's exchange: "'It was a strange coincidence,' [Nick] said. 'But it wasn't a coincidence at all'" (78). So when Nick discovers that Daisy was driving "the death car," he thinks, "A new point of view occurred to me. Suppose Tom found out that Daisy had been driving. He might think he saw a connection in it" (144). The repetitions of *Gatsby*'s plot enable Nick (and the reader) to see a connection—to make sense of events that unfold according to error, chance, and sheer irrationality. This repetition makes the uncanny legible as part of a pattern.

Repetition with a Difference

These various instances of traumatic repetition intersect and reach a climax in chapter 7, which culminates in Myrtle's death. In this chapter, one by one Fitzgerald revisits earlier moments in the text and brings their possibilities to a close. Despite the novel's final insistence on ceaseless repetition ("So we beat on, boats against the current, borne back ceaselessly into the past" [180]), the repetitions that occur in chapter 7 make a difference. Death makes the difference: Daisy's accident leaves behind a very "tangible body," and others follow. Nick gets what he has expected all along, albeit in an unexpected way. Consequently, he changes as a narrator. It is within this episode that Nick's narration becomes more omniscient and inventive. In the presence of death, he becomes alert and purposeful.

In the beginning of chapter 7, this change has yet to happen. Nick accepts an invitation to lunch at the Buchanans', just as he had once accepted a dinner invitation, and on the way there, he has an experience that is by now deeply characteristic. On the train, the woman next to him drops her pocketbook:

"Oh my!" she gasped.

I picked it up with a weary bend and handed it back to her holding it at arm's length and by the extreme tip of the corners to show that I had no designs upon it—but everyone near by, including the woman, suspected me just the same. (115)

Once again, Nick reasserts his disinterest as a narrator: he is merely a casual bystander, with no desires of his own. The incident on the train repeats an earlier moment in which Myrtle Wilson literally points the finger at him:

> "Crazy about him!" cried Myrtle incredulously. "Who said I was crazy about him? I never was any more crazy about him than I was about that man there."
>
> She pointed suddenly at me and everyone looked at me accusingly. I tried to show by my expression that I had played no part in her past. (35)

As this pair of instances illustrates, Nick begins the novel's climactic episode by reiterating his pose of naïveté, which we have already come to expect and to distrust. Nick extends his own ostensible lack of design to the novel's action at large; a similarly unmotivated mood pervades the entire afternoon of Gatsby and Tom's confrontation. Things happen *in spite of* intention.

As the suspense culminates, it takes a toll on Nick, and his narrative voice begins to slide. He hallucinates (once again) about a dead body:

> Through the hall of the Buchanans' house blew a faint wind, carrying the sound of the telephone bell out to Gatsby and me as we waited by the door.
>
> "The master's body!" roared the butler into the mouthpiece. "I'm sorry, madame, but we can't furnish it—it's far too hot to touch this noon!"
>
> What he really said was "Yes. . . . Yes. . . . I'll see." (89; ellipses in the original)

In this dreamlike condensation, Nick remembers the interruption caused by Myrtle's telephone call, conflating her desire for Tom's body with George Wilson's gullible interest in Tom's car. He imagines Tom's body as an automobile: dangerous, metallic, hot to the touch. If the dinner foursome of chapter 1 is interrupted by the "shrill metallic urgency" of a "fifth guest's" (15–16)—the telephone's—presence, the same foursome is joined in chapter 7 by a literal fifth guest: Gatsby. Gatsby's presence makes the danger of sexual jealousy incarnate, and that danger intensifies Nick's anticipation of death. The latent violence of Nick's imagination asserts itself more stridently. Most interesting, that anxiety ceases to seem gratuitous and instead refers more obviously to the plot and characters around him. A page later, Nick's auditory hallucination is confirmed—Tom *does* receive a phone call from Wilson about the car:

> "The rumor is," whispered Jordan, "that that's Tom's girl on the telephone."
> We were silent. The voice in the hall rose high with annoyance: "Very well, then, I won't sell you the car at all. . . . I'm under no obligations to you at all . . . and as for your bothering me about it at lunch time, I won't stand that at all!"
> "Holding down the receiver," said Daisy cynically.
> "No, he's not," [Nick] assured her. "It's a bona-fide deal. I happen to know about it." (116; ellipses in the original)

Nick's morbid imagination becomes oracular rather than merely fantastic, and in the process, he becomes increasingly allied with Tom. Nick covers for Tom, even though he might as well be on the phone with his "girl," since he has only cultivated a business relationship with Wilson as a pretense for stopping at the garage. Tom never intends to sell anything to George "at all," as he almost hysterically repeats. At this moment, we begin to see how intricately Fitzgerald overdetermines Nick's unreliability: it is impossible to say whether Nick extends his own alibi of good faith and honesty to Tom out of naïveté or because his premonitions of conflict are being uncannily confirmed. Nick, in fact, "happen[s] to know" a good deal more than his testimonial suggests, but defining the nature and limits of that knowledge is a complicated task. In the instance of his hallucination, and throughout chapter 7, Nick's knowledge exceeds the normal conventions of realism. He possesses an increasingly uncanny prescience, or what Ron Neuhaus criticized as an untenable first-person "Omniscient-I."[85] And while critics have alternately faulted Fitzgerald for this narrative inconsistency or explained it away as part of the novel's retrospective frame, no one has considered the role that traumatic memory and expectation seem to play in Nick's contradictory perspective. In fact, his preoccupation with death finally begins to fit the plot.

One reason it may be difficult to appreciate the odd cast of Nick's expectations is that Fitzgerald, through his use of thematic repetitions, insistently recalls and fulfills the reader's own expectations in great detail. Evocative repetitions abound: once again, Jordan and Daisy "lay upon an enormous couch" in white dresses (115); Tom promises (and fails) to show his stables; Tom garbles his apocalyptic anxiety ("I read somewhere that the sun's getting hotter every year . . . —or wait a minute—it's just the opposite—the sun's getting colder every year" [118]); the descriptions of Daisy's voice; the stop at Wilson's gas station. In all these repetitions, Gatsby's presence makes a difference, bringing them to an end. When Nick struggles (again) to describe Daisy's voice, Gatsby finishes his sentence for him:

> "She's got an indiscreet voice," I remarked. "It's full of—"
> I hesitated.
> "Her voice is full of money," he said suddenly.
> That was it. I'd never understood it before. (120)

This instance exemplifies the kind of difference Fitzgerald brings to the novel's tensions throughout this chapter: they are resolved in a way that undoes, at least in part, the romantic possibility that their suspension had enabled. Identifying the quality of Daisy's voice so explicitly with money—rather than with magic or with some ethereal femininity—effectively cheapens it. Fitzgerald makes explicit what had until now been only hinted at, suggested, latent.

Nick's expectations are fulfilled according to an uncanny logic in which actions are simultaneously inevitable and yet unintended, pregnant with meaning and yet "apparently pointless" (121). Action unfolds irrespective of intention: the relationship between Daisy and Gatsby becomes obvious despite Gatsby's intention to repress it. Tom, "astounded," hustles them all off to the city, despite the fact that no one wants to go (119). For no apparent reason, Tom insists on trading cars for the drive. Fitzgerald's plot requires both the departure and the switching of cars, but he refuses to provide compelling explanations for either. Things just *happen* that way out of "restlessness." As they meander through New York on their way to the Plaza, Tom keeps a close eye on Gatsby driving his wife in his car, and Nick speculates:

> I think he was afraid [Daisy and Gatsby] would dart down a side street and out of his life forever.
> But they didn't. And we all took the less explicable step of engaging the parlour of a suite in the Plaza Hotel. (126)

Nick imagines alternative narratives that would fulfill expectations. Those alternatives demonstrate, by contrast, that what actually happens is "less explicable." Thus, Fitzgerald thematizes the surrender to an irrational, machinelike logic. Tom, for instance, loses his equilibrium with the knowledge of his wife's affair and gives himself up to "instinct":

"There is no confusion like the confusion of a simple mind and as we drove away Tom was feeling the hot whips of panic. His wife and his mistress, until an hour ago secure and inviolate, were slipping precipitately from his control. Instinct made him step on the accelerator" (125). Tom has become a machine, merging with the car he drives: he is himself driven by an irrational impulse. Events begin to take place at a rate that no one seems able to alter or stop, and the action of the novel picks up speed.

Gatsby's depiction of this mystification of agency as a surrender to machine logic mirrors the ways in which numerous accounts mystified accountability for the war. In all combatant nations, government communiqués and propaganda represented the war as a large machine, driven by the enemy, which acted on them from outside. Individuals and nations—consciously or not—refused to represent the war as something they had created and willingly perpetuated. Interpreting the war as one of self-defense, in which individuals and nations were compelled to act, served ideological purposes. But interpreting the war in those terms over time fundamentally changed the way in which human agency was collectively imagined. Atavistic tendencies to destroy seemed to be inherently more powerful than the will to make and execute ethical decisions.

Nick's interpretation of Tom's aggression evokes wartime and postwar intellectual attempts to understand why the war happened, in which human "instinct" came under special scrutiny. For instance, in Bertrand Russell's analysis of the human responsibility for the conflict in *Why Men Fight*, he divides human activity into a "civilized" part, motivated by desire, and an impulsive part, motivated by an atavistic "instinct." He argues that if wars are to end, the instinctual aspect of human nature must be brought under control:

> All human activity springs from two sources: impulse and desire. The part played by desire . . . involves an interval of time between the consciousness of a need and the opportunity for satisfying it. . . .
>
> But desire governs no more than a part of human activity, and that not the most important but only the more conscious, explicit, and civilized part. In all the more instinctive part of our nature we are dominated by impulses to certain kinds of activity, not by desires for certain ends.[86]

Tom's surrender to "instinct" connects him to the war's destruction—destruction that was increasingly seen as having been wrought by humanity's instinctual, irrational, and "uncivilized" aspects. As Tom himself announces, "Civilization's going to pieces" (12). *Gatsby* describes the surrender to "instinct" as a process of becoming mechanized, active, and mobile, rather than human, reflective, and moral. But *Gatsby*'s ironic rhetoric—particularly Tom's garbled accounts of "civilization"—offers a more pessimistic account of the notion that rational intention might be successfully brought to bear on "instinct."

This paradox—this disturbing questioning of human intentionality—becomes the central oxymoron of the novel's climax. The plot takes shape as a terrible coincidence, masterfully but perversely logical. Daisy herself mows Myrtle down, unknowingly—unconsciously—killing her rival. This action illustrates both the uncanny logic of human violence and the tendency to mystify inflicted injuries as coincidences (or "collateral" damage). Or, rather, it suggests that the most powerful human logic is one of primal and unwitting destruction. Modernity, repeatedly embodied by the automobile, seems to privilege the primitive. The advent of machine culture is pictured as upsetting the fragile balance humans had struck between their destructive and rational capacities. But rather than simply asserting the end of human agency, *Gatsby*'s plot makes a more sinister suggestion. In *Gatsby*, a reduced capacity for agency abets a violent consolidation of power. Tom Buchanan—the character whose masculinity, whiteness, and class position place him at the top of the most traditionally configured power structures—profits from the novel's neat climax, without having to claim responsibility for its violence. This analogy has particular relevance to America's postwar situation, in which the war "to make the world safe for democracy," led by a president who had adopted the Progressive platform, gave way to a Republican victory, the return of privilege to big business, and the violent repression of organized labor and political "radicals." David Kennedy describes the failure of progressive politics in the postwar years as a result of chance, politics, and Republican and capitalist savvy, all of which were oddly favored by the ways in which the war was waged. But worse was progressives' disillusionment with their own cause, which might be akin to the deidealization and criminalization of a figure like Gatsby. As Kennedy puts it, "Disillusion with Wilson and disappointment at their own failure to protect the reform cause were not the only wounds the war inflicted on progressives. . . . One of the casualties of the war for the American mind thus seemed to have been the progressive soul."[87] The highly publicized rise of crime during Prohibition, to which Fitzgerald connects

Gatsby, made it less and less possible to idealize the common man, even if he had demonstrated uncommon leadership and heroism.

Doing the Work of Death

Despite the disillusion that the novel's plot engenders on its own terms and in the extent to which it alludes to recent historical damage, it changes Nick for the better. Seeing death gives him a new narrative authority. To the extent that he is a passive witness to the novel's climactic violence, Nick seems to be caught up in a cycle of uncanny repetition. But in its aftermath, Nick performs parts of what Drew Gilpin Faust has called the "work of death": he hears some of Gatsby's last words, takes charge of contacting his friends and burying his body, and tries to secure his memory. Rather than traumatizing Nick further, seeing death gives him a chance to reencounter the paradigmatic elements of war experience—death and loss—in a peacetime setting. Nick performs mourning rituals for Gatsby that soldiers at war rarely can. In narrating his experiences as a witness to the car accident and the crime scene, and in giving narrative shape to the end of Gatsby's life, Nick comes into his own as a storyteller. Some critics have found the changes in Nick's narration at this point troublesome and clumsy; others, such as W. Russell Gray, liken Nick to a detective who "observes and interprets with . . . acuity" and "reconstructs events."[88] He takes liberties with point of view, enacting an omniscience that violates the conventions of first-person narration. This, I argue, is Fitzgerald's way of marking a partial "cure" from Nick's trauma—he can finally remember what happens in detail.

The complex temporality of this change makes it impossible to isolate one particular moment of cathartic transformation. Instead, Fitzgerald's narrative suggests that both seeing Myrtle's dead body and taking responsibility for Gatsby's influence Nick's change. Indeed, Nick begins to lay claim to his story in a new way even before the car accident occurs, when he tells Tom and Jordan, "'I just remembered that today's my birthday.' I was thirty. Before me stretched the menacing road of a new decade" (135). The return of Nick's memory, however, seems strangely related to the accident that he is about to encounter. Fitzgerald uses the language of a car accident ("menacing road") to describe how Nick feels to be thirty, and follows the imagery with the action of the accident that leaves Myrtle dead. As Nick becomes a witness to death, his expectations of violence (of a "menacing road") become consciously available and are fulfilled. When, pages later, he returns to the fact of his birthday with the war-weary comment, "I'm thirty," he says, "I'm five years too old to lie to myself and call it honor" (177)—five years older than he was when he went to war—we as readers can attach his lost innocence to a plot and a character development that suits it. Nick's tone finally seems appropriate to his story.

When Nick leaves New York after the confrontation with Gatsby in the Plaza Hotel, he has new access to the past and future of his narrative. Instead of seeming to search for the right rhetorical mode, he chooses just the right one ("So we drove on toward death through the cooling twilight" [136]). At the scene of the accident, Nick's point of view becomes strangely mobile in both time and space:

> She rushed out into the dusk, waving her hands and shouting—before [Michaelis] could move from his door the business was over.
>
> The "death car" as the newspapers called it, didn't stop; it came out of the gathering darkness, wavered tragically for a moment, and then disappeared around the next bend. Michaelis wasn't even sure of its color—he told the first policeman that it was light green. The other car, the one going toward New York, came to rest a hundred yards beyond, and its driver hurried back to where Myrtle Wilson, her life violently extinguished, knelt in the road and mingled her thick dark blood with the dust.
>
> Michaelis and this man reached her first, but when they had torn open her shirtwaist, still damp with perspiration, they saw that her left breast was swinging loose like a flap, and there was no need to listen for the heart beneath. The mouth was wide open and ripped at the corners, as though she had choked a little in giving up the tremendous vitality she had stored so long. (137)

Nick's point of view synthesizes Michaelis's, the anonymous driver's, and perhaps even T. J. Eckleberg's. Time is simultaneously immediate and retrospective. This description echoes the accident after Gatsby's party, and, again, time bends to create an eerie blend of abrupt disaster and denouement (the speeding car "[comes] to rest"). Notably, the violence of the impact of metal on flesh remains couched in euphemism as "the business." Michaelis's witnessing dwells on facts that distract him from and delay the sight of Myrtle's dead body. But ultimately Michaelis sees, and Nick describes, a detailed vision of embodied death.

The spectacle of Myrtle's dead body, which Gatsby later asks Nick not to tell him about, acts as the first catalyst around which Nick's point of view transforms. Spectacles of blood and human injury call forth acts of meaning-making, of signification. Barbara Ehrenreich and Elaine Scarry describe in their meditations on war a powerful phenomenological response to seeing blood. They argue that blood, injury, and killing call forth terror, powerful emotions, and a need for sacralization.[89] Nick's account illustrates both horror and the need to make sense of it, since he provides grotesque details and draws on a rhetoric of religious sacrifice. That rhetoric transforms Myrtle into a kneeling penitent: "Myrtle Wilson, her life violently extinguished, *knelt in the road and mingled her thick dark blood with the dust*." This metaphor transforms a hit-and-run accident, somewhat improbably, into a sacramental rite that mingles life with death, blood with earth, in which Myrtle is imagined as offering ("giving up") her life ("vitality"). While the secular deity, Dr. T. J. Eckleberg, looks over the Valley of Ashes from his faded billboard, Myrtle becomes the sacrificial lamb in a regenerative rite at the novel's climax. But Fitzgerald immediately undermines that aura of sanctification when, in the next paragraph, he describes Myrtle's "left breast . . . swinging loose like a flap" (137). This grotesque detail—which makes the novel's violence horrifyingly tangible—asserts the unremittingly physical aspect of death. It functions as a remainder, evidence of what cannot be spiritualized.

The spectacle of Myrtle's dead body, both in its grotesqueness and in its sanctification, can best be interpreted with reference to the ways death was depicted during the war. Fitzgerald announced as much in his draft when Gatsby tells Nick not to tell him about it because he "saw enough of that in the war." Certainly, Nick's language of sacrifice evokes that used to describe soldiers killed in the war. Both entrenched governments and bereft mourners made their losses meaningful during the war by speaking of them in a language of sacrifice for the nation. That discourse made death more tolerable. Fitzgerald's description of Myrtle as a kneeling penitent echoes that wartime script in a way that shows how threadbare it had become. Myrtle obviously does not go willingly to her death, and the enumeration of her torn breast undercuts any notion of regenerative renewal.

Myrtle's dead body evokes New Death by defining the border of representability. Fitzgerald's editors urged him to revise his description of it. But he defended its violence: "*I want* Myrtle Wilson's breast ripped off— it's exactly the thing, I think, and I don't want to chop up the good scenes by too much tinkering."[90] Fitzgerald's refusal to "chop up" his description of Myrtle's ripped breast suggests that he wanted the scene to convey a certain shock. Given how subtly Fitzgerald renders the violence of Nick's memories, his insistence on this detail stands out for its explicitness. Put another way, this negotiation with the publisher also provides a clue to the editorial climate in which Fitzgerald made cuts to his manuscript. Too much violence and explicit language, he learned, drew censorship. Myrtle's ripped breast pushed, and therefore demarcates, the boundaries of what the publisher thought readers would tolerate.

One reason Fitzgerald may have "*want*[ed] Myrtle Wilson's breast ripped off" is that her wounded body receives the descriptive detail that Fitzgerald withholds elsewhere. Myrtle Wilson's breast receives the detailed description lacking in both Gatsby's and her husband's gunshot wounds. In this, she becomes a stand-in for a more painful sight. Indeed, as Greg Forter has shown, elsewhere the novel depicts Gatsby himself "through tropes of beneficent femininity," including breast imagery.[91] But when the image of the breast is torn and bloodied, it belongs to Myrtle. This gendered relocation recapitulates patterns of representation during the war. Myrtle's dead body recalls some of the most violent images from Allied propaganda campaigns, in which German military aggression was depicted in sexualized terms as violence done to female victims. For instance, American painter George Bellows repeatedly pictured indoor, domestic scenes of sexual violence in his popular lithograph series devoted to the war. In "The Cigarette" (1918), a German soldier pauses to smoke after killing and mutilating a woman, whose shining white body is nailed to the wall in the center of the image (see figure 8). Her breast has been torn off. The mutilated breast and the postcoital cigarette suggest a rape that Bellows does not show directly. He does not need to, since "the Rape of Belgium" was a phrase in wide circulation. Beyond rape, mutilation, and killing, Bellows's title invites his viewer to see a crime in the soldier's cool nonchalance, the utter lack of concern or remorse for what he has done. We hear a similar condemnation in *Gatsby* in the witness's condemnation that the "son-of-a-bitch" who ran Myrtle down "didn't even stopus car" (139). The violence done to the female body in both cases happens twice: once in physical action but again at the level of the gaze, in this case, the averted gaze: the utter denial of the dead body's pathos. This is what the viewer is asked to restore and compensate for through his or her angered response to Bellows's lithograph; it is also what so outrages Tom Buchanan, who whimpers, as they drive away, "The God damned coward! He didn't even stop his car" (141).

As I have argued elsewhere, propaganda depicting wounded women functioned to mobilize viewers and to sanitize war wounds at the same time. "The realities of warfare—the injury [the soldier] risks himself

FIGURE 8. "The Cigarette," George Bellows, black and white lithograph, 14 1/2 × 19 1/4 inches, 1918. (Amon Carter Museum of American Art, Fort Worth, Texas, record number 1985.63; used with permission)

and the injury he would inflict on others—are elided in such images"; instead, "vulnerability" becomes "a female predicament."[92] Such images reinscribe war wounds—done in most part to male bodies—on female bodies. The same logic is at work in the economy of description in *Gatsby*: the blood shed by men and women in chapter 7 appears most explicitly as Myrtle's. Her femininity makes the display of carnage possible. Her female body takes the place of men, whose deaths are, in comparison, highly sanitized. But despite its difference, her dead body provides evidence of the new human capacity for violence that the war left in such excess. Machinery mows her down in midstride, catching her by surprise, in the midst of a (mock) heroic gesture—her dash for freedom.

In *Gatsby*'s reenacted rather than recounted war, Myrtle's blood and torn flesh stand in not for soldiers' but for a veteran's: Gatsby's. The ugliness of death is asserted and circumscribed in advance of Gatsby's murder and Wilson's suicide, which are described as unfolding in a peaceful, pastoral landscape. At the most superficial level of the plot, of course, Myrtle's death triggers her husband's mistaken revenge. At a deeper level, it also restores the bond between Daisy and Tom Buchanan and brings Nick into a new relationship with Gatsby. Her death gives Nick a premonition, which is to say it calls on his memory. It impresses Gatsby's vulnerability on him and leads him to prepare for Gatsby's death. After Myrtle is wounded and dies, Nick begins to do the work of putting Gatsby to rest. He seeks Gatsby out and hears, once and for all, his life story. Nick gets the information that he needs and has lacked all along in order to fully believe in Gatsby, and that transforms him from a doubter into a believer. He says "good-by" to Gatsby and takes a final leave by saying the words that he is "always glad" for having said, the compliment that allows him to remember his relationship with Gatsby as purposefully finished (154).

In contrast to Myrtle's death, *Gatsby* portrays violence's effects on male bodies with decorous modesty. In telling about Gatsby's and Wilson's deaths, Nick spares his audience the bloody details and pictures the climactic crime scene in something akin to cinematic soft focus:

> I have an idea that Gatsby himself didn't believe [Daisy's call] would come, and perhaps he no longer cared. If that was true he must have felt that he had lost the old warm world, paid a high price for living too long with a single dream. He must have looked up at an unfamiliar sky through frightening leaves and shivered as he found what a grotesque thing a rose is and how raw the sunlight was upon the scarcely created grass. A new world, material without being real, where poor ghosts, breathing dreams like air, drifted fortuitously about . . . like that ashen, fantastic figure gliding towards him through the amorphous trees. . . .
>
> There was a faint, barely perceptible movement of the water as the fresh flow from one end urged its way toward the drain at the other. With little ripples that were hardly the shadows of waves, the laden mattress moved irregularly down the pool. A small gust of wind that scarcely corrugated the surface was enough to disturb its accidental course with its accidental burden. The touch of a cluster of leaves revolved it slowly, tracing, like the leg of a [compass], a thin red circle in the water.
>
> It was after we started with Gatsby toward the house that the gardener saw Wilson's body a little way off in the grass, and the holocaust was complete. (126)[93]

Although Nick feels belated in his arrival, that delay allows him to idealize Gatsby's death. As we have seen, he has already said "good-by." Nick assigns an order to everything about Gatsby's death. Gatsby gets to swim in the pool at last—something he had been waiting to do all summer. Nick imagines him as possessing a kind of complete and mature self-knowledge about himself and the meaning of his life up until that point and as possessing a readiness to die. He even pictures Gatsby living on in the knowledge of his own death, looking at the world from a new and different, less "warm" perspective, looking up through the trees as if from a grave, at a world inhabited by "ghosts." In this tableau, death unfolds according to a beautiful order, free of fright and trauma. Gatsby's wound appears not in terms of what it rips open but of what it does not: as Matthew Bruccoli points out in his notes to the novel, the air mattress is not damaged by the shot that kills Gatsby, and his body floats on undisturbed. Far from grotesque, the wound leaves its symmetrical trace, a "thin red circle" of continuity, in the water.[94] One might reasonably recall Clyde Wheeler's "clean death" on the trench parapet in *One of Ours*.

Nick's narrative imagines Gatsby's death as a Good Death, in which he is spiritually and physically at peace. Here, Fitzgerald recapitulates a pattern from his first novel, *This Side of Paradise*, in which one traumatic death by car accident is followed by and ransomed by a Good Death. In that novel, Fitzgerald contrasts Dick Humbird's traumatic death with the funeral of Amory's other role model, Monsignor Darcy. As I have already mentioned, Dick's abrupt death traumatizes Amory Blaine. Later in the narrative, Darcy dies at a mature age and in a state of grace. Fitzgerald signifies the fact that the Monsignor's death is spiritually "good" in aesthetic terms: his funeral is a beautiful combination of music, setting, costume, and ritual. "Monsignor would have enjoyed" it, Amory reflects. In death, his body looks peacefully at rest, as he lies "in his coffin, with closed hands upon his purple vestments" and with his face "not changed."[95] While Humbird's dead body evokes the grotesque memory of "a cat that had lain horribly mangled in some alley of [Amory's] childhood," viewing the Monsignor's presumably embalmed body at rest in its open casket gives Amory a "sense of security."[96]

In *Gatsby*, Nick does more than merely attend a funeral. Given his paradigmatically passive stance, Nick assumes a somewhat remarkable personal responsibility for Gatsby's body. He moves into the house and guards over the body for three days. This is no small matter. He need not—Gatsby is no kin to him. Moreover, by 1920, it was increasingly customary to have a dead body removed from the home and taken to a funeral home, where it was embalmed, laid in a "sightly and comfortable casket," and, after a viewing, taken to the cemetery for burial.[97] By 1922, "undertakers" had professionalized and restyled themselves as "funeral directors." They presided over a cultural shift in rituals of death, making funerals shorter, less doleful, and more aesthetically pleasing. Funeral directors increasingly took on the roles once played by family:

> The modern funeral director established a plan for the funeral and
> followed it in detail. He contacted the preacher and arranged for
> music; he selected flowers and lights; he prepared the body and
> provided the casket; he prepared the rooms and opened the win-
> dows. At the time of the funeral, he greeted guests and seated them,
> arranging for their conveyance to the cemetery. "Some will say I
> was a stage manager, and not an undertaker," wrote one funeral
> director. "Really it is much the same. I work for effect—for consol-
> ing, soothing effect."[98]

Despite the availability of such professional services, Nick performs them himself. He presides over the preparations and the event itself and tells the minister when to start. In doing this, Nick acts as both mourner and director. Though Gatsby's father eventually arrives, Nick works as much to console himself and to assuage Gatsby's ghost, who speaks to him repeatedly and urgently. Gatsby's body itself impresses this responsibility on Nick, who explains, "as he lay in his house and didn't move or breathe or speak, hour upon hour, it grew upon me that I was responsible" (164).

Nick's care for Gatsby's body and his internal dialogues with Gatsby's voice domesticate accounts from soldiers who lost comrades during World War I. As Winifred Kirkland put it, "Many a record from the trenches reveals how constant a presence a slain comrade remains to his mate."[99] While Nick suffers more than once in the novel from "savage, frightening dreams" of death (*The Great Gatsby*, 147), Gatsby's continued presence does not frighten him. Instead, it motivates him. Gatsby's voice speaks matter-of-factly, but urgently, spurring Nick to take action and to do what he thinks is right. Kirkland's description of the New Death's effects on the living is apt: "We [mourners] long to know ourselves in line with them, our dead." Loss creates a profound need among the living for "direction for [their] energy" and a "standard of valuation."[100]

Even after Nick takes care of Gatsby's immediate needs to be buried, his entire narrative seems bent on finding the lesson, the spiritual value, signified by his death. In saying this, I am not arguing that Nick's story represents adequate mourning or that he manages (or even tries) to relinquish his bond with Gatsby. Mitch Breitwieser, Greg Forter, and Seth Moglen all make persuasive cases for Nick's melancholia. In Freud's famous opposition between mourning and melancholia, the first is a way of grieving that allows the mourner to realize his or her losses and then forge new connections in the world, while the second involves an incomplete articulation of loss and a clinging to the lost object. The novel's famous closing passage leaves the reader with an impression of permanent fixation to loss, of perpetually being "borne back ceaselessly into the past" (180). But, as Moglen points out, "the distinction between mourning and melancholia should not be understood as a binary opposition: rather, they are two psychological tendencies on a continuum of grieving."[101] My point is that, read in the immediate aftermath of World War I, Nick's reaction to Gatsby's death reads like that of one soldier's response to the loss of another: he does his best to bury the body, to see that his grave is marked, and rededicates himself to the memory of the dead. Conditions at the front often made such actions impossible. The relative ease with which Nick can keep his vigil, care for the body, and see it safely buried, when contrasted with what such a character would have experienced at the front, goes a long way toward accounting for Nick's relieved sense that "Gatsby turned out all right at the end" (2). His mourning may not be complete, but it does bring him *some* consolation.

Losing Gatsby, in other words, is not just a loss but an opportunity: it allows Nick to claim and bury his dead. Though he admits to still being "haunted" and having "fantastic dreams" filled with "grotesque" houses and men carrying stretchers (176) after Gatsby's death, he returns to the Midwest and can look back on his past with clarity and precision that has been, up until that point, missing ("After two years I remember the rest of that day" [163]). Fitzgerald gives us adequate reason to read Gatsby's death as an objective correlative for Nick's war experience.

In addition to being meaningful to the novel's narrator, Gatsby's death functions more generally as a metaphor for all the men and beliefs destroyed in the world war. It is not just that Gatsby is "great" but that he signifies unrealized promise. Again, as Kirkland put it, "the boys killed in the trenches" left a persistent feeling of loss behind them because of their youth and unfulfilled promise; "there is something strangely persistent about any unfulfilled life."[102] The unfinished quality of Nick's grief seems most intelligible when it is considered not as a personal failing but as reflection of a collective response to the damages of war.

Fitzgerald's novel brings into focus what historians have only recently articulated, that in the aftermath of the war, "the mourning process was complicated, sometimes impossible"—that it was, in some senses, discouraged. Stéphane Audoin-Rouzeau and Annette Becker explain that often "the survivors were by and large not allowed genuinely to mourn; it was one of the hidden objectives of the post-war commemorations to forbid protracted mourning, which was seen as a betrayal of the men who had sacrificed themselves on the battlefield." Nick's failure to mourn in *Gatsby* needs to be read as a paradigmatic example of the many "impossible bereavements to come to terms with."[103]

One part of the mourning process that was blocked during and after the war that is particularly relevant to *Gatsby* is that of particularization and enumeration, or naming. In order to mourn, the bereaved must elaborate in specific detail what it is he or she has lost and, according to Moglen, the causes of that loss. Moglen criticizes *Gatsby* (and the canonical modernism it emblematizes) as "universalizing" loss, "gestur[ing] toward" a concrete social analysis of the damaging aspects of modernity only to "disavow" and "naturalize" it as part of a universal truth.[104] To the extent that the novel enacts this gesture, Fitzgerald gives narrative shape to a shared cultural experience of forbidden, frustrated mourning. This is not a failure of his imagination, though it may reveal the confusion of his political commitments. *Gatsby* registers a feeling that what had been lost was too great and too intangible to name specifically and that naming the causes and means of its destruction in all its gory detail would be too overwhelming.

In particular, *Gatsby* draws its reader's attention to a desire to justify death as "sacrifice" and to sanitize killing as "accident." Myrtle is hit by accident, then kneels as if in a sacrificial rite; Nick describes Gatsby's body as an "accidental burden" weaving an "accidental course" in the pool and calls his and Wilson's deaths a "holocaust"—a sacrifice (162). This language mystifies the fact that Gatsby is murdered, just as the newspapers' description of Wilson as "a madman" takes his actions out of the realm of what can be rationally judged (163). Fitzgerald represents these mystifying tropes as both personal to Nick and widely shared. Nick struggles to confront the causes of Gatsby's death. He confronts Tom about what he said "to Wilson that afternoon" (178)—sending Wilson to kill Gatsby. But he fails to take action. He imagines Tom's power as absolute, as something that cannot be successfully challenged: "They were careless people, Tom and Daisy—they smashed up things and creatures and then retreated back into their money or their vast carelessness, or whatever it was that kept them together, and let other people clean up the mess they had made. . . ." (179; ellipsis in the original). Nick shakes hands with Tom, and although he offers the reader a vision of himself as morally superior to Tom, Fitzgerald marks the limits of Nick's perspective in terms, once again, of unspeakability: the "truth" is, for Nick, strangely "unutterable" (178). Despite his new authority, Nick seems constrained. Though he can bury Gatsby, he allows the agents of his loss to remain secret and, in Forter's and Moglen's terms, mystified. Accusing Tom will not bring Gatsby back. Indeed it will only make his death seem more futile. Nick's predicament captures the terrible position occupied by masses of mourners. To revisit the scenes and actions of the war often made death seem less worthwhile, even meaningless. To indict the particular actors would require admitting the extent to which everyone—soldiers and civilians alike—consented to participate in the war. It might even mean holding the dead themselves accountable. Instead of engaging in such an anguished process, Nick, like the masses of people who survived the war, looks for ways to sanctify the dead and to avoid the uncomfortable problem of culpability.

Specifically, what remains "unutterable" for Nick is the question of agency. Nick feels that he cannot tell Tom that Daisy was driving, because Tom might think Daisy intended to murder Myrtle. The decision to kill has to be obscured: Wilson *decides* to kill his wife's lover; Tom *decides* to tell Wilson that Gatsby owns the yellow car. But Nick glosses over those decisions. His language in the passage quoted in the preceding paragraph implicitly compares Tom and Daisy to cars, turning them into weapons of war while avoiding the question of their ethical responsibility.[105] Being like a car means not having control ("Instinct made him step on the accelerator"; "It was all very careless and confused. . . . They smashed up things and creatures and then retreated"). Nick's own moral failing can only be broached in similarly evacuated terms, when Jordan rebukes him for being "a bad driver" instead of the "honest, straightforward person" he pretends to be (177).

Nick's complicity in leaving Gatsby's death a mystery is, then, another factor that makes it difficult for him to mourn Gatsby. He profits from Gatsby's death in a strange way, in that it gives him an experience of loss analogous to the one he claims not to have had in the war. Nick's expectations of violence, so impossible to trace to an original event, find fulfillment in the plot's culminating "holocaust." In a strange way, the mystification of Gatsby's murder as an "accident" necessitates and justifies his act of narration, because only he can offer an account—however partial—of the "unutterable fact[s]" (178).

The extent to which the novel obscures and sanitizes its violence may be the most important way in which its postwar story functions as an analogy for war. As it brings tensions to a culminating and irrevocable point, the accident enacts a kind of fate and thus becomes akin to an expression of the dominant—and disavowed—public will. The accident functions in precisely the way that Kenneth Burke describes war operating in modern society. He identifies war as an imperfect but representative expression of what the public intends—a "public enactment, to which all members of a given social body variously but commonly subscribe." He continues, "Unfortunately, in the modern state, . . . the act that comes closest to the totality of tribal festivals" and communal social rites "is the act of war. But modern war ('total war') itself is so complex, that we could hardly use it as our representative [example for illustrating the workings of social motive in action]." Although he hesitates to use war as such an example, he declares that "if it is the culminative we want, we must grant that war draws things to a head as thoroughly as a suppurating abscess, and is usually, like revolution, the dramatic moment of explosion after an infinity of minute preparatory charges."[106] War is too complex to be recognizable simply as an expression of the public will, but it is the closest modern society comes to one. For the most part, this is something we disavow. We tend to mystify and deny the extent to which we consent to war.

In *Gatsby*, the accident is climactic and seems to express a public will to order. Nick's language of sacrifice enlists Gatsby and Myrtle Wilson in the will that executes them, making their deaths seem consensual. But despite the language Fitzgerald attributes to his narrator, he makes it clear that the novel's logic depends on the exclusion of Gatsby's, Myrtle's, and George Wilson's desires. Their working-class bodies are counted cheap and yielded up in the interests of preserving "Civilization" (12), "family life and family institutions," and the social order preferred by Tom Buchanan (a world where "Mr. Nobody from Nowhere" is violently excluded [130]). Fitzgerald narrates the injury caused by a concentration of power held by the like of the Buchanans. To say this is to find oneself on familiar critical ground. Thus, many readers have recognized that while the novel mystifies the Buchanans' power as "fate," that mystification is partial, not complete. Fitzgerald brings traumatic violence into a coherent narrative under the rubric of "accident"—as an event without direct agents, for which responsibility remains elusive. But he makes the novel's use of accidents so logical, so convenient, that he invites the reader to "see a connection in it" (113)—to see the workings of power and wealth. The "accidents" illustrate the kind of violence the rich are capable of doing to those who want to claim a larger share of the wealth.

We might even see a connection between the recent war, the wartime "sacrifices" for democracy, and the social violence of the resumption of "normalcy."[107] Fitzgerald suggests that although Americans might not want to recognize the suffering of soldiers in wartime, they could not help but witness the war's transformation of the civilian world. The political implications of Fitzgerald's novel are also domestic: violence done and experienced by soldiers gets refigured along gendered and class boundaries in a civilian, postwar context. The novel, then, subtly condemns the war by describing its violent legacy and aftermath.

The repetitive structure of war trauma in *Gatsby* invites a reconsideration of the violence that punctuates the home-front, postwar world. This postwar and home-front focus avoids some of the clichés and limits of war writing: while many war writers insist on the untranslatability of the experience in the trenches into language and the impossibility of representing it in a way that noncombatants can understand, Fitzgerald makes its terrors visible through postwar analogies. By cutting references to war and refiguring it as an analogy, he brings its damage into a narrative that haunts us, collectively and deeply, even if we have not always appreciated why.

3 / Regendering War Trauma and Relocating the Abject: Catherine Barkley's Death

War is human, it is something that is lived like a love or a hatred and could be told like the story of a novel.

—MARCEL PROUST

Open any number of books about World War I and you will find the same quote from Ernest Hemingway's *A Farewell to Arms*. This one quote has become the canonical articulation of postwar disillusionment, the clearest statement of the "lost generation." Historians use it to illustrate the crisis of belief brought on by the massive slaughter made in the name of God, country, civilization, and democracy. In this passage, the novel's narrator, Frederic Henry, muses about the gap between official language and the reality of death in war:

> I did not say anything. I was always embarrassed by the words sacred, glorious, and sacrifice and the expression in vain. We had heard them, sometimes standing in the rain almost out of earshot, so that only the shouted words came through, and had read them, on proclamations that were slapped up by billposters over other proclamations, now for a long time, and I had seen nothing sacred, and the things that were glorious had no glory and the sacrifices were like the stockyards at Chicago if nothing was done with the meat except to bury it. There were many words that you could not stand to hear and finally only the names of places had dignity. Certain numbers were the same way and certain dates and these with the names of the places were all you could say and have them mean anything. Abstract words such as glory, honor, courage, or hallow were obscene beside the concrete names of villages, the numbers of roads, the names of rivers, the numbers of regiments and the dates.[1]

Since the novel's publication, this passage has epitomized its antiwar (or at least "antimilitary") stance.[2] It appears, often in full, in general studies of war, in both popular and scholarly accounts of World War I and its cultural impact (see, for instance, Fussell, Norris, Kennedy, Buitenhuis, Traxel, Braudy), and in accounts of American modernism (traceable from Hugh Kenner's classic *Homemade World* to Keith Gandal's recent *The Gun and the Pen*).[3] The passage has long functioned as a touchstone for Hemingway scholars who consider the narrator's protest against propagandistic language, his disgust for "what Malcolm Cowley termed the 'big words' of war," central to the novel's meaning.[4] Beyond the boundaries of Hemingway criticism, the passage tends to stand alone and to stand for the whole of *A Farewell to Arms*, for all of Hemingway's writing about war, perhaps for Hemingway's entire oeuvre, and not infrequently for the entire "lost generation." The synecdoche invites us to assume that the novel itself puts into practice the values it espouses here: verbal frankness, willingness to expose the death at the center of war, disillusionment with the cult of heroic masculinity conjured up by cant terms such as "brave" and "sacrifice" and the expression "in vain."

This chapter develops a different account of how the novel handles the problem of communicating soldiers' deaths in war. I join other critics such as Margot Norris in arguing that "we should be wary of trusting Frederic's demystification of patriotic cant."[5] Norris distrusts Frederic Henry altogether and describes him as a highly ironic figure, whose narration "shields the reader from unappealing and appalling images of war."[6] Though my argument differs from Norris's, we begin from an equally skeptical position. Put simply, the novel's representation of death and war trauma is far less forthright than its famous protest leads us to expect. Norris ultimately traces the novel's failure to disclose the ugliness of war to its readers, whose squeamish aversions Hemingway "challenges," "maneuvers" around, and ultimately makes available for critique. In contrast, I argue that much of its depictions of the ugliness of war was, in the process of revision, omitted. The novel "shields" the reader from war, I suggest, both by excising gross details and by refiguring its wounds as female. The novel, like the propagandistic language Frederic condemns, sanitizes the violence of war. For when *A Farewell to Arms* renders the death and injury of war directly, in unvarnished language and in realistic reportage from the front, it does so briefly and in passing. In contrast, the more vivid and memorable death in the novel is Catherine Barkley's. Her climactic death stands for the war. It is bloody, prolonged, frightening, and wasteful. She is a casualty of professional incompetence. She is young and has everything to live for. Her death epitomizes many of the shameful aspects of soldiers' deaths during World War I.[7] But she is a woman, not a soldier. As bloody as Catherine's end is, her death is a metaphor that falsely assimilates the violence of war into a conventionally tragic love story. In so doing, it subtly reassures readers that modern violence punishes transgressive women rather than men. The metaphor uses the sexualized and gendered figure of the nurse to relocate vulnerability, death, and the abject away from the battlefield and away from men. This relocation occurs not only, as Norris would have it, according to the reader's desire but according to the novel's (and its author's) as well.

My argument's emphasis on substitution recasts one of the longest-standing objections readers have had to *A Farewell to Arms*: the apparent split between its love story and its war story. As Linda Wagner-Martin reminds us, "Whether to consider *A Farewell to Arms* primarily as a novel about war, or a book about the wages of passionate sexual love, has been a critical dilemma for the past fifty years."[8] Max Perkins identified this as a problem even before the book's publication. He famously complained in a letter to Owen Wister, "The serious flaw in the book is that [its] two great elements . . .—one of which would make it a picture of war, and the other of which would make it a duo of love and passion—do not fully combine. It begins as one thing wholly, and ends up wholly as the other thing."[9]

Both the novel's and Hemingway criticism in general has tended to reify this split. Early appreciation for Hemingway centered on his style's hard realism, its journalistic, detailed portrayals of war and violence, and his portrayal of the "hero's code" as a modus vivendi in a fallen world. His war fiction, which most readers and critics believed was based on direct personal experience, figured prominently in arguments that delineated these concerns. When Philip Young argued for a more complex and more tormented Hemingway, he nevertheless reinscribed the war's centrality to the author's life and work.[10] But following cultural shifts within the academy and the posthumous publication of Hemingway's unfinished—and profoundly gender-bending—novel, *The Garden of Eden*, in 1986, critics largely shifted their attention to questions of gender: to Hemingway's androgyny, his cross-gendered identifications, his depictions of masculinity as a fraught performance rather than a code-emanating essence.[11] From such later perspectives, previous emphasis on Hemingway's war experience seemed to have been exaggerated. James Nagel worked to separate fiction from fact in accounts of the author's experience at the Italian front.[12] Hemingway's biographer, Kenneth Lynn, argued that Malcolm Cowley (and others) were mistaken when they began proffering theories about the war's impact on the writer. According to Lynn's account, Hemingway later, and fraudulently, endorsed the theory because it filled his needs for a "heroic explanation for his life." Lynn argues that the war functioned as a convenient alibi for wounds Hemingway actually sustained in childhood.[13] Interest in Hemingway's war writing and experience largely receded as critics such as Lynn took up questions of Hemingway's gender formation and ambivalence. In contrast, this chapter, like other recent work, proposes to integrate the concerns of both these critical traditions. It reconsiders the ethics and aesthetics of the novel's depiction of war and pays special attention to Hemingway's use of omission in relation to his complex attitudes toward and performances of masculinity. This chapter, then, builds on Matthew Stewart's and Alex Vernon's recent arguments against binarizing war and gender in Hemingway's texts. Instead, those subjects are most often, in Hemingway, mutually constitutive. As Vernon writes, "images and talk of pregnancy, childbirth, and marriage in Hemingway . . . can be directly linked to war."[14]

But if the links between war and sexual love are sometimes direct, as Vernon states, they are also often slippery, metaphoric, and subtle. Both Hemingway's experience of and writing about death in war is tangled up with sexual substitution. One of his own first encounters with New Death came on around June 7, 1918, when he and other ambulance volunteers were put to work gathering the fragmented bodies—not of soldiers but of female munitions workers wounded in an explosion near Milan. It was shocking for him to handle the dead. Their bodies had been blown apart and scattered in pieces. Most appalling of all, they were women. For Hemingway, the strange world of New Death, where bodily integrity and the boundaries between life and death are violently and repeatedly transgressed, became tangible through what he called "the inversion of the usual sex of the dead," the death of women, rather than men, in war.[15] He makes this connection most explicit in his short and graphic essay "A Natural History of the Dead" (included in *Death in the Afternoon* and written not long after *A Farewell to Arms* and, perhaps, in response to the prudery of some of his novel's reviewers).[16] But if women can die—surprisingly, obscenely—in wartime, of course, men's deaths in peacetime can also be horrible and surprising, as Hemingway's father's suicide was in December 1928. His father's death was a preoccupation during the composition of *A Farewell to Arms*, and it undoubtedly informed his account of Frederic's loss. But whatever his personal experience was, the novel itself, I argue, minimizes the loss of men at war (and at peace) and focuses instead on the loss of a woman.

In *A Farewell to Arms*, I argue, Hemingway renders the horrors of men's war death through a sexual substitute. He worked to contain the spectacle of male wounds and abjection. Seeing how sexual substitution and death combine in the novel gives new insight into the novel's form, its appeal, and the cultural crises out of which it grew. By turning his reader's attention away from war experience and toward Frederic's tragic loss of Catherine, Hemingway found an objective correlative for the parts of the war that were too horrifying to convey. He found a figure for the war that would make its violence and abjection more tolerable. As we shall see, some of the endings Hemingway rejected would have drawn the two elements together more explicitly and reminded the reader about the war. But he ultimately chose an ending that focused his reader's emotion and attention exclusively on the love story. To put it baldly, Hemingway both did and did not want to reveal the horrors of war. As he famously told George Plimpton, "I always try to write on the principle of the iceberg. There is seven-eighths of it underwater for every part that shows. Anything you know you can eliminate and it only strengthens your iceberg. It is the part that doesn't show."[17] By the end of the novel, the war has been almost wholly submerged. It is what "doesn't show."

My emphasis on Hemingway's use of a gendered metaphor to naturalize and contain the troubling specter of the war's New Death runs counter to orthodox interpretations of the novel. With the sacrosanct passage's protest against the "big words" of war providing the central piece of evidence, most critical arguments emphasize the novel's lack of metaphor and tend to describe its use of irony and realism to condemn war. Before developing my argument, then, I want to reconsider in a bit more detail Frederic's denunciation of "abstract language" and the critical assumptions for which it has come to stand.

Frederic's Protest against the "Big Words" of War

When Frederic complains that "the things that were glorious had no glory," he echoes many wartime observers and participants who questioned the "glory" of war, as Alexander McClintock did in his memoir: "We lived in the muck and stench of 'glorious' war; those of us who lived."[18] The disjuncture between the experience of war and the ways it was represented in the media and popular press triggered a representational crisis, a crisis of how to speak and write truly and accurately. Hemingway, as others had before him, alludes to a very particular problem: how could the war's death toll be conveyed? The problem is stunning in its simplicity. "The main purpose and outcome of war is injuring," Elaine Scarry asserts, yet "though this fact is too self-evident and massive ever to be directly contested," it tends to "disappear from view along many separate paths."[19] Frederic indicts propagandistic language as just such a path. Romantic diction such as "glory" and "sacrifice" disguise the ugly facts of wounding, killing, and death. Before considering how this indictment has been assimilated in the decades since its publication, it is instructive to consider what provoked it.

During World War I, combatant governments censored news, letters, photographs, and films from the front. As Paul Fussell has described, the front was both very close and a world away.[20] Evidence of death came under particular rules. It was illegal to publish photos of dead British soldiers in Britain, for instance. This created a divide that Allyson Booth insists was fundamental: "Soldiers buried their dead and then encountered them again, . . . but British policy dictated that the civilian bereaved would never have anything to bury. Soldiers inhabited a world of corpses; British civilians experienced the death of their soldiers as corpselessness."[21] This is true to an extent. Unlike the United States, Britain did have a policy of burying soldiers where they fell and, later, of gathering their remains for reburial and commemoration in national cemeteries abroad. But this divide was surely more permeable than Booth allows. Many wounded soldiers were sent back to hospitals in England and died there. The soldiers' effects sent back to families could include blood-soaked uniforms and kits. It is true that attempts to document the war came in conflict with the censorship laws enacted as security measures and to maintain morale. Despite such rules, evidence of death and injury at the front did make it home, both in embodied forms as wounded veterans returned and in disembodied linguistic and visual representations. As Joanna Bourke attests, "Despite censorship regulations, photographs of dead soldiers were widely circulated."[22] Postcards with gruesome titles and corpses to match sold briskly. Though each combatant nation enacted rules to limit such images, the indignities of death at the front were an open secret.

In the process of getting through, representations of death and injury were often romanticized or sanitized. Consider a sequence from the wildly popular "documentary" silent film *The Battle of the Somme* (released in Britain and the United States in 1916).[23] Filmed by Geoffrey

Malins and J. B. McDowell and produced by the British propaganda unit known as the Trade Topical Committee, this film issued from the ranks of those who made, and thus could break, the censorship rules.

One sequence of the film is introduced by the following intertitles:

ROYAL FIELD ARTILLERY
MOVING UP DURING BATTLE OVER
GROUND WHERE THE GORDONS'
AND DEVONS' DEAD ARE LYING
AFTER A GLORIOUS AND
SUCCESSFUL CHARGE ON THE
RIDGE NEAR MAMETZ.[24]

That intertitle is followed by another:

THESE TWO BATTERIES
ADVANCED UNDER FIRE TO A
POSITION BEYOND MAMETZ
AND WERE FORTUNATE IN
HAVING NO CASUALTIES.[25]

The two intertitles tell the viewer what he or she is about to see in advance of the moving image they describe. In an era when film narrative and editing were in a nascent phase, intertitles gave audiences the verbal instructions they needed to interpret film footage. These two intertitles do more than orient the viewer, however; they work to contain the spectacle of death before its display. Both intertitles take the living as their subjects: the "Royal Field Artillery" and "these two batteries" will be doing the action in the footage. These living subjects occupy a ubiquitous position in narrative time: they exist simultaneously in a narrative present (they are "moving up during battle"), future (they "advanced" *after* this footage was taken to a new position and "were fortunate in having no casualties"), and past (this footage was all taken and edited together already). This complex temporality underlines, above all, the survival of its subjects. Such complex temporality pervades wartime and postwar cinematic representations of World War I, where it, according to David Williams, gives rise to a new structure of memory and a new sense of time. Williams attributes this new, modern way of perceiving and remembering the war to several "interlocking elements" that include "the immediacy of the visual image; the invasion of the present by the past; the simultaneity of past and present; and the presentness of viewing."[26] The viewer's sense of chronology, in other words, merges the present and the past: in this instance, the still living subsume the recent dead. After receiving the intertitle's verbal information that the "two batteries advanced," viewers see moving-picture footage of a cavalry officer leading a horse-drawn carriage toward the camera across the visual field to the viewer's left (see figure 9, a still from this sequence). Yet despite the verbal cues that what matters here are the troops who are moving up, the visual frame presents the viewer with other evidence as well. In particular, we see the dead body of a British soldier in the picture's foreground. It is both out of focus and immobile. Verbally, it has been generalized as plural ("the Gordons' and Devons' dead") and demoted to a modifying clause describing the terrain, merely a feature of "the ground" over which the sequence's real subjects advance. The intertitles assimilate the dead body into a "glorious" and "successful" past that has already been won and is no longer at issue. Still, the figure of the dead body resists that assimilation. It draws the viewer's eye as an object that is visually central to the frame yet supposedly peripheral to the action. Despite Joanna Bourke's warning that "the contrast between the anonymous, mutilated corpse on the battlefield and the personalized, integrated corpse at home should not be exaggerated," this frame documents the sharp contrast between the way corpses were treated at home and their necessary neglect on the battlefield.[27] At home, dead bodies are cleaned, laid out for visitors, usually ritualized in some way, and buried. Human beings treat their dead, except when they cannot afford to, according to a variety of rituals. In the nineteenth century, the unclaimed corpses of the poor were often dissected or buried in a pauper's grave. In this frame, a similar or even worse fate has befallen a body that itself symbolizes the nation. Despite the camera's focus on it, the central corpse in this image receives no recognition from the other subjects in the scene. The cavalry ignore it— they just keep on going. Although it is not bloody or blown apart, its awkward position looks uncomfortable—this body does not look to be "at rest." Moreover, the viewer's eye strains to identify other dark lumps in the surrounding field, which may or may not be other dead bodies. In other words, this image's unidentified, unnamed, and unburied dead betray what the intertitles and the moving figures work to downplay: that life has been lost and that the dead remain unburied and perhaps unidentified. Though the intertitles describe what happened before this footage was taken as "a glorious and successful charge," there is nothing "glorious" about the visual disposition of its central unburied corpse or the remainders of others around it.

FIGURE 9. Frame from *The Battle of the Somme* (1916). (Imperial War Museum, London)

The viewer of this sequence—and the film had millions of viewers in 1916–1917—is put in Frederic's position: the audience encounters a contradiction between visual evidence of death and its verbal description. Though one part of the film arguably does show a "glorious" charge in which several British Tommies leave a trench, it is faked (it was staged and filmed behind the line) Meanwhile what the camera authentically captures is often either dull or decidedly more grim and outstrips the intertitles' romantic descriptions.

The way that *The Battle of the Somme* has been described is, itself, a testament to the way in which knowledge about and consent to what the war did to male bodies has been sanitized over time by historians. Allyson Booth develops an argument about the home front's "corpselessness" using evidence from *The Battle of the Somme* and its ostensible lack of death. She writes, "In this wildly popular movie, the most famous scene (and the only representation of death) involves one soldier sliding back down into a trench while his companions continue 'over the top' and into no man's land. This 'death,' however, is the one scene in the film that is not authentic. Filmmakers staged it—a staging that speaks tellingly of exactly how much civilians were allowed to see."[28] She draws her account of the film apparently not from viewing it but from Samuel Hynes, whose more detailed account of it includes the assertion that "death in battle is represented only once," during this one staged scene. Hynes admits that the film drew criticism for being suited to "a chamber of horrors" rather than a cinema, that some theater owners refused to show it, and that others likened watching it to seeing a public hanging. But he surmises that such reactions were evoked by this same melodramatic and faked scene.[29] But in fact, the film contains several long takes that focus on dead bodies. Some of them look posed and have melodramatic intertitles (including one dead soldier with his dog, also dead, by his side). But others are ugly, awkward, and torn. The film includes an entire sequence showing a group of soldiers at work burying the dead. They struggle and look tired in the mud and grasp at ungainly, stiff corpses. Rigor mortis shapes the bodies into weird masses and makes them hard to handle. The soldiers throw the corpses into a mass grave. Much of this appears, sequence after sequence, without commentary by intertitle. While it is true that the technology and the danger made it impossible for Malins and McDowell to film men going over the top without resorting to theater, they showed plenty of death.[30] Once the fighting stopped, they found abundant opportunity to document and convey the physical damage incurred by soldiers. Millions of contemporary viewers in the United Kingdom and the United States saw a much grimmer film than either Hynes or, following him, Booth describes.

The cognitive dissonance that troubles Frederic, then, was a ubiquitous and structuring feature of representations of the war, even ones with official sanction and popular appeal. His perspective is anything but unique. Vincent Sherry has argued that "the effort to legitimize" the war in the popular press, mass media, and government documents led to a crisis in "public reason" and "civic rationality"—in people's willingness to believe what they read. Modernist writers—including Pound, Eliot, and Woolf—were "representatives of a vanguard awareness" that was widely shared and that emerged in response to duplicitous public discourse.[31]

So why, we might justifiably ask, has Hemingway's protest been so singled out? Despite the fact that Frederic's interior monologue occurs within the mind of a character who never explicitly becomes a writer, many critics refer to it as a self-reflective statement, a "prolegomenon," by Ernest Hemingway. Malcolm Cowley identified it as "the classical statement of ... revolt" against the war, which, though not original to Hemingway, was "brilliantly stated" and "likely to be echoed for a long time."[32] Paul Fussell uses this passage to illustrate the war's primary effect on language: it made irony a popular idiom. As Fussell puts it, "It was not until eleven years after the war that Hemingway could [make this declaration] in *A Farewell to Arms*.... In the summer of 1914 no one would have understood what on earth he was talking about."[33] For Fussell, Hemingway speaks through this passage for a whole generation of writers for whom war experience had driven such a wedge between conventional language and truth that it became possible to speak, or write, only with irony.

There are several ironies here. The first involves chronology. The reaction against the war's misrepresentation began earlier than Fussell suggests, within months of the war's outbreak. Hemingway's protest, itself, echoes the words of an older writer, spoken in the first year of the war. Hemingway specifically considered making an epigraph of this quote from Henry James:

HENRY JAMES IN CONVERSATION WITH PRESTON LOCKWOOD NYT
MARCH 21, 1915

"One finds it in the midst of all this as hard to apply one's words as to endure one's thoughts. The war has used up words; they have weakened, they have deteriorated like motor car tires; ...... and we are now confronted with a depreciation of all our terms, or, otherwise speaking, with a loss of expression through increase of limpness, that may well make us wonder what ghosts will be left to walk."[34]

James's complaint that war had "used up" language sounds a lot like Frederic's. Indeed the comparison between the deterioration of language and "motor car tires" would be an apt one for an ambulance driver to make. The presence of this fragment as a potential epigraph reveals that Hemingway himself considered it worthy of quotation and repetition, foreshadowing the way his own words would, in turn, be used. In the published novel, of course, the insight does not appear in an epigraph, nor is it attributed to this other noncombatant writer involved in ambulance relief. The rare interview with James from which Hemingway took the quote had been granted by the older writer during the war, when he put fiction aside to organize and fund-raise as the chairman of the

American Volunteer Motor Ambulance Corps.[35] Not only was such war work not the sort with which Hemingway wanted to align himself, but he had openly impugned James's masculinity in 1926.[36] In *A Farewell to Arms*, James's name is gone, and instead the epiphany about language is framed as a result of being at the front: "*I had seen* nothing sacred." The novel's final iteration privileges those who, like Frederic (and Ernest Hemingway), have experienced war for themselves and therefore understand how to write and speak about it. As a result, Hemingway avoids comparison with other men of letters, loses the reference to ambulance driving, and instead emphasizes the value of masculine war experience. From this vantage, the passage works from within the text to consolidate the author's public persona with the authority of first-person war experience. The passage decries some myths only to shore up another: that of Hemingway, the war hero.[37] Frederic's famous protest served Hemingway's self-interest as a supposedly authentic observer of war. Commentators ever since have invoked the passage to illustrate the split between combatant and noncombatants, between those who wrote about the truth of war and those who stayed at home, read newspapers, and generated propaganda. But recognizing that Hemingway's text echoes Henry James's complaint about the war's effect on language underscores just how well home-front observers and noncombatant writers understood the problem.

Fussell's paradigmatic interpretation of the protest is also ironic in that "irony" itself is not the solution Frederic imagines. It is true that he has an ironic perspective on propaganda. "Abstract" words and images have been so misused that they have surpassed cliché to become morally reprehensible. Frederic condemns romantic diction and hackneyed images of heroic masculinity (such as those offered in *The Battle of the Somme*) as vehicles used to misrepresent human slaughter. By alluding specifically to the war posters "slapped up by billposters," he complains not only that lies have been told but that they have been told *in order* to seduce more recruits. What he has seen at the front betrays the lie of propagandistic images and words. Having seen war's violence up close, he insists on the difficulties of representing it ethically. Death should not be euphemized or disguised as something beautiful. Language that masks killing and blood is "obscene." But if the problem itself was not new, neither is Frederic's solution. He suggests that the war can be represented not with *irony* but by *names*: "finally only the names of places had dignity." Names—"the concrete names of villages, the numbers of roads, the names of rivers, the numbers of regiments and the dates"—can still signify; they are all you have if you want to "mean anything." As Bernard Oldsey argued decades ago, Frederic's declaration aligns him with a nominalist philosophy that rejects abstraction for realism, universals for particulars.[38] In this account, not all language is suspect; the "irony" for which Fussell makes Hemingway the spokesman does not actually apply to proper names.

Scholars attentive to that aspect of Frederic's protest have read it as a justification of *A Farewell to Arms*'s realism, particularly its concrete descriptions of settings and landscape and its pared-down dialogue. In the lectures that Glenway Westcott gave with Malcolm Cowley, Westcott pointed to this paragraph to explain what he saw as Hemingway's "substitution . . . of factual realism for great sentiments."[39] Put this way, Hemingway's presentation of particular details is what makes his novel a compelling, and compellingly antiwar, World War I narrative. Michael Reynolds has gone furthest not just to celebrate this realistic aesthetic but to authenticate it, to corroborate that Hemingway's "concern was for 'the way it was,' which he loosely defined as 'the people, the places, and how the weather was.'" Reynolds credits Hemingway's scrupulous use of "books, maps, and firsthand sources" for his achievement in "recreat[ing] the Austro-Italian front more vividly than any other writer."[40] From this perspective, Frederic's interior monologue still speaks accurately and self-consciously for the novel as a whole and for its aesthetics, but it justifies factual authenticity (particularly the depiction of *places*), not irony.

Reynolds's emphasis on accurate details, however, also constitutes a subtle departure from Frederic's protest, which justifies the use not just of facts but of *names*. Henry advocates a trope, common during and after the war in newspapers, in ceremonies, on monuments, and to some extent literary texts, described by the historian Thomas Laqueur as a kind of "hypernominalism," in which individual proper names predominate over allegorical figures, which are either absent altogether or subordinated to place names and lists of the dead.[41] The ubiquity of lists of names on war memorials suggests that they appealed to survivors as the most meaningful way of representing the deaths of soldiers and, by extension, the collective sacrifice and suffering of the war. Several writers incorporated this signifying practice into their prose. William March's *Company K* provides a clear instance: both its title and table of contents (which lists soldiers by name, indicating the narrator of each chapter) put Frederic's theoretical insistence on the "dignity" of proper names into literary practice. Hemingway himself uses names in a minimalist and therefore powerfully evocative way in *The Sun Also Rises*.[42] If

Frederic's protest accurately reflected the novel's aesthetic practices, we would find *A Farewell to Arms* using character, regimental, and place names to convey important meaning, to recall war casualties, and to make their losses felt.

In fact, the opposite is true. Factual detail functions to distract the reader from injury and death in *A Farewell to Arms*. As Margot Norris puts it, "Frederic's narration does not explicitly lie, but its factualism riddles it with holes and blindnesses."[43] Scarry asserts that "the act of injuring in war" tends to "disappear" through various rhetorical paths, including omission and redescription.[44] In *A Farewell to Arms*, factual accuracy acts as such a path, despite its celebrated reputation as one of the novel's primary sources of authenticity. When Michael Reynolds published *Hemingway's First War* in 1976, he argued against the "symbolic value" previous scholars had ascribed to Hemingway's "mountains and plains" and established the factual veracity of the novel's settings, chronology, and even weather. He traced its power to its evocation of "the way things were" and away from its metaphors. So, for instance, "not once during Book Three of *A Farewell to Arms* does fictional rain fall when actual rain did not. . . . The historical facts of the weather conditions during the retreat match Hemingway's fictional account in every respect."[45] To be sure, Reynolds points out that this "actual rain" did not fall on Hemingway himself, since he was still a teenager in the United States. He draws a welcome distinction between Ernest Hemingway's autobiographical experience and his narrator Frederic's fictional experience on the Italian front. But despite the distinction, Reynolds reinforces the tendency to interpret the novel as a literal transcription, rather than a metaphorical translation, of historical experience. In *A Farewell to Arms*, as in *The Sun Also Rises*, according to John Atherton, names provide "access" to some aspects of the war but also work "as a form of denial."[46] For while they establish the authenticity of the setting, they also suggest Frederic's status as a rational, unemotional, unimpaired witness of the war's events. Focusing on the war as a series of events that Frederic relays as simple facts in accurate detail wholly overlooks, as Norris has shown, the problems of witnessing and narrating traumatic experience: particularly in instances of violence, Frederic's narration "stops at an empirical level, giving evidence but no witness, no testimony to the self's vision or feeling that could endow the incident with significance or meaning in the story."[47] The text leaves the reader to puzzle out the meaning and long-term ramifications of wounding, killing, and death. Trevor Dodman makes a case for reading Frederic as a sufferer of post-traumatic stress disorder (PTSD), who "suffers from the compulsion to remember and retell his past" even though he is "both unable and perhaps unwilling to put that very past into words."[48] His suggestive reading highlights the narrator's lack of affect in traumatic episodes and his need to retell them. I, too, suggest that the flat tone Frederic manifests in scenes of violence is symptomatic of a split between words and their meanings. He sounds like the ideal soldier Samuel Hynes describes in *The Soldier's Tale*, one who "has no feeling for the men he kills" and who injures others without compunction or regret and who needs no "inflating terms of romantic war—'glory' and 'courage' and 'heroism' and all that" to justify or sanctify what he has done.[49] Like Dodman and Norris, I argue that these affectless moments in Frederic's story set the stage for the return of profound regret and a sense of punishment later in the narrative. We must reconsider, then, the novel's factual accuracy and its presentation of "concrete" details, and we must dispute the assumption that Frederic's protest can be read as an accurate statement of authorial intent.

Frederic Henry, in other words, is a factually accurate but emotionally unreliable narrator.[50] Accurate, seemingly objective descriptions evoke the Italian front but work to downplay the killing that occurred there. Reynolds demonstrates, for instance, that Hemingway evokes the retreat from Caporetto in geographically, temporally, and meteorologically accurate terms.[51] And yet those terms do very little to help the reader weigh the impact of the retreat and its instances of violence. How should we respond to Aymo's death when he is shot by retreating Italians or to the fact that Frederic and Bonello kill an Italian sergeant for very little reason at all? Despite the fact that we can locate these deaths on a map, we do not know what to make of them. They are passed over briefly and seem to have almost no effect on the narrator. This minimizes their significance. Certainly, these deaths are not described with false heroics; but nor is their "dignity" or weight established. Killing, being wounded, and fearing for one's life all seem too easy, even banal.[52]

Here, I want to connect these other moments with Frederic's famous protest—not just to what it says but to how it works, through paired omission and metaphor: "I had seen nothing sacred, and the things that were glorious had no glory and the sacrifices were like the stockyards at Chicago if nothing were done with the meat except to bury it." The *things* Frederic has seen cannot be specified except through negation (they were not "sacred" or "glorious") or through the approximation of a simile drawn from peacetime which is itself not quite right ("the stockyards at Chicago" *if* they produced only waste). Instead of as a statement of authorial intention, we would do better to read this passage as a cryptic, even wishful, narrative utterance, whose symptomatic elisions and omissions demand closer scrutiny.

Frederic's war story is one of displaced affect. The abjection at the heart of it is minimized in his accounts of receiving and inflicting wounds. "The things" he has seen and done and felt are perhaps never fully disclosed, as if their meaning can never fully be reckoned or conveyed. But where the novel does represent the abjection at the heart of war most explicitly, it relies on the brutal and wasteful end of its love story, in Frederic's account of Catherine's death.

Refiguring the War through Metaphor: From Wounded Soldiers to Catherine Barkley

When Frederic begins his story in *A Farewell to Arms*'s famously economical first chapter, he describes the Italian front in realistic detail and with few metaphors or figures of speech. "In the late summer of that year we lived in a house in a village that looked across the river and the plain to the mountains. In the bed of the river were pebbles and boulders, dry and white in the sun, and the water was clear. . . . Troops went by the house and down the road and the dust they raised powdered the leaves of the trees" (3). In this pasage, a dispassionate and knowledgeable observer recalls the setting's physical details. As Reynolds has shown, the chapter's details render Gorizia, its panoramas, and its place in the front with considerable historical and "geographic accuracy."[53]

When a simile appears on the second page, it is striking and odd: "[The troops'] rifles were wet and under their capes the two leather cartridge-boxes on the front of the belts, gray leather boxes heavy with the packs of clips of thin, long 6.5 mm. cartridges, bulged forward under the capes so that the men, passing on the road, marched as though they were six months gone with child" (4). The comparison between soldiers marching in the rain and pregnant women is both far-fetched and uneasy. On the one hand, it suggests that soldiers head to war bearing life, not instruments of death. On the other, it foreshadows, as other critics have noted, where the novel's depiction of war wounds will go: it looks toward the front but comes to dwell on labor and the delivery room.[54] Men carry weapons that they will use to kill each other, and those weapons are identified in precise detail. But the meaning that those weapons have for bodies and lives—namely, risk of wounding and death—is conveyed not through the specificity of detail but through the gendered metaphor. Looking at the marching soldiers, Frederic must know that many of them will die in the offensive and not return. But that is not what his words say directly. Instead, that knowledge hovers just beneath the surface, in a metaphor that conveys their vulnerability by comparing their bodies with the soft and vulnerable body of a pregnant woman.

Chapter 1's strange simile illustrates the pattern that structures the text at large: the uneasiness that male vulnerability provokes is managed through a process of feminization that directs the narrator's (and the reader's) attention away from vulnerable male bodies and toward a vulnerable female one. Alex Vernon argues that this simile conveys soldiers' loss of agency, their emasculation, and their feminization under military discipline.[55] But given the text's ultimate representation of pregnancy as fatal, the simile suggests not just a loss of power but a loss of life. The process begins here with this simile and proceeds through the repetition of imagery and words such as "rain," "hemorrhage," and "bravery," which appear in relation first to soldiers but increasingly, and fatally, to Catherine. Chapter 1's emblematic metaphor reverberates later in the novel: the soldiers who march off to fight and die and who look as if they are "gone with child" do not reappear, but Catherine's friend Ferguson repeats the phrase when she chides Catherine for being "god knows how many months gone with child" (247). The mantle of danger that the phrase threw over the soldiers has, in this later echo, a more direct and nonmetaphorical object: Catherine.

If the soldiers who look as if they are "gone with child" seem unmanly, so, it turns out, is death in the army. In chapter 1's last lines, Frederic tallies the number of soldiers who died not from wounds but from sickness: "At the start of the winter came the permanent rain and with the rain came the cholera. But it was checked and in the end only seven thousand died of it in the army" (4). These unnamed soldiers die a drawn-out and messy death. Diarrhea offers no chance of heroic exploit; it makes no distinction between the brave and the cowardly, the cunning and the stupid, the upright and the stooped. A traditional interpretation of this line would gloss it as a prefiguration of Frederic's protest, since in it Hemingway deflates the "glory" of war. And of course that is true. But we would do well to compare these briefly noted deaths in the rain to the novel's final depiction of death in the rain: Catherine's. Frederic avoids a detailed description of how rain produces the conditions that allow cholera to spread or how cholera affects the human body. "Permanent rain," in other words, is not simply realistic. "Rain" matters here because it initiates the imagery that links together so many instances of death and dying in the novel.

The status of rain in the novel provides an illuminating interpretive crux. Certainly, rain's meaning in the novel is overdetermined. Hemingway uses the traditional pathetic fallacy to convey the suffering of humankind through nature's apparent hostility. Early Hemingway critics drew attention to this and other instances of his romantic symbolism. Yet as historically minded critics have insisted, rain is also realistic. Reynolds has insisted that there is no "fictional rain" in the novel. He rejects the rain's symbolic meaning in favor of Hemingway's realism: for him, what matters is Hemingway's intent to depict the weather accurately. As a corrective to dehistoricized interpretations, Reynolds's point is crucial: "actual rain" matters in accounts of the war. Rain brought mud, and mud was deadly—literally—in those places on the Western Front where troops were mired in it to drown or be shot. Rain made the retreat from Caporetto more costly in ways exemplified by the loss of Frederic's ambulances. Rain flooded trenches and camps and carried fecal and decaying matter into drinking-water supplies, spreading cholera and other sickness. Hemingway himself remembers rain as a fickle agent of the work of New Death, who "washed [the dead] clean when they lay in it and made the earth soft when they were buried in it and sometimes then kept on until the earth was mud and washed them out and you had to bury them again."[56] In literature about the war, rain needs to be considered not just in relation to conventional literary symbolism but as a circumstance that impinged on events and influenced experience. However, in *A Farewell to Arms*, rain is not reducible to a detail of historical accuracy. If in chapter 1 rain falls on soldiers and makes them miserable, then brings the deadly cholera, it also falls whenever the fictional lovers' fortunes are in decline (when they part in Milan, when they flee the police in Stresa, and when Catherine dies). Early on, Catherine confesses to being "afraid of the rain because sometimes [she sees herself] dead in it" (126). Her prophecy makes explicit the fear and death the rain symbolizes as it falls throughout the novel, foreshadowing the rain that falls on Frederic when he walks home from the hospital after her death. Rain is both a realistic aspect of the retreat from Caporetto and a novelistic simile that conveys the tragedy of the central love affair. When it appears as the very last word of the novel, rain has been gradually, unbearably, freighted with meaning.

Tracking rain's meaning across the novel reveals an important novelistic shift. Noting the difference between Frederic's voice at the end of chapter 1 and the end of the novel reveals how Hemingway gradually replaces irony with symbolism. Certainly, Frederic's comment that "only seven thousand" died of the cholera is a classic instance of the wartime irony Fussell describes. His utter lack of affect manifests his distance from death and an avoidance of its gory detail. This is true throughout the text at large in its direct depictions of the war. War wounds and deaths are conveyed in this same oddly objective, flat, and affectless tone. Frederic's comment about the number of dead and the ingloriousness of their deaths minimizes their meaning. It is not here but through the novel's use of repetition and its structuring gendered metaphor that Hemingway portrays the emotional devastation caused by war's unsightly death. When Frederic loses Catherine, he expresses it in a voice of anxiety and emotional suffering (332).

As Hemingway's novel intertwines the war story with the love story, the narrative effects a subtle replacement. Catherine's dying female body comes to stand for the vulnerable bodies of male soldiers. In this way, Hemingway superimposes the love conflict on the war. As that process unfolds, the reader is invited to reimagine the physical vulnerability to death as something that belongs more essentially to women. Catherine's death binds together the most discomfiting strands of the war story and in so doing allows Frederic to encounter its death and abjection in a displaced and, as we shall see, a more narratable form. By displacing blood, fear, death, and their attending emotions in this way, Hemingway hews to the line of his culture's notions of war and masculinity.

Making New Death Old: The Inexact Analogy between War and Death in Childbirth

Catherine Barkley dies for a long time. Unlike the instances of soldiers' deaths and wounding in the novel, her death has an entire chapter devoted to it. Hemingway renders it with a repetitiveness that suggests a longer stretch of time than the twenty hours or so covered by the chapter. She claims to live "past where [she] was going to die," only to die hours later (319). In fact, we prepare for her death from very early in the novel. Catherine announces that she is "afraid of the rain" because she sometimes sees herself "dead in it," and it rains intermittently for the rest of the novel. Ferguson unwittingly predicts where Catherine's "trouble" will lead and becomes hysterical: "'I'm not crying,' Ferguson sobbed. 'I'm not crying. Except for the awful thing you've gotten into'" (247). Nurses endured notoriously difficult conditions during the war, working grueling hours at intensely physical labor, living in unheated tents and receiving smaller food rations than their male counterparts in the armed forces, and seeing a great deal of suffering and death. Their lives were often in danger. They had little time to cry, sob, name call, and get angry in the way Ferguson does in this episode. Her uncharacteristically overly emotional response is, however, paradigmatic: although there would be little time in the rush of a "push" to stop and cry over dying soldiers, Catherine's pregnancy is a different story. It admits sentimental reactions that war deaths forbid. It calls forth the melodrama Hemingway avoids when describing war.

Hemingway foreshadows Catherine's death in multiple ways. Unlike the shell that explodes randomly near Frederic, her ordeal follows a predictable calendar. Warnings sound repeatedly that childbirth poses a threat to her life. Her doctor ominously observes her to be "rather narrow in the hips" (294) and prescribes beer "to keep [the baby] small" (293). As the months pass, Frederic and Catherine's conversations invoke an uncertain future. Hemingway limits the reader's imagination of that future, restricting what can be known of their preparations to bare statements such as "Catherine bought the things she needed for the baby" (310). What "things"? Where will they live? Why will they not meet each other's families? Such questions hang fire. Though Catherine and Frederic discuss marriage, their repetitive conversations take on the aspect of a set piece, making their marriage seem just as hypothetical and in fact unlikely as it ever had. It becomes increasingly impossible to imagine their lives beyond the moment of childbirth. As the time of the narrative passes, as the characters move down off the mountain to be closer to the hospital, Hemingway draws his reader inexorably toward the last page of the novel, where we know it must, in some sense, end. As Frederic and Catherine prepare, the very actions that they undertake to prepare for the baby's arrival portend disaster. "We knew the baby was very close now and it gave us both a feeling as though something were hurrying us and we could not lose any time together" (311). Hemingway thus conveys a sense of impending doom to the reader, and when the pains come, we turn the page with anxiety.

As different as childbirth is from battle, this structure of feeling resembles what soldiers experience in anticipation of an attack. If war brings death and injury in maddeningly unpredictable ways, it also brings them with maddening reliability in situations of particular danger. Large-scale frontal attacks during World War I provide notorious examples of predictable, devastating slaughter. The lead-up to such a "push" often inspired a range of fears in soldiers: inklings of superstition, rational knowledge that some—indeed many—would be dead within hours, dread. Many soldiers took time as an attack approached to write what might be a last letter home. So, too, Catherine intends to write Frederic "a letter to have if anything happens" but does not (330). Hemingway describes her labor with the same foreboding that pervades accounts of the war. Fear can produce either bravery or cowardice. Untested soldiers often endure a terrible suspense about how they will respond when the time comes to perform, and war literature often explores and dramatizes the moment of mystery that precedes battle. In this chapter, Hemingway does likewise with childbirth. As Catherine's labor begins, anxiety makes it possible for her to demonstrate her excitement, to earn Frederic's praise for being "a good, brave girl" (313). Catherine's initially counterintuitive response to pain (she calls the bad pains "good ones" [314]) shows her relief that, at least, the waiting is over. Just as Frederic wants to go ahead and have his knee operated on as soon as possible, Catherine shows a desire to face the danger once and for all.

But if Catherine faces labor like a "good, brave" soldier in battle, its pain breaks her. It happens quickly. Here we find some subtle and important differences between the way Hemingway represents war experience, soldiers' responses to wounds, and childbirth. In contrast to Mark Spilka, who argues that Catherine "dies bravely, like a true Hemingway hero," and other critics who emphasize her heroism and resemblance to Hemingway's "code hero," I would highlight the differences between their sufferings, which amount to cowardice.[57] Catherine's suffering is more verbal, is more explicit, and takes up more space on the page than other accounts of injury and suffering in the novel. She calls for gas on only the second full page of the chapter and becomes, by the facing page, "a fool about the gas" (317). Her complaints of pain punctuate the chapter. She calls for gas in fourteen separate instances, and her call in each instance is often repeated and italicized for emphasis. Hemingway finds ways to make each call for help not only a repetition of the one that came before but also more urgent and intense. In this way, he portrays pain destroying Catherine's world: "I'm going all to pieces. *Please give me that. It doesn't work. Oh, it doesn't work!*" (322, emphasis in the original). This is both similar to and different from Frederic's experience after being wounded. He, too, feels intense physical pain. But he endures it more stoically, suggesting the medics tend to other wounded men before him. Frederic sweats and swears ("Good Christ!") but otherwise gives little verbal evidence of his suffering. When he goes under for his surgery, he says nothing "silly," "not a thing" (106). The surgery itself is unnarrated and occurs off-page between the end of chapter 16 and the beginning of chapter 17.

In contrast, Catherine's time as a patient in the hospital, though drastically shorter than Frederic's, contains one conversation after another in which Catherine begs nurses and doctors for help. She is repeatedly the subject of others' conversations, which often take place in her absence. Doctors and nurses shield her from the knowledge of and responsibility for her own and the baby's condition and thus imply a fragility that contrasts starkly with Frederic's autonomy throughout the ordeal of his own wound, surgeries, and recovery. Frederic manages his own care, from the moment he supervises his removal from the battlefield to the moment when he seeks a second opinion and chooses his own surgeon. Catherine becomes caught up in a theatrical scene designed and controlled by others. When at last the doctor and Frederic decide that she will have a Caesarian operation, her body is wheeled into an amphitheater. Hospital staff rush to the gallery, as if to a show: "We're just in time. Aren't we lucky?" (324). Her body becomes a spectacle that Frederic finds it difficult, but not impossible, to watch: "under the light, the doctor was sewing up the great long, forcep-spread, thick-edged, wound. . . . It looked like a drawing of the Inquisition. I knew as I watched I could have watched it all, but I was glad I hadn't" (325). Throughout the scene, Hemingway emphasizes her passivity, her being looked upon as if she is already dead: "I thought Catherine was dead. She looked dead" (325).

What are we to make of the differences between Catherine's suffering and male suffering? Does the novel denigrate women for their weakness? In Judith Fetterly's landmark feminist reading of the novel, she underlines its misogyny and takes its measure in the "disparity between the treatment of Catherine's death and the treatment of deaths of men at war." For her, Catherine "presents that *reductio ad absurdum* of the female experience: she feels guilty for dying and apologizes to the doctor for taking up his valuable time with her death," while the man who, "analogously, hemorrhages to death in the ambulance sling above Frederic does not see himself as stupid, bad, or irresponsible."[58] In other words, Hemingway makes men seem superior: they suffer valiantly, while women seem silly because they cannot take pain. This shows, Fetterly argues, that "male life is what counts."[59] This is right, but only half right. What counts is male life *and* male death. But representing male fear, male suffering, and male death encroaches on what is taboo. Hemingway needed a stand-in: Catherine. I suggest we read her not as a representation of woman but as a man in figurative drag, whose femininity allowed Hemingway to show, even almost camp up, what otherwise would be shameful. My point is not to deny the misogyny Fetterly identifies but to trace it to the specific historical codes that produce it in this instance.

Let us look more closely at the deaths Fetterly identifies as analogous. After Frederic receives his wound, he first is seen at a dressing station near the front and then is taken in an ambulance to a field hospital. On the ride, a man in the stretcher above him hemorrhages to death (61). Catherine, of course, also has "one hemorrhage after another" until she dies (331). They die in the same way, with the same word. In the ambulance, the man's blood drips onto Frederic:

> I felt something dripping. At first it dropped slowly and regularly, then it pattered into a stream. I shouted to the driver. . . . "The man on the stretcher over me has a hemorrhage."
>
> "We're not far from the top. I wouldn't be able to get the stretcher out alone." He started the car. The stream kept on. In the dark I could not see where it came from the canvas overhead. I tried to move sideways so that it did not fall on me. Where it had run down under my shirt it was warm and sticky. I was cold and my leg hurt so that it made me sick. After a while the stream from the stretcher above lessened and started to drip again and I heard and felt the canvas above move as the man on the stretcher settled more comfortably.
>
> "How is he?" the Englishman called back. "We're almost up."
>
> "He's dead I think," I said.
>
> The drops fell very slowly, as they fall from an icicle after the sun has gone. It was cold in the car in the night as the road climbed. At the post on the top they took the stretcher out and put another in and we went on. (61)

Fetterly complains that this man, unlike Catherine, "does not see himself as stupid, bad, or irresponsible." But in fact, we should note, he does not "see himself" at all. True, he does not apologize for bleeding or dying. He cannot; he is unconscious. We know nothing of him—not his feelings, not what his wounds are, not his exact moment of death, not even his name. This death, to recall the terms of Frederic's protest, "has no glory," and worse, it has no name to give it meaning.

In other words, the bleeding soldier is different from Catherine, but the difference is not as positive as Fetterly's comparison implies. His body is an anonymous figure of the abject. In Julia Kristeva's essay on abjection, she suggests that the corpse epitomizes the abject because it confronts us with our own mortality. Bleeding, oozing bodies threaten our own sense of health and physical integrity. She writes,

> A wound with blood and pus, or the sickly, acrid smell of sweat, of decay, does not *signify* death. In the presence of signified death— a flat encephalograph, for instance—I would understand, react, or accept. No, as in true theater, without makeup or masks, refuse and corpses *show me* what I permanently thrust aside in order to live. These bodily fluids, this defilement, this shit are what life withstands, hardly and with difficulty, on the part of death.[60]

Though Kristeva's description emphasizes smells and textures, she ultimately offers a more abstract explanation of the abject. It is "what disturbs identity, system, order. What does not respect borders, partitions, rules. The in-between, the ambiguous, the composite." The corpse epitomizes this because it "no longer signifies anything"; in it, we behold "the breaking down of a world that has erased its borders": it is "death infecting life."[61] Kristeva's account helps explain several aspects of this scene's power. All the details combine to transgress any sense of order. Most upsetting, obviously, are the unnamed man's gradual death and his unstoppable blood flow. Blood should be inside the body, not outside. If blood transgresses that border and runs down one's skin, it should be one's own, not someone else's. But in this scene, another man's blood flows onto Frederic's body, producing a confusing blend of "warm and sticky" and "cold and sick" feelings. Other senses and rubrics are confused as well: the blood drips in the dark, where Frederic cannot see; they are in transit, neither up nor down the hill, neither here nor there; the man seems both dead in life (he is already unconscious) and alive in death (he continues to bleed *after* Frederic feels him settle "more comfortably"). Frederic's experience is disordered on many levels simultaneously.

But if Kristeva's definition of the abject fits the bleeding body in the upper bunk quite well, her account of abjection—the involuntary, sharp, repulsive reaction against the abject—hardly describes Frederic's response in this scene. Seeing a corpse or feeling its fluids drain onto his own wounded body would, according to Kristeva, move Frederic to "the border of [his] condition as a living being"; in general, facing such a confrontation, the "body extricates itself, as being alive, from that border."[62] Being wounded and strapped in himself, Frederic cannot move out of the stream of blood that drips down onto him.

He tries to, but when he cannot, he does not vomit, panic, or become hysterical. His internal narration remains remarkably calm. With the objectivity of a watch, he notes the rate of the drips. When the driver stops and calls back to him, Frederic's response is matter-of-fact. What becomes striking, then, as we apply Kristeva's term to this passage, is the minimalism of Frederic's response. That minimalism, combined with the man's namelessness, invites readers to pass over this scene and to attribute little significance to it. As Frederic himself describes the events in this chapter, "all that was happening was without interest or relation" (60); it is difficult, as a reader, to interpret what the bleeding man's death means. It exists in a narratological no-man's-land, without a clear import in the narrative as a whole or in Frederic's development. That confusion leads many readers to ignore it altogether. This is a paradox: the event is horrific and disturbing but also random and meaningless. The unnamed leaky body is removed from the ambulance and the narrative simultaneously. It leaves behind a trace of blood, which will ultimately be recalled by and bound into the novel's later, climactic hemorrhages. Catherine's hemorrhages have an excess of narrative meaning, because they both bring the novel to its conclusion and evoke such a different response from Frederic.

The analogy between Catherine's death and the soldier's death is inexact. Both deaths are bloody. But his death is a short, disconnected episode; hers is the novel's climax. His death calls forth little comment; hers, as we shall see, provokes Frederic to long, feverish internal monologues. His is silent; hers is voluble. His is unseen and witnessed only by Frederic, in the dark; hers occurs with a large cast of attending characters and actors, following her surgery in a hospital theater. He dies a soldier; she dies out of uniform, in another country. He is a man; she is a woman.

This comparison reveals how gender is used to contain the uncomfortable topic of vulnerability. The analogy *has* to be inexact, and for particular reasons. The differences between their deaths reflect the cultural tendency to deny the abject in men or, more generally, to separate maleness from any kind of bodily fluid, particularly blood. In Elizabeth Grosz's analysis of corporeality, of how members of Western culture have understood what it means to live in a body, she identifies an aporia: "There is virtually nothing," she reports, "virtually no phenomenological accounts of men's body fluids."[63] She attributes "men's refusal to acknowledge the effects of flows that move through various parts of the body and from the inside out" to "their attempt to distance themselves from the very kind

of corporeality—uncontrollable, excessive, expansive, disruptive, irrational—they have attributed to women. By excluding men's body fluids from
their self-representation, or rather, by exerting a quasi- or apparent control
over them," she continues, "men demarcate their own bodies as clean and
proper."[64] Grosz's work aptly describes the tradition Hemingway inherited.
It offers very limited means for representing male blood flow, the abject
and uncontrolled seepage of male bodily fluid. Writing about war from
within this tradition, Hemingway pushes against and makes visible certain boundaries. That is, traditional Western literature about war positively
asserts the "glory" of male fighting. Wilfred Owen bitterly condemns war's
motto, "*Dulce et decorum est / Pro patria mori*," as "the old lie" in his Great
War poem.[65] Even in attempting to depart from this tradition, to avoid "the
old lie" and to portray male bloodletting as other than sweet and beautiful, Hemingway nevertheless comes up against its negative limits: how can
men bleed abjectly? According to a deeply ingrained cultural logic, they
do not; the less said about it, the better. From this perspective, Frederic's
lack of response is the only one that seems credible. In *A Farewell to Arms*,
Hemingway repeatedly takes us to the edge of the sayable and often arrives
somewhere beyond it, as he does in the scene of the hemorrhaging soldier.
Frederic often finds himself where there is "nothing to say"—a phrase that
appears repeatedly in the novel as, precisely, a stand-in for what cannot be
said, at least not directly. In this way, Hemingway's narrative reinforces the
gender code and puts it into question at the same time: he makes us aware
of compulsory silences, without breaching them completely.

Hemingway's confrontations with the cultural taboos surrounding male bodies' abjection left hatch marks all over the manuscript of
A Farewell to Arms. The struggle began long before the narrative of
Frederic Henry and Catherine Barkley took shape. The earliest-known
fragment of the novel begins with the narrator's pain upon arrival at a
hospital in Milan: "They carried the stretcher into the hospital and set
it down. . . . At the moment of lifting him off the stretcher there was the
pain and he waited, knowing it never went past a certain point. That
was his theory but the pain kept on and passed that point and he was
suddenly sick cold inside and in back of his ears, far inside between
the bones."[66] The narrator, Emmett Hancock, occupies the realm of the
abject. Pain knows no boundaries and instead overflows its theoretical
limits. Feelings blur into compounds ("sick cold") and penetrate into
undefined parts of the body. Once the narrator is in his room, the pain
recedes and he sleeps. In the morning, it returns when the nurses arrive
and wash him. The pain, however, cedes to shame:

They put a clean pajama jacket on him and left him under the clean sheet. When they were gone and he was alone in the bright sunny room suddenly that muscle over which he had no control relaxed. He called but no one came. He lay quiet under the sheet and let it happen. He felt better but ashamed. A new nurse came in to see him and he told her he had made a mess. She said he was a poor boy and it did not matter. Another nurse came and they changed the sheet [and] cleaned him off and washed him clean with soap and warm water. They left him alone again. He felt better and then there was a sharp griping pain and it had happened again. They had fixed a bell for him to call with beside the bed. They came in and were as nice about it as they had been the first time but they gave him a rubber sheet.

"I'm awfully embarrassed," he said. "I wish I could help it."

It happened twice more that day and it did a great deal to make him feel less like an officer [and a gentleman]. He had liked the nurses and hoped to make a good impression and instead all he did was ruin bed sheets and have to be looked after like a baby.[67]

Thus begun, the novel went nowhere, and Hemingway apparently abandoned it for quite some time. (Notably, this handwritten fragment is stored apart from the manuscript of *A Farewell to Arms*, though scholars have unanimously agreed that it is that novel's earliest beginning.) Frederic Henry's arrival in Milan contains nothing about uncontrollable bowels, messy sheets, or feeling like a "baby." This depiction of the abject male body would, as the narrator notes, go a long way toward denigrating war and its hierarchies of value. War is experienced not as doing things that make a man feel "cool and clear," as Krebs (in "Soldier's Home") recalls it,[68] but the opposite: it brings loss of control and continual self-soiling. Acting like a soldier and imposing physical discipline on oneself leads, in this account, to eventual and humiliating surrender—not to the enemy but to one's own bodily functions.

Other depictions of abject male bodies appear in some of the most heavily revised passages in Hemingway's typescript pages. Some, like the scene just described, he wrote only to omit entirely. Most involve blood rather than feces. For instance, in the typescript, when Frederic goes in search of food for his ambulance crew, his conversation with the Major is interrupted:

Outside something was sat down /beside the entrance & One of the two men who carried it looked in.

"Bring him in," said the major. "What's the matter with you. Do you want us to come outside and get him?"

The two stretcher bearers picked up the man under the arms and by the legs and brought him in. His head hung on one side and his tongue was out. There was dirt blown into his /$^{pallid\ brown}$ face and /^{dust} $^{in\ his\ eyes}$ ~~ears and as he breathed a very light scarlet red foam bubbled made bubbles where his tunic was ripped and torn along his chest (as though it had been rubbed against an emory wheel).~~[69]

In this and other similar passages, we glimpse the difficulties Hemingway encountered as he focused his narrative on wounded male bodies. While most of his typescript looks clean and has few corrections, this passage betrays effort precisely where it touches on physicality. Despite those efforts, Hemingway eventually marked it out with a large "X," and it does not appear in the finished novel. Deciding just where and in what detail to include such "things"—the oddly objectified and inanimate burdens that male bodies seem to become in passages such as this one— seems to have constituted a recurring problem in the typescript. Finding the right language with which to describe male bodies as they leak, bubble, and bleed caused Hemingway to create what looks like a written record of stuttering, interrupted speech, one that alternates between gushes of hastily written phrases and the halting stops of individual letters, half-words, and scratch-outs.

The novel's most sustained and detailed description of male injury occurs in the episode of Frederic's wound. In it, he and his companions are eating in a dugout when a shell hits and explodes. Frederic loses consciousness; then awakens to witness his driver Passini's noisy, painful, bloody death ("One leg was gone and the other was held by tendons, . . . and the stump twitched. . . . 'Mama mama mia.'"); then realizes that he himself has been badly wounded ("I knew that I was hit and leaned over and put my hand on my knee. My knee wasn't there") (55). This episode is, I would argue, the event in the novel most in need of narrative redaction. Frederic's wound occasioned a great deal of trouble and effort; those pages are among the most heavily revised in the entire typescript. What eventually became four or five finished pages was carved out of a dozen or more pages of draft. Perhaps it is the terror and violence of this episode that left Hemingway temporarily stranded. On the one hand, he wanted to show the extremity and meaninglessness of war, its absolute destruction. On the other hand, it does not destroy Frederic. The narrator manages to maintain both psychological and physical integrity in the face of war's destruction. Caught in the crossfire of this narrative contradiction, Hemingway struggled over how to end the episode of Frederic's wound.

The conclusion of this episode suggests that Frederic's abject experience needed a surrogate. Hemingway turns away from Frederic as a victim of war and toward the depiction of other wounded bodies, exhibiting in this episode what becomes the novel's paradigmatic strategy for representing male trauma. It was when he had trouble finishing the chapter with Henry's wound that Hemingway invented the unnamed soldier bleeding to death in the ambulance. That episode marks a breaking point in the typescript and in the novel's composition. After its densely penciled pages comes a clean page marked both "New Chapter" and "End of Chapter," followed by another marked "New Chapter Illustration." He planned, at least at one point, to end the chapter with Frederic's pain: "I knew had never felt pain before. I hoped there would be a limit" was planned but omitted; another drafted chapter end concludes, "[I] let the pain ride."[70] As we know from the novel's earliest beginning, one of Hemingway's possibilities here would have been to turn to a depiction of Frederic's arrival in hospital and an account of his repeated self-soiling. Instead, the author develops Frederic's account of being underneath another man, whose blood distracts him—and the reader—from the originally penciled account of his narrator's pain. Hemingway ends the chapter not on Frederic's pain but on a surrogate's. The man above Frederic bleeds to death, is removed, and then is replaced with yet another nameless body. Pain disappears, blood appears in its place, and the stream of blood is traced elsewhere and, ultimately, taken away.

After writing about these wounded male bodies, Hemingway again faltered. "I did not return to the war for three months," declares Frederic on an ensuing draft page. On another draft page following this section, Frederic offers a lengthy, self-reflective account of the problem the entire episode poses to his story:

I do not like to remember the trip back to Milan. ~~The train got into the station early in the morning. if you have never traveled in a hospital train there is no use making a picture of it. This is not a picture of war, nor really about war. It is only a story. That is why, sometimes, it may seem there are not enough people in it, nor enough noises, nor enough smells. There were always people and noises~~ /unless it was quiet ~~and always smells but in trying to tell the story I cannot get them all in~~ /always ~~but have a hard time just sticking~~

~~keeping~~ ~~to the story alone and sometimes it seems as though it were all~~
~~quiet and nothing going on but what happened~~ ~~But it wasn't quiet~~ ~~If you~~
~~try and put in everything you would never get a single day done~~
~~and then the one who made it might not feel it so I will try to tell~~
~~it straight along and hope that the things themselves will give the~~
~~feeling of the rest. Besides when~~ ~~Also when~~ ~~you are wounded or a little~~
~~crazy~~ ~~a little out of your head~~ ~~or in love with someone the surroundings are~~
~~sometimes removed and they only come in at certain times. But I~~
~~will try to keep the places in and tell what happened. It does not~~
~~seem to have gotten anywhere and it is not much of a love story so~~
~~far but it has to go on in the way it was although I skip everything I~~
~~can.~~[71]

Describing war wounds and abject male bodies prompted Hemingway
to take stock of the novel's purpose and methods. As Michael Reynolds notes, "it sounds more like Hemingway talking to himself than
anything we might expect Frederic to say."[72] This voice searches for a
narrative thread. Is the novel "really about war" or not? Having had
difficulties producing the corporeal account of how war feels, sounds,
and smells over the past several pages, Hemingway here voices doubts
that it can be done. He starts to explain the compromises an author
finds himself making: certain "noises and smells" cannot be fit in; not
all the important people can be included; a writer has to "skip everything [he] can" and leave important things out. He has to hope that the
"things themselves will give the feeling of the rest" or, in other words,
that select details will successfully stand in for the whole of war. But
from the midst of this mea culpa issues a solution, of sorts: "it is not
much of a love story *so far*" (my emphasis), but from this point on,
it becomes one. The record suggests that Hemingway began, at this
point in the writing process, to scale back his plans for developing the
significance of Frederic's male comrades (the priest and Rinaldi, first
and foremost, as Reynolds has shown).[73] Instead he began to develop
the part of the whole that he could: at this point, the tragic love story
increasingly begins to bear the burdens of representing the war. In fact,
several tensions from the novel's opening section are simply left hanging. Too many stories cannot be told; too many events defy the process
of narration and the assignment of significance it entails. Does Rinaldi
have syphilis? What does the priest know that Frederic only learned
later and was able to ignore? What happens to the other drivers and
the various soldiers who receive and inflict wounds in the war? These

multiple narrative detours are signaled but left unanswered as the narrative increasingly shifts to the romance plot.

In the novel's final published version, it portrays male wounds in war but in brief moments and stripped-down language. The ensuing experience in the hospital bed (once described as a site of repeated, involuntary shitting) is cleaned up and romanticized. The manuscript allows one to see the laborious production of Hemingway's famous economy, to catch another glimpse at what lies below the tip of his proverbial iceberg. His experience as a journalist gave him a tactic for dealing with the unwieldy task of representing war and its wounds. As he whittled his words away to produce a more laconic text, certain words received special emphasis. Just as important, as he repeated them across disparate scenes, he linked the instances of the abject across the novel. What was hard to represent in one place found other outlets. So, as Linda Wagner-Martin points out, various scenes (Henry's wounding, the man who dies in the stretcher above Frederic, and Catherine's death) all contain the repetition of the words "*hemorrhage, warm, dead.*"[74] When Wagner-Martin asserts that the death of the soldier in the ambulance "foreshadow[s] . . . the romance denouement, the proof of medical inability to save life, the randomness of hemorrhage and death," she notes, as Fetterly had, the resemblance between two of the novel's scenes of death.[75] Extending their arguments, I broaden the comparison to include still other depictions of death and abjection. Hemingway omits, truncates, and defers those aspects of the war and then revisits them in the scene of Catherine's death. Through a series of details, her death becomes an inexact but powerful analogy for a whole range of male wounds and male shame.

Narrating Catherine's death allows Frederic to revisit several previous moments in which his narrator finds little to say. In some cases, as in the case of the man who bleeds to death, unspeakability can be traced to a taboo about male wounds. In other instances, silence has other valences. Sometimes, those valences are multiple and invite conflicting interpretations. Such is the case with the episode in which Frederic shoots the sergeant during the retreat and then lends his pistol to Bonello so that he can "finish him" off (204). To some critics, he has to—it is his job as an officer. To others, Frederic's act is "cold-blooded murder."[76] Perhaps, as Ellen Andrews Knodt argues, he "panics in the face of his inability to exert his leadership," feels "fright," then "recognizes his embarrassment as the sergeants size up the situation," and so "chases after the sergeants, pleading with them to come back."[77] In short, he loses control. As Knodt and previous critics all agree, however, the problem this incidence poses stems from the absence of "direct comment on how Lt. Henry feels about the shooting."[78] Hemingway avoids ascribing a feeling and thus a *meaning* to male violence, whether endured or inflicted. But if it has no clear meaning, it is also not clearly *meaningless*. In other words, the narrator's lack of emotion is not simply a reiteration of his condemnation of slaughter in his famous statement. Instead, the sergeant's dead body continues to draw Frederic's gaze as an abject thing in "dirty long-sleeved underwear," distinctive in its unseemly presence (206). It becomes, in a sense, a sign of the unburied, unmourned dead at large and of the unfinished business of New Death.

We can consider Frederic's reaction to losing his friend Aymo in similar terms. In that instance, too, he exhibits little emotional response. He registers the responses of the other drivers, which allow the reader to infer something about what it means to them to lose Aymo: Piani swears (in a phrase that was omitted and replaced with a dash), Bonello "sa[ys] nothing," looks away, and covers Aymo's face with his cap (213, 214). These gestures bespeak anger and a need to mourn. By comparison, Frederic seems calm. He reasons about who would have shot at them. For him, Aymo's death seems to have meaning only as a sign that, properly deciphered, has bearing on their survival. As they leave, Frederic observes the scene in the concrete detail we have come to expect from him: "I looked back. Aymo lay in the mud with the angle of the embankment. He was quite small and his arms were by his side, his puttee-wrapped legs and muddy boots together, his cap over his face. He looked very dead. It was raining. I had liked him as well as any one I ever knew. I had his papers in my pocket and would write to his family. Ahead across the fields was a farmhouse" (214–15). As readers who share Frederic's perspective, this passage should arouse our curiosity. If Frederic had liked Aymo so much, why have we not heard more about him? Why has he been such a minor character? The detail in this passage is deceptive, because it forestalls that curiosity—it seems to give us many "concrete details" but tells us precious little. We know what Frederic sees but nothing about what he feels. Though Aymo's death is narrated rather precisely (where the bullet goes in and how the body is placed, for instance), we know almost nothing about what his death means to Frederic. In his account, the fact that he "had liked" Aymo is related alongside and with no more emphasis than the fact that Aymo was wearing puttees or that it was raining. Frederic's flat tone makes Aymo's death, like the sergeant's, almost banal.

The disjunction between the violence of these events and the calmness of Frederic's tone could be glossed with reference to the novel's famous protest. His lack of affect may be the retrospective product of his postwar disillusionment: he "[does]n't say anything" because language itself has been too corrupted. Frederic's refusal to use language can be read in these terms: as an ethical choice, as the decision not to lie. (He says, "I did not say anything," not just before his protest statement but on other occasions as well [see 19, 20, 332].) In the relation of Aymo's death, minimalism provides a way to manage the contradiction that here lies a friend whom he "had liked . . . as well as anyone [he] ever knew" but whose death has no meaning within the war's larger historical narrative. It does not occur in battle but in retreat. There is nothing particularly brave about skirting Udine. Aymo seems to have been killed by a fellow Italian rather than an enemy. Frederic does not lie about any of this. But he does not tell the full truth about it either, because all this should be hard to bear if he "had liked Aymo" as much as he says; as well as mother, father, brother, sister, grandfather, friend; as well or better than the priest and Rinaldi; as well, even, as Catherine. Elsewhere he condemns mean-ingless death as absurd or, to use his own language, "obscene." Given his response to loss elsewhere in the novel, Frederic should experience Aymo's death with outrage and sadness. But we see nothing of anger or of fear or of a sense that the world is somehow a diminished place in which to live. We see a farmhouse and a body placed a certain way in a certain location. This may be accurate, but it is also deeply unsatisfactory.

This dissatisfying silence offers other interpretive possibilities, including the difficulty of speaking about bonds between men. From that perspective, the most important part of this episode is the story of the friendship that death interrupts and brings to an end. That story is left out. Aymo's name, which, as Robert Martin suggests, "derives from the Latin root *amor* (to love) reduced to the first-person singular amo or 'I love,'" hints at intimacy.[79] The full story of Frederic's friendship with Aymo is alluded to but permanently deferred when Frederic says he will write a letter to Aymo's family but, to our knowledge, never does. What would such a letter say? Would it assure Aymo's parents of their son's "honor" and "courage" or tell them that his "sacrifice" had not been made "in vain"? Would it tell them that he loved their son dearly but had to leave his body unburied, in haste? What is there, finally, to say about his death?

Answers to this question are difficult, since they require interpreting things that are not there—the blanks produced by the narrator's lack of affect and his projected but unwritten letter. A commonsense interpre-tation would see Frederic's response to losing Aymo as an instance of realism, consistent with the novel's attempt to represent the experience of the retreat with psychological accuracy. In other words, Frederic does not have the time to respond to Aymo's death—he has to keep moving. This is one of the places in the novel where its retrospective frame disappears, where the reader is invited to focus on Frederic of 1917 rather than on the older Frederic who remembers and tells the story. Hemingway, we assume, wants to accurately record what conditions are like for men at war. Still, Frederic's cold-bloodedness seems extreme. As I have noted, critics have debated whether it is pathological or not, whether it is the sign of emotional damage or a sign of emotional maturity. My argument shifts the debate. Rather than interpreting Frederic's composure on its own or with reference to the "thousand-yard stare" famous from other wars, we should instead compare it to his very different response to death at the end of the novel. His narration of Catherine's death in childbirth is detailed and emotive in a way that all previous instances of wounding and death are not. Cumulatively, these earlier instances are the "before" against which "after" takes its meaning. Regendering death makes it tolerable. Frederic can grieve for a dead woman in a way he cannot grieve for a man.

The differences between Frederic's responses to death are subtle but profound. After Catherine's death, just as after Aymo's, Frederic finds little to say publicly. When the doctor tries to talk to him about Catherine's death, Frederic cuts him short: "There's nothing to say. . . . I do not want to talk about it" (332). He tries to mourn in private, alone with Catherine's body, but that too fails: "After I had got them out and shut the door and turned off the light it wasn't any good. It was like saying goodbye to a statue. After a while I went out and left the hospital and walked back to the hotel in the rain" (332). Yet, while Aymo's death is abrupt and meaningless, Catherine's is the opposite. The impossibility of placing Aymo's death in a narrative context that allows for the expression of emotion is solved in Frederic's narration of his loss of Catherine, belatedly and indirectly. The reader's curiosity about how it feels to walk away in the rain from a loved one whose already "very dead" body must be left behind is deferred in the scene of Aymo's death but is reawakened and satisfied in the novel's conclusion.

Frederic's account of losing Catherine revisits both previous losses and his own previous wound. It functions as a version of what Reynolds would call an "echo scene," in which Hemingway "run[s] the same scene past the reader twice."[80] Earlier scenes in the novel undergo a narrative transformation as they reappear in a feminized form far from the theater of war. What Hemingway renders in such frightening and unconventional language when it happens to Frederic also occurs to Catherine, who slips in and out of consciousness and has to confront the fear of her own death several times. But again the repetition is inexact. Potentially terrifying aspects of Frederic's wounding return as parody in Catherine's labor. His out-of-body experience is terrifying. But as he watches Catherine fade in and out of consciousness, deliberately asking to be put out, she seems "a little drunk" and "a fool" (318).

The most extreme example of this repetition-as-parody occurs when Catherine tries and fails to maintain her responsibility toward others despite her pain, just as Frederic had. Before looking at this aspect of Catherine's dying, let us recall some comparable details from the episode of Frederic's wound. When Frederic survives the shell explosion, he hovers above his body on the edge of consciousness but then recovers his wits and begins to look for the other drivers. He sees Passini, who has been horribly wounded. The spectacle of his wounded comrade paradoxically spurs Frederic to regain his composure and to reassert a leadership role. Frederic tries to stabilize himself by focusing his attention on others' wounds:

> Then I heard close to me some one saying "Mama Mia! Oh, mama Mia!" I pulled and twisted and got my legs loose finally and turned around and touched him. It was Passini and when I touched him he screamed. His legs were toward me and I saw in the dark and the light that they were both smashed above the knee. One leg was gone and the other was held by tendons and part of the trouser and the stump twitched and jerked as though it were not connected. He bit his arm and moaned, "Oh, mama mia, mama Mia," then "Dio te salve, Maria. Dio te salve, Maria. Oh Jesus shoot me Christ shoot me mama mia mama Mia oh purest lovely Mary shoot me. Stop it. Stop it. Stop it. Oh Jesus lovely Mary stop it. Oh oh oh oh," then choking, "Mama mama mia." Then he was quiet, biting his arm, the stump of his leg twitching.
> "Porta feriti!" I shouted holding my hands cupped. "Porta feriti!" I tried to get closer to Passini to try to put a tourniquet on the legs but I could not move. . . . I saw there was no need to make a tourniquet because he was dead already. I made sure he was dead. There were three others to locate. I sat up straight and as I did so something inside my head moved like the weights on a doll's eyes and it hit me inside in back of my eyeballs. My legs felt warm and wet

and my shoes were wet and warm inside. I knew that I was hit and leaned over and put my hand on my knee. My knee wasn't there. My hand went in and my knee was down on my shin. I wiped my hand on my shirt and another floating light came very slowly down and I looked at my leg and was very afraid. Oh, God, I said, get me out of here. I knew, however, that there had been three others. There were four drivers. Passini was dead. That left three. (54–56)

The narrator's experience of wounding goes back and forth between an awareness of his own damaged body and his spectatorial relationship with Passini, whose wound is depicted in far greater detail and is, of course, fatal. Passini suffers in a way that Frederic does not. Passini regresses to a primal language of childhood, calling at once for both earthly and heavenly mothers. Hemingway's irregular capitalizations, run-on sentences, and verbal repetition signal Passini's psychic breakdown. Not so Frederic, who, despite his initial confusion and separation from his own body, does not lapse into his mother tongue but continues to use his appropriate, and nonnative, Italian. In contrast to Passini's hysterical appeal to a trinity of "mama Mia," Mary, and "Jesus shoot me Christ," Frederic's prayer is simple, unified, and brief; it lacks the emphasis of capitalization, irruptive expletives, quotations, or exclamation points. Frederic's use of the past tense to describe his prayer creates another kind of distance: the temporal distance between the Frederic who prayed and the Frederic who recalls having prayed. While he does report that he "felt very afraid," the passage's stylistic elements imply something else altogether: that Frederic's wound evokes a relatively limited amount of anguish from him, that despite his wound, Frederic maintains a calm, rational coherence. He engages in a step-by-step evaluation of his and Passini's situation; he registers objective evidence of their wounds; he thinks in quantitative terms about the soldiers in his command ("There were four drivers. Passini was dead. That left three.") and so seems to maintain his sense of authority. Frederic even registers his own wound in matter-of-fact, if repetitive, terms: "My legs felt warm and wet and my shoes were wet and warm inside. I knew that I was hit and leaned over and put my hand on my knee. My knee wasn't there. My hand went in and my knee was down on my shin" (55). This gives way to his one expression of emotion: "I looked at my leg and was very afraid. Oh, God, I said, get me out of here. I knew, however, that there had been three others. There were four drivers. Passini was dead. That left three. Some one took hold of me under the arms and somebody else lifted my legs. 'There are three others,' I said. 'One is dead'" (56). In this passage, Hemingway presents his narrator as supremely stoic and brave, manly despite his injury and his need of rescue. This wound, as with those Debra Moddelmog speaks of generally in Hemingway, "marks [Frederic's] inner worth, especially his virility"; "the disabled hero's body performs as an able one, as 'normal'" in comparison with others around him.[81] Even though he cannot lift himself or walk, Frederic continues to act in his mind as a commander, as someone who is responsible for others. In narrative terms, Passini's wounds emphasize Frederic's physical and mental survival.

Aspects of this moment get reworked in the episode of Catherine's death. She, like Frederic, attempts to look beyond her pain and to reassume a role of responsibility. "I so want to be a good wife and have this child without any foolishness," she tells Frederic (315). She puts his needs before hers. In the episode of his wounding, Frederic does something similar when he insists that others get medical treatment before he does ("I'd rather wait. There are much worse wounded than me" [58]). He conducts himself as a man, as a superior officer who can withstand any necessary pain. But what seems unremarkable in his case bothers readers when Catherine tries it. During her labor, Catherine repeatedly minimizes her own needs and tells Frederic to go have a meal ("Go have another breakfast," she tells him [317]) and not mind her pain. She tries to spare his suffering. She tries to maintain a normative feminine solicitousness for the needs of others ("You must go have something to eat, doctor. . . . I'm so sorry I go on so long" [317]). Yet these are precisely the moments that Judith Fetterly finds so offensively absurd. Male stoicism, when relocated to a feminine body, seems ridiculous. In these moments, Catherine's ordeal parodies Frederic's. (It even parodies Emmett Hancock, who has to apologize to the nurses for repeatedly soiling the bed.) The switch in gender takes the portrayal of attempts to cope with physical suffering away from a context of war, with its expectations of heroism, and allows us to see, if we will, how preposterous those conventional expectations are. Catherine's male impersonation is like an instance of reverse camp, in which her performance of exaggerated masculinity underscores the artificiality, the unnaturalness, of its routine poses and roles.[82]

This particular parody does not provoke laughter so much as tears. Regendering embodied suffering and death calls forth a different kind of response from Frederic. Of course, Catherine's suffering and death are also removed from the front. This dual transformation makes Frederic

more tender and Catherine abject. My understanding of how Hemingway uses gender to order affect and vulnerability in this instance is, in
other words, precisely the opposite of that described by Mark Spilka. We
are not, as he suggests, "witnessing a historic flight from tenderness, or
from tender aspects of male humanity."[83] Frederic regains a tenderness
he had to disavow in the war theater, but only and precisely because the
body whose breakdown he witnesses is female.

Away from the war, Frederic seems to experience a different range of
emotion than previously. Specifically, Catherine's impending death provokes a range of anger, hope, and despair in Frederic that Hemingway
portrays in a series of interior monologues:

> Maybe [the child] was choked all the time. Poor little kid. I wished
> the hell I'd been choked like that. No I didn't. Still there wouldn't
> be all this dying to go through. Now Catherine would die. That was
> what you did. You died. You did not know what it was about. You
> never had time to learn. They threw you in and told you the rules
> and the first time they caught you off base they killed you. Or they
> killed you gratuitously like Aymo. Or gave you the syphilis like
> Rinaldi. But they killed you in the end. (327)

The despair he feels over losing Catherine reaches back retroactively to
encompass his feelings about losing Aymo and Rinaldi and his anger
toward military autocracy. What could not be felt or uttered then finds
its place in the narrative alongside Catherine's dying body. The hysterical
edge we heard before in Passini's prayer but not in Frederic's now takes
over the narrator's calm:

> Everything was gone inside of me. I did not think. I could not
> think. I knew she was going to die and I prayed that she would not.
> Don't let her die. Oh, God, please don't let her die. I'll do anything
> for you if you won't let her die. Please, please, please, dear God,
> don't let her die. Dear God, don't let her die. Please, please, please
> don't let her die. God please make her not die. I'll do anything you
> say if you don't let her die. You took the baby but don't let her die.
> That was all right but don't let her die. Please, please, dear God,
> don't let her die. (330)

These feverish interior monologues convey Frederic's anguish and
suffering and allow the reader to hear what he will not tell the doctor
because there is "nothing" to say. The death of his child and his fear that
Catherine will die too prepares the occasion on which and the *means* by

which Frederic begins to ascribe meaning to his earlier losses, including that of Aymo: he rails now against its gratuitousness and expresses, at least to himself, the outrage and emotional injury that had previously gone unmentioned. Catherine's death sets up a retrospective chain of association that enables Frederic to express anger and fear. As a result of death's indirect and inexact repetition, he lays belated emotional claim to the experience that had initially passed by without feeling, affect, or meaning.

Some critics have explained this aspect of return in Frederic's narration with reference to contemporary trauma theory, as it is described by Cathy Caruth and others.[84] Dodman's account of Frederic's narration as a belated laying-claim to traumatic experience, discussed earlier, offers useful insight. But I hope that my discussion here also shows the role *gender* plays in Frederic's experience of trauma and in his belated attempt to lay claim to it. Masculine wounds, shame, and death are difficult to verbalize in this novel. Only when refigured as feminine can they be described as meaningful. Frederic has a relatively easier time articulating his own suffering over the body of a female surrogate. Trauma is a cultural event. Though its underlying structure may be consistent, its experience and expression are idiomatic and vary according to time, place, culture, and subject position. Attending to its split temporal structure (that it breaks experience between an unapprehended traumatic event and its delayed apprehension), however useful, is not enough: the cultural and historical codes that shape our apprehensions must themselves be a part of any full exploration of what makes an experience traumatic and how, if, and when it might be "claimed." Despite Hemingway's willingness to portray wounded men, his depiction of abject death seems fullest when it takes female form.

In an instance of revision that has become the stuff of scholarly legend, Hemingway rewrote the novel's ending approximately forty times. Once again, this long-recognized issue becomes newly legible in light of our reconsideration of its attempt to represent and feminize war trauma. In many of the rejected endings, Hemingway attempted to bring the war back into the novel and to make it more explicitly a war story. Rereading these various endings (as one can do partially in Oldsey's *Hemingway's Hidden Craft* or completely in the Hemingway archives) demonstrates Hemingway's ongoing attempt to connect Catherine's death with the suffering of soldiers in wartime. The novel's first published ending (published by *Scribner's Magazine* when the novel was serialized) makes that connection explicit:

It seems she had one hemorrhage after another. They couldn't stop it.

I went into the room and stayed with Catherine until she died. She was unconscious all the time, and it did not take her very long to die.

There are a great many more details, starting with my first meeting with an undertaker, and all the business of burial in a foreign country and going on with the rest of my life—which has gone on and seems likely to go on for a long time.

I could tell how Rinaldi was cured of the syphilis and lived to find that the technic learned in wartime surgery is not of much practical use in peace. I could tell how the priest in our mess lived to be a priest in Italy under Fascism. I could tell how Ettore became a Fascist and the part he took in that organization. I could tell how Piani got to be a taxi-driver in New York and what sort of a singer Simmons became. Many things have happened. Everything blunts and the world keeps on. It never stops. It only stops for you. Some of it stops while you are still alive. The rest goes on and you go on with it.

I could tell you what I have done since March, nineteen hundred and eighteen, when I walked that night in the rain back to the hotel where Catherine and I had lived and went upstairs to our room and undressed and slept finally, because I was so tired—to wake in the morning with the sun shining in the window; then suddenly to realize what had happened. I could tell what has happened since then, but that is the end of the story.[85]

In this ending, Frederic lists Catherine's death among the postwar doings and fates of soldiers he remembers from the war. She becomes one casualty among many. Frederic's incantatory evocation of "March, nineteen hundred and eighteen," links Catherine's death, both in its original occurrence and in the way it could be remembered, with the war. ("Finally only the names of places and the dates had meaning.") This ending made those connections explicit in a way that Hemingway ultimately decided to occlude. His choice suggests that, as Linda Wagner-Martin puts it, "war is both background and foreground"; the war "was the iceberg he was so consciously aware of"[86] and that he worked to imply, evoke, and symbolize, rather than wholly reveal. Hemingway's ultimate decision to edit his ending and to eliminate the other characters and the allusions to the war reveals something about what he wanted the ending to evoke and how he thought that could best be done. Naming them does not make us feel for the suffering of the soldiers and the vets. Bringing them up makes their fates seem banal. The dates do not mean anything, despite the insistence in the famous protest. What hurts is walking away from a dead woman in the rain.

4 / The Missing of *Sartoris*

*It always needs all the accompaniments of visible sickness and slow
dissolution quite to convince us that our living have become our dead.
The boys killed in the trenches are still a present force because our brains
cannot believe them dead, when our eyes have not seen them die.*

—WINIFRED KIRKLAND, *NEW DEATH*

Monuments to the Missing

Rising above a plain in the Valley of the Somme in northern France,
a large monument stands in commemoration of "the missing of the
Somme" (see figure 10). The monument at Thiepval is subtly modeled on
the triumphal arch. It is inscribed with names of the dead and backed by
a large cemetery. Designed by the architect Sir Edwin Lutyens, it has been
called a "silent scream"—a work of pacifism protesting the deaths in the
Battle of the Somme and, by extension, the whole of World War I. In *Sites
of Memory, Sites of Mourning*, Jay Winter emphasizes its minimalism,
which allowed Lutyens "to express the inexpressible nature of war and
its human costs." Winter reads the monument's geometrical structure
of arches within arches as "an embodiment of nothingness." Lutyens, he
suggests, "took the form of a triumphal arch, and multiplied it. . . . The
progression [of arches and framed empty spaces] extends upward, from
smaller arch, and therefore smaller area of emptiness to larger arch, and
larger area of emptiness, to still larger arch in the centre of the monument, to nothing at all."[1] Rather than triumph, the monument focuses
one's awareness on emptiness. Its "sequence of staked arches," insists
Allyson Booth, frames "empty space" so that "absence is rendered in a
way that constitutes gigantic presence."[2] The huge monument draws the
visitor's eye to what is simply not there.

Expressing the inexpressible and symbolizing nothingness are difficult
charges for the artist in any medium. But in a very real sense, making

FIGURE 10. Thiepval Memorial to the Missing
of the Somme (Somme, France), designed by Sir
Edward Lutyens. (Photograph provided by and
used with permission of the Historial Museum
of the Great War [Péronne, Somme, France])

"nothing" concrete was Lutyens's goal. The monument stands in the
place of bodies that were never recovered or, if recovered, never identified. During the war, the Western Front moved backward and forward
across the Somme River Valley, churning up the landscape and littering it
with human remains. Bodies interred behind the lines one month would
be relocated within no-man's-land by subsequent fighting. John Keegan
explains that during the Battle of the Somme, which went on from July to
November 1916, the area became an "arena of attrition" and a "holocaust"
of human life where over a million soldiers died. Britons recall it (especially July 1, 1916, the battle's opening day) as their "greatest military tragedy" and continue to make pilgrimages to the site today.[3] The Thiepval

monument was built not simply to honor the dead but to embody those who were never found. The monument signifies not just a euphemistic "loss" of individual soldiers to death but their actual material disappearance. It draws attention to the missing through its geometry and through the inscriptions on its surface—the names, dates, regiments, and ranks of the dead. These inscriptions allow visitors who come to the battlefield to visit not the physical remains of the dead but their *names*—disembodied traces of men who have been, quite literally, lost.[4]

Despite the monument's impressive size and evocative design, one might feel that it offers, in fact, precious little to a mourner: not because Lutyens failed but because of the inherent difficulty of representing the missing dead—what the monument invokes as "the missing of the Somme." The particular means by which people waged World War I challenged traditional mourning practices and languages of commemoration, such as the triumphal arch. Modern artillery, trench warfare, and the unprecedented scale of mobilization enabled men to do new violence to the human body:

> Many of those who died in battle could never be laid to rest. Their bodies had been blown to pieces by shellfire and the fragments scattered beyond recognition. Many other bodies could not be recovered during the fighting and were then lost to view, entombed in crumbled shell holes or collapsed trenches or decomposing into the broken soil battle left behind. . . . At the war's end, the remains of nearly half of those lost remained lost in actuality.[5]

In addition, governments of Germany, France, and the United Kingdom all buried their soldiers where they fell or in cemeteries near the front; they did not pay for or even allow families to claim their dead. Mourning in the absence of physical remains thus posed a problem during and after World War I. As Winifred Kirkland put it, "our brains cannot believe them dead, when our eyes have not seen them die."[6] Cultural historians have recently focused on mourning practices and aesthetic vocabularies developed in the face of this reality: for instance, the overwhelming British response to the Tomb of the Unknown Soldier can be understood as a result of the fact that so many dead were never found.[7] Modernist writing and architecture, according to Booth, often work to bridge the gap between the "corpseless" world of the home front and the corpse-strewn world of the front.[8]

Although the Battle of the Somme occurred in 1916, before the United States entered the war, how to represent the missing became an

American problem as well. After the war, the United States also conse-
crated an unidentified body in a Tomb of the Unknown Soldier.[9] But the
physical distance between the United States and France added another
dimension to the question. Earlier wars left a complicated tradition, and
it seemed for a time that all Americans, like Britons, might have to for-
feit their dead. Whether to leave American soldiers buried in Europe or
to take on the unwieldy and expensive task of bringing home decom-
posing bodies became the subject of national debate. Did one *need* a
body in order to mourn? Echoing the logic of Rupert Brooke's "The Soldier," some people justified leaving the bodies in Europe as a reminder
of American sacrifice, so that there would be "some corner of a foreign
field / That is forever" America.[10] Predictably, given Americans' national
history of isolationism, many of them countered that their dead should
not be left abroad to become "hostages" in future European conflicts.
As Kurt Piehler has shown, families, the War Department, Congress,
and other interested parties (including the funeral industry organization the Purple Cross) eventually reached a compromise: survivors
could choose whether to have bodies buried abroad, in Arlington Cemetery, or in a family plot. A large majority (70 percent) asked to have the
bodies of their dead returned to the United States. Another twenty-five
thousand families chose to leave their loved one's body in a European
grave. Some of those who left their dead in Europe eventually visited
the foreign graves, either independently or, in the case of the "Gold Star
Mothers," courtesy of the U.S. government.[11] Others refused. In other
words, how to mourn those who died at a distance posed a problem
to which no one solution seemed adequate. Lisa Budreau describes
the various compromises, which were difficult to reach and make
good. "The anxious uncertainty" occasioned by the U.S. government's
"immediate postwar indecision over the disposition of its war dead was
a heartbreaking period for all concerned. Once resolved, the agonizing wait for the body's return could take years. For others, the decision
to leave their deceased overseas came at an equally high price. There
would be no funeral service, no headstone at a local cemetery, nothing
left to venerate, and no closure so necessary in the grieving process.
For those whose sons or husbands were officially termed 'missing' or
'unknown,' . . . time seldom offered any solace," since "countless bodies remained unidentifiable, and scores of others were never found."[12]
Survivors' various responses suggest that many felt the actual body to
be important, if not essential, to the mourning process. In thousands of
cases, that piece of the process was missing.

The problem of how to mourn those killed in World War I preoccupied not only the families of American soldiers but also American writers and artists. At roughly the same time that Lutyens was designing the Thiepval monument, William Faulkner was at work constructing a narrative to evoke the missing dead of the recent war. This problem prompted him to innovate the modernist narrative strategies that would make him famous. Only a few scholars have considered World War I as the crucial context for Faulkner's development as a modernist writer.[13] This chapter focuses in particular on his third novel, *Sartoris*, which has been neglected by readers and critics in favor of his later novels. (*Sartoris* has been in and mostly out of print for most of the time since its publication in 1929.) Yet it is in *Sartoris* (or, more properly, in *Flags in the Dust*, the manuscript out of which Faulkner's friend Ben Wasson carved *Sartoris* for publication) that Faulkner invented Yoknapatawpha County and in which he began to develop the aesthetics that define his work.[14] The challenge of making a distant war seem near, making its invisible wounds apparent, and portraying the problems associated with mourning the missing dead are what spurred Faulkner to innovate his signature modernist narrative strategies. Faulkner's fiction emanates from what critics have increasingly understood as a point of origin for diverse modernisms: loss. The Compsons' loss of Caddy; Sutpen's loss of innocence; the Brundrens' loss of their mother—the difficulty of mourning the disappeared and the dead pervades Faulkner's mature fiction. Seth Moglen places Faulkner's writing alongside that of other American modernists in his canon of "melancholic" modernism, because it tries, but fails, to mourn the losses and wounds of modern industrial capitalism. Both Moglen and Greg Forter find that Faulkner's works naturalize historical trauma.[15] Certainly, *Sartoris* depicts a melancholic world that is doomed to repeat the traumas of its historical past. But the central wound in *Sartoris* is inflicted by war, not only capitalism. Moreover, in contrast to Moglen and Forter, I argue that the novel's depiction of failed mourning offers its reader an opportunity to move beyond the melancholia it portrays. It is, in other words, a critique of melancholia and traumatic repetition as responses to traumatic loss. Faulkner invites his reader to do what *Sartoris*'s characters cannot: reckon, articulate, and mourn losses incurred in World War I. This has not been appreciated, precisely because, as in Lutyens's monument, the wounds in *Sartoris* are evoked rather than detailed.

Faulkner, like Cather, Fitzgerald, and Hemingway, wrote about the war repeatedly.[16] Before *Sartoris*, his first novel, *Soldiers' Pay* (1926), tells the story of a wounded veteran who comes home to die. Faulkner eschews depictions of glamorous combat in order to focus on the trauma of war, felt at home and after the fact by demobilized soldiers and civilians in turn. Faulkner returned to the figure of the returning soldier in a manuscript for a third novel, *Flags in the Dust*, which tells the story of Bayard Sartoris's return and delayed death. Bayard Sartoris, unlike Donald Mahon, the protagonist of *Soldiers' Pay*, suffers psychological rather than physical wounds. Though his wounds are invisible, they are just as deadly: he reenacts his war experience continuously through a repetition compulsion and ultimately commits suicide. He gives himself the death he wishes to have had in the war. In both novels, Faulkner compels his reader to take stock of war damage as it was felt after the fact, in American locales and by American civilians and veterans alike. He portrays the invisible wounds born on the home front. In contrast, his final novel, *A Fable*, depicts the Western Front directly. And lest we assume that World War I is mostly absent from his other novels, we may need to think again: John Limon persuasively reads *As I Lay Dying* as "very nearly a perfect specimen of the Great War novel," despite the apparent fact that "the Great War is nearly irrelevant to it."[17]

Though more obviously relevant to the war, *Sartoris*'s preoccupation with war damage also ventures into territory that is at once insistently concrete and more abstract, even metaphysical. Not only are Bayard Sartoris's wounds invisible, but so is their cause: his psychological trauma opens around the loss of his twin brother, whose body literally disappears into thin air during an aerial combat mission. This provokes a metaphysical problem. Witnessing his brother's death is traumatic because he is there but not there; seeing his brother disappear, Faulkner suggests, is worse than seeing him die. How do we know what we know? How can Bayard accept the psychologically unacceptable fact of his brother's death without the evidence of a body? He knows his brother cannot have survived, but he also has no direct knowledge of his death. What is the nature of his experience as a witness, given that what he most needed to see went missing? Faulkner frames Bayard's crisis not as a universal one but as the result of particular historical experience in modern warfare. Just as Lutyens's monument uses architectural form to evoke an awareness of "emptiness" and "the missing of the Somme," so too is Faulkner's *Sartoris* constructed around the missing. The narrative's omissions, silences, interruptions, Bayard's stream-of-consciousness-like speech, and multiple distracting plot lines foreground the difficulty of representing the war's damage. The difficulty Bayard has in telling his story reveals the silence imposed on men in the name of masculine stoicism.

Faulkner himself, of course, felt the war to be a missing experience. He brought fictions of the war to life in his writing but also in his masquerade as a wounded aviator. As Fitzgerald had, Faulkner had been close to going overseas when the war ended. As his biographer, David Minter, records, "For five months he performed calisthenics, practiced marching, and studied principles of flight" as a cadet in the British Royal Air Force. "When the war ended on November 11, 1918, Cadet Faulkner was stationed at the School of Military Aeronautics in Toronto, in the third and final phase of pre-flight training, almost in reach of an airplane. Though he had seen many planes and heard many stories, though it is possible that he had flown, it is certain that he had seen nothing of the skies over France."[18] Famously, he tried not to let this opportunity for glamour slip through his fingers altogether. After being demobilized, he returned to Oxford, Mississippi, wearing an officer's uniform, affecting a limp, and cultivating a local legend about his war wounds.[19] Faulkner's lie has been read variously, as a young man's prank, as a budding novelist's research into the lives of returning veterans, and as an elaborate psychological-defense strategy.[20] Doreen Fowler suggests the masquerade was a way of coping with "a psychic disjunction that is universally experienced and universally repressed. . . . Faulkner [attempts] to represent, to signify, with disguised representations in both his art and his life," the "loss at the core of being."[21] The challenge of understanding Faulkner's relationship to an imagined, but not actual, war experience has preoccupied critics for years—a testament to the consistency with which he advanced the impression of having been to war.[22] Philip Young reads "the combat fantasies of Fitzgerald and Faulkner as meaningful" and insists on "the importance and validity of vicarious experience," although, he admits, it is not "the same as being there in the vulnerable flesh."[23] Most recently, Keith Gandal has posited that Faulkner did receive a psychological wound in 1917–1918: the wound of rejection, inflicted by the army for what it deemed his physical inadequacy. In Gandal's terms, Faulkner suffered a mobilization wound rather than a combat wound.[24]

In contrast to Gandal's account, however, the present argument addresses neither Faulkner's biographical experience nor his representations of cross-ethnic romance. I draw out the war's effects on another aspect of his aesthetics. He chose as a central conceit a realistic and not-uncommon problem: how to mourn an American soldier whose body had gone missing. He complicated this problem by making one of the survivors a soldier who himself would rather have died in the war. In *Sartoris*, witnessing New Death both provokes and frustrates storytelling. The novel's aesthetics respond to and reflect the difficulty of representing and mourning World War I's modern violence. Specifically, Faulkner represents the trauma of losing someone not just through death but through disappearance. The novel describes the psychic and social processes through which that common traumatic experience was disavowed, repressed, and reenacted. It makes its reader aware of the unsaid and the missing—the parts of the war which veterans and civilians conspired to forget.

Raising Ghosts of the Past

In *Sartoris*'s opening paragraph, Faulkner raises the specter of the dead. Old Man Falls pays a visit to another old man, Bayard Sartoris, and brings with him, "like an odor, . . . the spirit of the dead man," Bayard's father. These men do not merely remember the dead. Instead, they "sit for a half an hour in the company of him who had passed beyond death and then returned." The ghost of John Sartoris is "far more palpable than the two old men" who are, in Faulkner's language, perched themselves somewhere between life and death.[25] Faulkner uses a variety of rhetorical strategies (most notably, synaesthesia, the blending of different sensory appeals) to make the past more tangible than the present, the dead more alive than the living. The past, "like an odor"—the sensual vehicle most associated with memory—is "palpable" despite the fact that it cannot be seen. Despite Bayard's deafness, he hears his father breathing. In ways that anticipate *Absalom, Absalom!*, Faulkner here announces *Sartoris*'s central rhetorical mission: bringing the disembodied and absent past into a present narrative and, in so doing, making its continuing impact apparent. But if Sutpen's ghost haunts a voice rather than a house, the ghost of John Sartoris haunts silence. The novel opens with a soldier who has "passed beyond death and then returned" to haunt the living.

Though Faulkner opens his novel by raising the ghost of the southern past in the spirit of John Sartoris, who fought in the American Civil War, the novel unfolds around a more recent past and a younger John Sartoris, who died in World War I less than a year before the novel opens. Colonel John Sartoris haunts his son Bayard; the dead aviator John Sartoris haunts his twin brother, Bayard. As the repeated names suggests, these two Sartoris losses mirror each other; the recent traumatic past resonates with other pasts, other plots, and other traumas. Faulkner hints at patterns of traumatic repetition and forces his reader to encounter one historical layer in the midst of another. Despite the similarities between the stories of the distant and recent pasts, there is a difference: the distant past can be pleasurably recounted. Faulkner begins with what can be discussed and with stories that have been crafted into familiar and amenable shapes. The distant past is welcome inside the "citadel of silence" (literally, deafness) within which the living (such as Old Bayard) protect themselves (2).

In contrast, the novel's trigger incident is the return not of the ghost of Colonel John Sartoris but of a flesh-and-blood, still-living man: young Bayard Sartoris. The novel opens on the very day that he arrives in his hometown of Jefferson, Mississippi. Young Bayard brings the ghost of his twin brother, Johnny, lost in the war, home with him. Although this return triggers the novel's plot, Faulkner defers the scene of his homecoming for over forty pages. In fact, although the plot is essentially young Bayard's, Faulkner includes many characters, episodes, and subplots that compete for the reader's attention. This is striking considering that *Sartoris* is itself the streamlined version of an even more complex manuscript, *Flags in the Dust*, which Faulkner had difficulty publishing. The rich confusion of his novel in its original form (which Wasson preserved to some extent in the editing process) provided Faulkner with a wealth of material to which he would return in years to come. Faulkner called *Sartoris* "the germ of [his] Apocrypha," for it was in this novel that he invented Yoknapatawpha County, his own "postage stamp" of land, as a subject for his fiction.[26] Consideration of the textual variations between *Flags in the Dust* and *Sartoris* is beyond the scope of the present inquiry and has been undertaken elsewhere.[27] However, my argument does make sense of the single most important difference between the two versions: *Sartoris*, in comparison with *Flags in the Dust*, focuses more particularly on the returning World War I veteran, Bayard.[28] *Sartoris* offers its reader fewer distractions from his story of return and (lack of) readjustment. Emphasizing its postwar plot, then, made the novel intelligible to Ben Wasson and to publishers in a way that Faulkner's original manuscript was not.

The obscurity of Bayard's story, which may have led so many publishers to reject the manuscript, was inherent to Faulkner's design. For although the story of Bayard's return organizes *Sartoris*, it is neither easy to tell nor easy to understand. On the contrary, Faulkner withholds it, only revealing bits and pieces of it in a discontinuous fashion. The novel's modernist difficulty—its paradoxes, divergent subplots, omissions, semantic irregularity, stream-of-consciousness-like speech, and the extreme mobility of its narrator—becomes the vehicle of a story that is, Faulkner insists, nearly impossible to tell and to hear. In this sense, what seem like distractions serve an important and organic function: they indicate possible ways of understanding—and of *refusing* to understand—Bayard's story. That is, the spatial and temporal leaps taken by the novel's third-person narrator among the various characters and their various memories all work to delay the novel's central mystery: what happened to Bayard? Although characters (and, in turn, readers) want the answer to this question, its pursuit is forestalled, silenced, and interrupted. Faulkner's novel takes on the shape of resistance: Bayard resists telling, and characters resist hearing, the details of his war experience. It is precisely by withholding or delaying the story of what Bayard lost that Faulkner is able to tell the story of *Sartoris*—the story of the effects of that loss. *Sartoris* exemplifies Faulkner's early interest in what John Limon has emphasized in the later novels, particularly *As I Lay Dying*: the difficulty of writing, *after* war—of representing not just war experience but what it means to survive it.[29] The story unfolds around the various perceptions among the living of what it means to have lost Johnny, around their collective failure to mourn his death and disappearance.

Bayard's Audience

Before revealing what happened to Bayard, Faulkner establishes the various expectations and anxieties that his story arouses in the people he left behind on the home front. Cumulatively, these instances trace connections between what happens to soldiers "over there" and to the people who stay home. Though civilians have not left, they have vicarious imaginary experience of the war in their anxiety for their loved ones. They also have more direct encounters with its damage when survivors return. Faulkner suggests that the stories of soldiers need to be understood not in isolation but in the way they are alternatively imagined, romanticized, silenced, and unwillingly encountered after the fact. Revealing Bayard's story of "foreign" war from within a postwar and domestic context undoes the spatial (front and home front) and chronological (wartime and postwar) binaries traditionally used to make sense of war.

To this end, before introducing Bayard himself, Faulkner uses the characters' suspense and speculations both to pique and to forestall the reader's curiosity about Bayard's war experience. Simon, the black coachman of the Sartoris family, informs Bayard's grandfather (also named Bayard) of his return:

> "He got offen de two o'clock train. . . . Wouldn't even git off at de dee-po. . . . He never even had on no sojer-clothes. . . . Cunnel, you reckon dem foreign folks is done somethin' ter him?"
> "What do you mean?" Bayard demanded. "Is he lame?" (5)

The question of Bayard's physical injury is deferred—Simon makes no answer. This vagueness both creates suspense and hints at a different kind of injury—one that is psychological and social, rather than physical, in nature. Bayard is not lame, but that may not be reason for relief. In fact, his condition is more difficult to diagnose and recover from than a physical injury.

In the same conversation, Faulkner broaches other controversies Bayard's homecoming reopens:

> "Dem foreign folks done done somethin' ter him, er dey done sot dey po-lice atter him. I kep' a-tellin' him when he fust went off to dat 'ere foreign war him and Mr. Johnny neither never had no business at—"
> "Drive on!" Bayard said. "Drive on, damn your black hide." (5)

Old Bayard's interruption of Simon's speech abruptly ends the conversation. Its harsh racial depersonalization contrasts with the narrator's patronizing but fond attitude toward Simon.[30] This abrupt moment, then, draws the reader's attention to the present and away from the subject of "foreign war." Old Bayard's verbal lashing of Simon's "black hide" replaces a distant violence with a nearer hostility, distracting both himself and the reader away from his grandson. His abruptness signals anxiety. Bayard silences Simon because he does not want to hear about the "foreign war" his grandson had "no business" fighting and because he cannot bear to be reminded of "Mr. Johnny." Though the vague awareness that the war "done" an unspecified "somethin' ter" Bayard invites the reader's suspense, his grandfather's negative reaction foreshadows the resistance and the interruptions that he will encounter in telling his story.

The rumor of Bayard's return provokes a similar response from his great-aunt Jenny. Again, anxiety emerges in a language of racist hostility. When Simon gives her the news, Jenny storms, "You damn fool nigger! . . . You went and blurted a thing like that to Bayard? Haven't you got any more sense than that? . . . Drive on!" (34). Once at home, Aunt

Jenny fills the silence with "a wealth of trivialities," as if to distract old Bayard from his reverie, despite the fact that "it was very seldom that she descended to gossip" (39, 40). These interrupted and gratuitous conversations constitute characters' attempts to cover over the uncomfortable gaps that open in anticipation of Bayard's return.

Long before Faulkner introduces Bayard's story, the expectations it must fulfill are outlined, even more specifically, by Sartoris stories from an earlier war: the American Civil War. The narrator recounts the Sartoris family's war stories as recalled by Aunt Jenny, Old Bayard, and Old Man Falls. These stories, like the parlor "constantly in use" in Colonel John Sartoris's day, are memorials to a "jovial but stately masculinity" (59). Faulkner's narrator suggests that the masculinity of the Civil War has become enshrined and idealized, forming a central part of what Olga Vickery describes as southern "myth."[31] This ideal of white southern masculinity—which Susan Donaldson describes as a "curious combination of chivalry and violence, honor and self-destruction, physical derring-do and introspection"[32]—is the standard against which Bayard's war story will be measured. This code requires "asserting aggressive behavior and authority at an early age, knowing one's place in the midst of an elaborate hierarchy of inferiors and superiors, venerating one's father, defending one's family and taking violent revenge for offenses, and guarding the reputation of one's mother, sister, wife, and daughter."[33] Since war traditionally provides a proving ground of masculinity, war stories traditionally celebrate heroes who fight and die according to such a code. Thus, the comparison between Bayard's own war story and those of the past promises a figurative measurement of his manhood. But New Death changes the experience of warfare and thus antiquates the codes and narratives Bayard shares with his family. Or, to put it another way, the recent and as-yet-unassimilated damage at the center of Bayard's war experience is framed and bracketed by a different past, one which has already undergone the romanticization of repeated narration. The codes of masculine conduct in warfare—bravery, stoicism, heroic exploit and daring—are reasserted and recounted in advance of their possible disruption in the telling of young Bayard's modern combat experience. Stories from the past establish the inherited idiom through which Bayard must communicate his war story. Although the Civil War was traumatic, Faulkner suggests that by the time Bayard returns from World War I, a romanticized version of it had become assimilated through story.

Delaying the scene of Bayard's return, then, allows Faulkner to do more than create suspense and establish the novel's setting. Initial instances of omission and proliferation—the omission of Bayard's story and the consequent proliferation of avoidance strategies that anticipate, bracket, and obstruct its telling—epitomize the narrative logic at the heart of *Sartoris*. "Faulkner is not unaware of our impatience," Jean-Paul Sartre wryly notes; instead, "he plays upon its effects"; he follows "a certain formula: it consists in not telling, remaining hidden . . .—telling *a little*."[34] This is the heart of the novel's self-conscious modernism. Sartre discusses its formal innovation as a development on novelistic realism; he takes it as evidence of Faulkner's individual writerly talent (his signature as a modernist), rather than seeing it as paradigmatic or situating it within a larger cultural response to recent historical experience. But its omissions and delays map psychological and social resistance to the awareness of historical trauma: the narrative unfolds around the repression of an experience that cannot or will not be articulated.[35] The repression occurs largely because the experience does not fit into shared assumptions and narratives. In the process of delaying or withholding information, Faulkner's novel draws attention to what characters do not ask and do not tell. This suggests that some knowledge is intolerable and that characters work actively to exclude it.

Making Bayard's story unspeakable in this way allows Faulkner to make the reasons for its unspeakability precise and historical, rather than universal. *Sartoris* locates the repression of Bayard's story not only at the threshold of his own internal psychological mechanisms (which do play a role, as we shall see) but also at the site of communication with others, which occurs through shared social codes (particularly, southern ideas about the natural heroism of aristocratic white men). His audience, then, has definite expectations about what a war story should sound like. It is not only that Bayard keeps himself from knowing his own war story but that he knows his family will not hear it. The division between these two locales of awareness—one interior and psychological, the other exterior and social—is permeable and overlapping. Faulkner's narrative about Bayard's war story invites us to trace a complicated negotiation between these two sites of realization and communication.

The subject of Faulkner's novel (a returning soldier traumatized by war) and the confusion this subject engenders (particularly over how and why his war experience continues to haunt him) resemble the evidence that prompted Freud's speculations in "Beyond the Pleasure Principle." As Freud notes, veterans and other sufferers of traumatic neurosis often fail or refuse to speak of or recall the scene of their wound because, he suspects, they "are more concerned with *not* thinking of it."[36] In other words, "*not* thinking of it" is an activity in and of itself. In many ways, *not* thinking of or talking about Johnny's disappearance is what *Sartoris* is about. But while both Freud and Faulkner examine the lingering aspects of war trauma for veterans, Faulkner emphasizes its social aspects and in particular how codes of American masculinity put some stories under erasure. Before describing his protagonist's story and his (in)ability to tell it, Faulkner forces his reader to encounter Bayard's audience—the Sartoris family—with all their prejudices, limitations, and imperfectly mourned historical experiences.

The problem with Bayard's audience is not that they do not know anything about war but that they know too much about it. The Sartoris family wholly identifies with the "Lost Cause," the southern myth of the American Civil War, as a doomed and therefore all-the-more-gallant effort. Loss is at the center of their forebears' imagined glory. Faulkner's postbellum South is structured around loss. He makes this apparent through the routinized and defensive behavior of his characters. One of those behaviors is the racialization of others by whites—the routine performance of racial difference and discipline ("Drive on, damn your black hide"). The older Bayard's asserting his power allows him to fend off intolerable awareness. But the performance's well-worn tone betrays it as a practiced and familiar one. Faulkner's depiction of the stereotypical pantomime between the aged white aristocrat and his long-suffering black retainer is Faulkner's self-conscious display of inherited literary and cultural tropes. But it is more than that. Old Bayard, Old Man Falls, and even Simon cling to their traditional roles. That clinging suggests how necessary the roles are to those who play them. These roles, like the house's "memorials" to the "jovial masculinity" of an earlier cultural moment, enshrine not its continued presence but its loss. Faulkner suggests this through tropes of hauntedness, memory, and the loss of hearing that define Old Bayard. His physical deafness materializes his psychological enclosure in a guarded, defensively constructed world.

Old Bayard's entire routine seems constructed to maintain a fragile link with the past. Arriving home after his exchange with Simon, Bayard goes riding, as he does every afternoon. Faulkner's description of Bayard's afternoon ride emphasizes its ritualization: "The negro lad waked easily and untethered the mare and held the stirrup. Old Bayard mounted and remembered the cigar at last and fired it. The negro opened the gate into the lot and trotted on ahead and opened the second gate and let the rider into the field beyond. . . . A ticked setter came up and fell in at the mare's heels" (24). The boy, the horse, and the hound all pose in a

landscape where time stands still. In their ordered positions, they maintain Bayard's place in the world and assure him of its continuity. His
daily habits maintain his identity within an ideal of aristocratic white
masculinity: he is master over black servants; he lives in a pastoral scene
of ample land, loyal mounts, and hunting dogs; he commands well-made
artisanal goods. His world recalls the Sartoris stories of the Civil War,
which are all cavalry episodes. But just as the cavalry did not survive
World War I as a meaningful unit, so its heroic aura does not survive
in *Sartoris*. These trappings, and the masculinity they signify, are all
threatened by young Bayard's return from the war. Faulkner's nostalgic
evocation of this "richly static" world signifies that its time has, in fact,
already past; modernity will soon change it. Faulkner signals modernity's incursion into this world through young Bayard's purchase of the
fast car that antiquates the family's use of horses, that he uses in various
suicide attempts, and that literally frightens his grandfather to death.

Faulkner's portrayal of the home front suggests that it is already, even
before Bayard's return, marked by and defended against awareness of
loss. In ways that mirror Freud's opposition between mourning and
melancholia, Faulkner describes a melancholic southern culture, where
mourning is perpetually deferred. For although almost sixty years have
passed, those who survived the Civil War continue to exhibit a "loss of
interest in the outside world," a "turning away from any activity that is
not connected with thoughts of" what was lost.[37] They knit the present
to the past with anecdotal references to, for instance, the "bed of salvia
where a Yankee patrol had halted" and the leaded window panes that
"Jenny had brought from Carolina in a straw-filled hamper in '69" (6, 8).
These storied objects do more than suggest a sense of history. They play
a more insidious function, as object lessons used to pass a melancholic
attachment to the Civil War on to subsequent generations. Through such
references, young southerners learn that what counts as significant is
what has passed and that their own exploits will never measure up. The
"doom" that stalks the Sartoris twins in France has its origins in the
stories of that earlier American war.

Many critics have described Faulkner's use of temporality as modernist
"because its interest lies not just in recounting the past, but in interrogat-
ing the terms of that recounting within a self-conscious examination of
the possibilities of writing."[38] Often overlooked in such discussions of his
modernist interrogation of temporality, however, is the social function it
serves here, where he first puts it to use. Faulkner's temporal overlap—
between Old Bayard and his memories of Colonel John Sartoris, young

Bayard and his memories of Johnny—structures the denial of losses incurred and exacted during successive wars. The failure to mourn the Civil War fully has begotten a nostalgia for the past that profoundly limits the extent to which the present can be understood on its own terms. Mourning, as Eric Santner reminds us, requires "a 'good enough' empathic environment.... It ... must be witnessed."[39] Bayard's community fails him because to witness his loss would require them to question the values enshrined in their own nostalgic stories of the past, the traces of their own melancholic memories of the Civil War. That they cannot do. Through Faulkner's depiction of their rigidity, he reckons the high cost of southern nostalgia. That nostalgia not only causes Bayard's postwar suffering but provided the Sartoris twins' bankrupt justification for going off to war in the first place. Unmourned historical trauma, he suggests, repeats itself.

Bayard's Story

After establishing the historical roots of Bayard's inability to mourn, Faulkner lets the reader overhear his testimony. But that testimony does little to gratify our curiosity about what has happened to him. Bayard's problem is primarily one of narration: he cannot tell his story in a coherent way. His speech resembles stream-of-consciousness narration, flowing associatively from one thing to the next without clear conversational markers. The first thing he says to his grandfather—not having seen him in over a year—is, "I tried to keep him from going up there on that goddam little popgun" (43). It is not surprising that he should speak immediately about his dead twin brother, Johnny. Indeed, we know that the death of "Mr. Johnny" comes to mind to all those who anticipate Bayard's return. What is surprising is his beginning in medias res: no greeting, no explanation for his late arrival, no account of his own survival and return. His grandfather asks him twice if he is "all right," and Bayard makes an evasive answer: "Why not? ... Takes damn near as big a fool to get hurt in a war as it does in peacetime. Damn fool, that's what it is" (44). Grammar indicates denial: the person who gets hurt is put under erasure, as an "it." In Bayard's speech, associations progress according to a highly personal frame of reference, which excludes the uninitiated reader. But if stream-of-consciousness narration invites meaning-making, Bayard's odd speech obscures meaning, acting to shield him and his listeners from the story he has to tell.

Rather than Bayard's answering his grandfather's question (whether he is "all right") or going into more detail about what is on everyone's mind (his brother's death), he launches into the story of his search for revenge. He appeals, in other words, to the definition of southern white masculinity that locates honor in revenge. He leaps from saying that he tried to stop Johnny to the end of the story and to his own attempts to even the score, which never seem to have been sufficient:

> "There was one I had to lay for four days to catch. Had to get Sibleigh in an old crate of an Ak. W. to suck him in for me. Wouldn't look at anything but cold meat, him and his skull and bones. Well, he got it. Stayed on him for six thousand feet, put a whole belt right into his cockpit. You could 'a' covered 'em all with your hat. But the bastard just wouldn't burn." His voice rose again as he talked on. . . . Young Bayard's voice went on and on, recounting violence and speed and death.
>   "Hush," old Bayard said again. "You'll wake Jenny." (44–45)

The narrator filters Bayard's words, letting some through while leaving others out, making sense of a narrative that tends to run on too long and lose us in its details. Just as old Bayard "hush[es]" his grandson, so too the narrator silences certain parts of the story. Censored, the war story loses its specificity after a certain point. It may seem that Faulkner uses indirection to invite the reader to imagine the details, to picture what the narrator refers to only as "violence and speed and death." And yet I do not think that we are to imagine that Bayard is giving *all* the details to his grandfather while Faulkner, through the narrator, withholds them from us. Other details are present but do not convey much meaning; we do not know who Sibleigh is or how an "Ak. W" flies. These details promise more than they deliver. For although they evoke the setting of Johnny's death with some particularity, they do not reveal what is most disturbing about the death. Bayard's story is unsatisfying because its central moment—the killing of Johnny—is left out. Instead of saying that, Bayard focuses on the question of the adequacy of his own response to his brother's death—an adequacy he wants to establish according to ideals of masculine exploit (a code the narrator glosses as "violence and speed and death").

Invoking this code ironically creates inconsistencies in Bayard's story. He accuses the pilot who killed his brother of being cowardly and unwilling to put himself at risk, of only attacking when he is sure of a victory ("Wouldn't look at anything but cold meat"). In contrast, he claims to respond according to an old-fashioned code of dueling and revenge and to kill his brother's killer through a feat of cunning, determination, and skill. But in order to establish the value of his revenge, he has to take back what he said about the pilot. "It was Plöekner. He was one of the best they had. Pupil of Richthofen's," he offers (46).[40] "Well, that's something," his aunt agrees (46). Telling the story the way it happened means calling the values of masculine exploit into question, but without those terms, it seems hard for Bayard to assign meaning to his story. He returns to the nostalgic code of masculine "violence and speed and death" despite its inadequacy.

Bayard cannot tell his story from beginning to end, and he leaves out the most important parts. His narration focuses on the moments before Johnny's death, as if to discover in its retelling an alternative ending.

> "I tried to keep him from going up there, on that damn Camel. . . . I couldn't keep him from it. He shot at me," young Bayard said; "I tried to drive him back but he gave me a burst. He was already high as he could get, but they must have been five thousand feet above us. They flew all over him. Hemmed him up like a damned calf in a pen while one of them sat right on his tail until he took fire and jumped. Then they streaked for home. . . . Streaked for home, with the rest of his gang," young Bayard said, "him and his skull and bones." (45–46)

When Bayard finally concludes his story, he does so just as he started it: "I tried to keep him from going up there on that goddam little pop-gun" (46). This verbal repetition signifies the story's unfinished quality: Bayard's story brings him right back to the beginning, and he is ready to start all over again.[41] Indeed, "him and his skull and bones" takes us back to the first part of Bayard's story: his own search for revenge. Perhaps Bayard wanted to do to the pilot of the "skull and bones" what he had done to Johnny, hence his disappointment in the fact that "the bastard just wouldn't burn." The visuality of certain images (fire, "skull and bones") conveys Bayard's complete absorption in the details of his story; he seems to relive rather than to remember it. Though Bayard is no modernist poet, his story's meaning seems to be condensed and encoded in a series of imagistic phrases. He does not make allowances for his audience by explaining his references. The recurrence of various phrases ("damn little pop-gun") establishes the circularity and repetitiousness of Bayard's story. Its internal repetitions correspond to the way Bayard tells it in the novel at large, over and over again. Each time he tells it, he reveals a bit more detail, comes a bit closer to formulating and bringing into available awareness whatever it is that makes this memory so haunting. The foolishness of Johnny's death—its lack of necessity—continues to outrage him, now almost as much as when it occurred. Bayard explains the scandal of Johnny's death as the fact that it occurred for no real reason. But more shocking is what Bayard cannot bring himself to say in this version of his narrative, which is that Johnny disappears, literally, into thin air.

The deferral and truncation of Bayard's story through avoidance strategies that interrupt its telling epitomize *Sartoris*'s narrative logic, which "consists in not telling" its story, in Sartre's famous formulation.[42] This structure maps what is paradigmatic about trauma: the narrative unfolds around the repression of an experience that resists articulation. This is what Donald Kartiganer defines as "Faulknerian modernism": "a fictional mode" in which "what is absolutely essential and missing is the given of the text."[43] Although Kartiganer does not discuss *Sartoris*, Faulkner invents this kind of "modernism" here, as a means of representing the traumatic legacy of World War I.

Because Bayard cannot tell his whole story, he seems haunted by Johnny's death. After the conversation has ended and his family has sent him to bed, Bayard enters the room he had shared with his brother and is immediately engulfed by memory, which lies "like dust everywhere in the room" and "stop[s] his breathing": "he [goes] to the window and [flings] the sash crashing upward and lean[s] there, gulping air into his lungs like a man who has been submerged and who still cannot believe that he has reached the surface again" (48). Just as the ghost of the first John Sartoris seemed "palpable," here the memory of Johnny takes on a stifling corporeality. Bayard is haunted not just in his mind but in his body. Faulkner depicts the physical reality of mental abstraction through Bayard's hysterical claustrophobia. The language suggests that Bayard's memory of Johnny shifts from this place, which evoked it, to France. The room in Mississippi brings Bayard back not to his childhood but to the war. Bayard's vertiginous physical sensations implicitly recall the story he had been telling just moments before. He feels "like a man who has been submerged": like one who has almost drowned, who has been gassed, or who has come near to death. The sensation of disbelief that Faulkner describes suggests both an incomplete assimilation of experience and a kind of desire—Bayard's failure to realize what has happened and his desire *not* to realize it. Bayard's anger and loss merge in his identification with his brother and become a fantasy that Johnny's death is not yet inevitable or that he—Bayard—may not have to survive it.

Faulkner's depiction of Bayard's anguished response to Johnny's disappearance emphasizes the kind of suffering undergone by those who, during the war, had to live in suspense about their missing dead. In Allyson Booth's account of home-front "corpselessness" as a trigger for modernism, she describes civilians as almost blissfully naïve about what it meant for soldiers to go missing. For them, "to be labeled 'missing' rather than 'dead' justifie[d] a certain amount of hope."[44] But in Faulkner's account, "corpselessness" leaves survivors in a painful suspension that precludes hope, indeed precludes any relationship to a future. Without a body to mourn, Bayard and his family remain fixated on the unresolved past.

Though Faulkner's descriptions allow us as readers to make such an interpretation, Bayard himself does not have access to it. Instead, his encounter with his memory in the passage quoted earlier illustrates that Bayard's past remains in his present as somatic symptoms (here, of breathless panic). If Bayard tried to tell the story of his brother's death with finality just a few minutes before or to lay his memories to rest when he visited the cemetery that afternoon (a scene that Faulkner announces but does not narrate directly), this scene signals the failure of those attempts to mourn. He goes to sleep, only to "wake himself" and his aunt "with his own groaning": "'What's the matter?' he said. 'That's what I want to know,' Miss Jenny answered. 'You make more noise than a water pump'" (48). Rather than speaking narrative, Bayard can only make unconscious noise about "what's the matter." Bayard's nightmares identify him as a classic sufferer of traumatic neurosis. His story emerges not just (or not even primarily) in his narration but in his actions, in his silences, in his dreams, and in Faulkner's thick descriptions of his state of being. Bayard's attempts to tell his story occur directly in relation to these other, more enacted, kinds of memory.

Remembering, Repeating, and Working-Through

Faulkner's portrait of Bayard Sartoris as a sufferer of traumatic neurosis corresponds in some obvious ways to Freud's descriptions of nightmare-ridden war veterans in "Beyond the Pleasure Principle." People with traumatic neurosis cannot remember, and so cannot articulate, the experience that psychically injured them. In "Remembering, Repeating, and Working-Through," Freud describes their characteristic "compulsion to repeat": "the patient does not *remember* . . . what he has forgotten and repressed, but *acts* it out. He reproduces it not as a memory, but as an action."[45] Bayard seems able to recall his experience and attempts to tell his story. He is, however, repeatedly interrupted. Unable to tell about it in a satisfying way, Bayard repeats his war experience. Not surprisingly, given his experience as a pilot, he compulsively seeks fast machines. He reenacts the speed of his war days in a new fast car and eventually in an airplane. Predictably, even intentionally, he gets into a series of "accidents" that return him to the war and to the death he cannot recall in narrative.

In these details, Faulkner's depiction of war veterans suffering from psychological damage repeats something hinted at in *Gatsby*'s attention to cars.[46] It was becoming increasingly possible to allude to veterans' postwar trauma by figuring them as "reckless drivers." Immediately upon *Sartoris*'s release, one reviewer explained that it "concerns itself with the fragment of life that is left young Bayard Sartoris, back from the war where he and his brother John were aviators and where John met his death. . . . Bayard sets out at once with a fast automobile to try to kill himself."[47] Another observed, "It is the nervous strain of war that causes the sickness of mind and the feverish thirst for activity that is finally destructive. . . . [Bayard's] melancholy is not bettered by the loss of his brother. . . . With no battles left to fight, Bayard dulls his misery with a series of meaningless anodynes: he speeds insanely along the country roads in a racing car, scaring negroes and keeping his family on edge; he rides wild stallions; he drinks fiery liquor. Literally he drives himself to death, for after he has tried all manner of machines which only wound and do not kill, he at last gets a full answer to his suicidal frenzy."[48] A veteran's wish to kill himself, then, had by 1929 become part of an established and recognizable pattern. The reviewer's language is at once insightful and unwitting: Bayard clearly suffers from war wounds, but those wounds are unspecified. They are only named within the vague condition of "nervous strain of the war." Why Bayard is nervous, or why he wants to die, is not spelled out. This vague term reflects the sense of mystery that surrounded "shell-shock" and its various iterations. The medical community then (as now) had difficulty pinpointing why a particular experience might be traumatic to one person and not to another or why a soldier can endure a great deal only to reach a particular breaking point. The difficulty of knowing and naming the specific origins of shell-shock finds its way both into Faulkner's form and, here, into commentary on it. My reading both proposes a very specific origin for Bayard's condition and interprets the difficulty of its revelation. This reviewer's shorthand, part of a well-worn and coded discussion of "nervousness," generalizes about Bayard's postwar trauma, tracing it to the war but glossing over its specifics.

Though many critics have returned to the question of Bayard's trauma, certain aspects of it deserve more attention.[49] *Sartoris* illustrates an attempt to bring traumatic loss to consciousness and to initiate mourning. Although Bayard's repetitions are self-destructive, they provide opportunities to restage, recall, and work through his loss. Freud announced this paradox and emphasized its potential, while admitting the difficulty of exploiting it: "Only when the resistance is at its height can the analyst, working in common with his patient, discover the repressed instinctual impulses which are feeding the resistance; and it is this kind of experience which convinces the patient of the existence and power of such impulses."[50] Faulkner offers a similar insight in his novel, because it is when Bayard repeats, when he catches himself in the act of doing something that takes him back to the scene of Johnny's death, that he tries again to tell his story.

The second time Bayard tries to tell his war story occurs when—and because—he has gotten into an "accident," actually a deliberate part of a joke he plays on Simon. Until this point, Simon has steadfastly refused to go, as he derisively calls it, "cyar-ridin'" (87). Others have been seduced, but he has held to his faith in "hosses" (231). Bayard finally lures Simon into the car, then speeds up to frighten him. Bayard callously observes this fright and continues to torture him: "Bayard glanced at him again, and Simon was watching him and the blurred irises of his eyes were no longer a melting, pupilless brown: they were red, and in the blast of wind they were unwinking and in them was that mindless phosphorescence of an animal's. Bayard jammed the throttle down to the floor" (116–17). Whether Faulkner is complicit in Bayard's denial of Simon's humanity or whether he is using free indirect discourse to reveal the racist and dehumanizing cast of Bayard's glance, he vindicates Simon's point of view at least insofar as Bayard is clearly not acting like "a gentleman." Bayard breaks his word, he lords power over someone weaker than himself, and he recklessly endangers not just himself (his prerogative as a Sartoris, after all) but his dependent and a wagonload full of "negro women" who are "moving drowsily and peacefully along the road" (116).

In Bayard's use of the car as a weapon, his manipulation of its power to terrify and injure, he repeats the violence of war. True, the repetition just misses being parodic. Throughout *Sartoris*, Faulkner's representations of African American characters verge on minstrelsy and "comic" racist stereotypes. But Faulkner portrays Simon's fear with undeniable pathos. And although no one is seriously hurt by Bayard's driving, the incident reifies his feeling that he is a monster: he convinces others, namely, Simon, that he is one. When Simon refuses to get back into the car, Bayard calls him "a fool" (just what he had called his brother) (118). Bayard feels "savage and ashamed" (119). Haunted by guilt for not adequately protecting his brother, he acts out that guilt, making it more palpable by compounding it with actual guilt. In an instance of transference, he carries out his war on civilians, who are by definition not rightfully his opponents. He is armed and they are not. Acting out his anxiety about his failure to be a hero in this way returns him to the event that haunts him, with a difference: he feels "savage and ashamed" toward someone who is still alive.

This repetition provides Bayard with an opportunity. He catches himself in the act of behaving irrationally and cruelly, against his better intentions. He can confront the feelings that his actions repeat. Faulkner emphasizes this opportunity by following this episode immediately with a depiction of Bayard's second attempt to tell his story. His audience this time is Rafe MacCallum, a man both he and Johnny knew before the war. Once again, both story and listener are inadequate. Before hearing the story, MacCallum gets himself and Bayard fairly drunk, deliberately inducing a kind of numbness. Again, Faulkner censors the details: "He fell to talking of the war. Not of combat, but rather of a life peopled by young men like fallen angels, and of a meteoric violence like that of fallen angels, beyond heaven or hell and partaking of both: doomed immortality and immortal doom" (127). Bayard's spoken dialogue returns with a lament: "That was the only thing Johnny was ever good for. Kept me from getting in a rut. Bloody rut, with a couple of old women nagging at me and nothing to do except scare niggers. . . . Damn ham-handed Hun. He never could fly, anyway. I kept trying to keep him from going up there on that goddam popgun" (127). Despite the obvious repetitions, this narration emerges precisely because Bayard has a new reason to feel guilty: he has been "scar[ing]" people. This new context evokes his unresolved feelings of guilt from his past, left over from not having succeeded in "trying to keep [Johnny] from going up there on that goddam little popgun." This repetition might have provided an opportunity to do what Freud called "working-through" the original instance of his loss. However, it passes him by. Telling this story in this way has no therapeutic value, in part because MacCallum gets Bayard drunk instead of listening. Instead of using repetitions as an occasion on which to tease out what remains inarticulate and unresolved about the past, this conversation allows boundaries between the past and present to be increasingly blurred and imprecise. Bayard's monologue drifts in and out of then and now, conflating into one inchoate mass the anger he feels toward the "old women nagging at [him]" (his aunt Jenny and his grandfather Bayard), his brother, who "never could fly" and acted like a fool, the "damn ham-handed Hun" who killed his brother, and himself, who has "nothing to do except scare niggers."

Bayard's speech betrays the perseveration (verbal repetition) characteristic of traumatic fixation. But although his linguistic repetitions ultimately signal a failure to work through, this failure need not be inevitable. Repetitions of language can enable a speaker to verbalize and claim experience and to embed it in a larger narrative and thus change its meaning.[51] When Faulkner rewrote the story of Bayard Sartoris in the screenplay *War Birds*, as Bruce Kawin has argued, he represents his character's repetitions within a process of successful working-through.[52]

In *Sartoris*, by contrast, Faulkner evokes this possibility in order to explore its failure. Here, narration never initiates mourning. Crucially, Faulkner links this failure not just to the inflexibility of the Yoknapatawpha community but to literary language more generally. As Bayard speaks, the narrator glosses his speech in a higher diction. Bayard's simple vernacular and the narrator's elevated imagery of "fallen angels" and "meteoric doom" make a strange duet. But Bayard's omissions are merely duplicated, rather than transformed, by this clichéd literary imagery. Faulkner's narrator reiterates the code of romantic masculinity, which limits the reader's ability to "hear" Bayard's story. "Meteoric doom" blankets the realities of modern warfare in Miltonic imagery. The difficulty Bayard has being specific about what happened when his brother died is thus mirrored by the narrator's diction. Faulkner makes literary language visible as a vehicle of denial.

Bayard does not speak this language himself, but Faulkner's use of it reminds us of the cultural repository of the masculine ideals a man such as Bayard would have internalized, against which his vernacular war story would be measured. When Faulkner's narrator breaks into these moments of high diction, they seem self-conscious and jarring. By juxtaposing them with vernacular speech and realistic description (of the greasy food in the restaurant where he tells his story, for instance), Faulkner draws our awareness to the discursive seams in the text—the places where he moves between one set of conventions and another. Heroic diction and southern tradition are, in Faulkner's novel, two overlapping idioms that overdetermine the *non*transmission of Bayard's story. Faulkner suggests that both censor narration according to falsely coherent, and ideologically inflected, systems of signs.

Heroic imagery offers a literary analogy for the myth of gentility and manliness that pervades *Sartoris*'s southern culture. The narrator's romanticism corresponds to Rafe MacCallum's assumptions about what men should do and what kinds of stories they should tell. The correspondence, again, is not exact. These characters do not talk this way in the novel. Rafe MacCallum, the man to whom Bayard tells his story this time, is plainspoken and has no formal education. However, the narrator's romanticism "speaks" for Rafe's code of masculinity.

As part of the MacCallum clan, Rafe embodies an even more rigorous version of the southern code of masculinity that Bayard encounters all around him (and within himself). This code of masculinity limits Bayard's ability to tell his story again, in a different way, when he goes to visit the MacCallums in the woods. He goes there to escape feelings of guilt following his grandfather's fatal heart failure, for which he feels responsible. (Once again, he has been driving recklessly and succeeded, this time, in frightening his passenger literally to death.) This time, he must feel even more "savage and ashamed." But the entire time he is there, he withholds this information from the MacCallums. He remains strangely silent. It is not manly to have run off, and in their company, Bayard cannot, or will not, admit having reneged on his filial responsibility.

Bayard's silence among the MacCallums contradicts the atmosphere they ostensibly foster. Faulkner figures the MacCallum place, as he later does the hunting lodge of "The Bear," as a masculine sanctuary, where men can retreat from modernity and find their rugged, "natural" selves. Except for a wizened servant, there are no women. It offers an escape from domestic comforts and from the bonds and responsibilities that come with them. And yet entrance into this domain comes at a price. It offers a more fragile shelter than one might assume. Bayard has to communicate according to an even more constrained set of expectations and tolerances.

Indeed, at the MacCallums', Bayard's is not the only story that cannot be told. He shares a bed with Buddy MacCallum, the youngest, who is, like Bayard, back from fighting in France. Buddy's war story emerges in the "inarticulate idiom of the war. It was a vague, dreamy sort of tale, without beginning or end and filled with stumbling references to places wretchedly mispronounced" (320). His speech, too, apparently sounds like stream-of-consciousness. Buddy literally cannot name where he was. When Bayard asks, he responds, "Up there, where them limeys was. Where they sent us. Flat country. Don't see how they ever git it drained enough to make a crop, with all that rain" (319). Perhaps, given the extent to which artillery bombardment disfigured landscape and geographical markings, Buddy's description is accurate enough. But there may be more reasons for his vagueness. This description all but names the Belgian sector of combat where Americans served under British command. As Mitchell Yockelson's *Borrowed Soldiers* shows, the two divisions under British command endured hard fighting and high casualty rates.[53] However vague, Buddy cannot tell his story within his father's hearing. Fighting for the "Yankee" army puts his experience out of the bounds of what can be discussed (320). The still painful experience of the Civil War has put some stories permanently off-limits, despite the fact that Buddy has distinguished himself as a soldier ("They gimme a charm"—a medal—he tells Bayard [320]).

If Buddy's apparently heroic war story cannot be borne, it is not surprising that Bayard's stories would have to be censored and mystified as well. When Bayard first tells his story to Rafe in the café, Rafe responds to it in a way that reveals his adherence to a code of masculinity according to which men are expected *not* to talk about emotion. According to that stoic code, one conquers, rather than articulates, feelings of inadequacy. Instead of listening, Rafe offers Bayard a chance to reassert his manliness by riding a wild stallion.

MacCallum offers the horse as an old-fashioned cure for Bayard's war neurosis. The wild horse symbolizes an earlier form of masculine exploit—the same tradition evoked, in fact, by the name Bayard, the famous hero of medieval France known to be *"sans peur et sans reproche."*[54] The horse's appeal stems from its place in an antiquated code of martial manliness that Bayard has betrayed by surviving the war, by driving cars, by "scaring niggers," and by generally undermining his position as a "gentleman." MacCallum imagines that the horse might cure Bayard's fixation to cars, which is consistently glossed as a symptom of modern degeneration. ("'De ottomobile,' Simon philosophize[s], 'is all right fer pleasure en excitement, but fer de genuwine gentlemun tone, dey ain't but one thing: dat's hosses'" [231].) If the horse fails to do that, it might at least kill him and allow him the manly death he missed during the war. That possibility seems to be the implication in MacCallum's insistence that the horse trader allow Bayard to ride it, despite the risk: "'That hoss'll kill him.' . . . 'Let him be. That's what he wants'" (132).

But Bayard's escape on horseback into a premodern past fails. When he mounts, "the beast burst[s] like bronze unfolding wings; the onlookers . . . hurl[] themselves to safety as the gate splinter[s] to matchwood beneath its soaring volcanic thunder" (133). Faulkner's description turns the horse into an airplane. He alludes to the scene of Johnny's death and suggests that once modern war has been experienced, one cannot recapture the heroic simplicity of cavalry days. While World War I had been mystified through comparison to crusades on horseback (see figure 11), the process works in reverse here. Faulkner derealizes this horse, suggesting that the actual physical sensation of riding it cannot compete with the psychological traces left by mechanized warfare.

Faulkner challenges one of the few myths of heroism to survive the war. According to Modris Eksteins, the war in the air was imagined as the last bastion of traditional combat. He argues that "many saw in the air a purity of combat that the ground war had lost. The 'knights of the sky' were engaged in a conflict in which individual effort . . . , romantic notions of honor, glory, heroism, and chivalry were still intact."[55] In *Sartoris*, Faulkner critiques such nostalgia. Flying leads directly to Bayard's disillusionment with his aristocratic roots, his gentlemanly ways, and his belief in chivalric mores. *Sartoris*'s deromanticization of flying seems striking given Faulkner's habit of masquerading as a wounded pilot. Indeed, some of the few satisfactions Hollywood afforded Faulkner were those that allowed him to use his fascination with flying, whether working on scripts about aviators or collaborating with Howard Hawks, director of the popular aviation war drama *Dawn Patrol*.[56] Nevertheless, in *Sartoris*, war in the air does just as much psychic damage as war on the ground. Bayard's search to recapture his war experience on the stallion, in his car, and ultimately in an airplane draws the three together as similarly unheroic. They become almost interchangeable as inadequate prostheses for male wounds.

Neither Bayard's accident with Simon nor falling off the wild stallion enables him to work through his repetition compulsion. Neither his family nor his friends can bear to listen to his story in detail. Perhaps because they share the same code of stoic masculinity, speech about fear, anxiety, and loss is inadmissible. Banished from the realm of the speakable, his traumatic memories continue to resurface in dream and in action. Having generated suspense by repressing Bayard's story, Faulkner gradually reveals clues about it, using elements of the detective story, as he did to such effect in later novels such as *Absalom, Absalom!*. These clues emerge in scenes that depict Bayard in the twilight between sleep and waking—a state of imperfectly guarded consciousness:

FIGURE 11. "Pershing's Crusaders," anonymous, color, 28 × 42 inches, 1918. (Hoover Institution Archives, Stanford University)

He still waked at times in the peaceful darkness of his room and without previous warning, tense and sweating with old terror. Then, momentarily, the world was laid away and he was a trapped beast in the high blue, mad for life, trapped in the very cunning fabric that had betrayed him who had dared chance too much, and he thought again if, when the bullet found you, you could only crash upward, burst; anything but earth. Not death, no: it was the crash you had to live through so many times before you struck that filled your throat with vomit. (203–4)

This language—feverish, symbolic, urgent, illogical—attempts a mimesis of the dream. Sleep returns him to the scene of Johnny's death, or "not death, no: it was the crash." There is something fixating about the crash itself. Bayard cannot articulate what it is, and so he returns to it repeatedly in dreams and, finally, in an automobile accident (which characters and the reader alike have all learned to expect as inevitable).

But even in giving, Faulkner takes away. He finally fulfills the reader's expectation that "the crash" will happen again, but he omits the scene itself. He gives the reader only belated access to it—we can know it only in retrospect and by its effects. Once again, we are left to interpret an aftermath. Two men discover Bayard lying face down in a creek, ribs broken, unconscious, the car's motor idling. Faulkner narrates the discovery from their point of view, maintaining a silence around the experience Bayard has finally achieved. They load him into their wagon and take him home.

Once there, Bayard gathers his brother's personal effects—Johnny's picture, hunting coat, hunting trophy, and Bible—and burns them in the backyard. Not surprisingly, this scene has received a great deal of attention from critics. Given that the novel is about Bayard's loss, this scene is central, because it is one of the only times he mourns in a ritualistic way. (That is, although Faulkner alludes to Bayard's visit to the cemetery upon his arrival, he omits the scene itself. Here, he doubles back and gives the reader access to an important but so-far-elided scene of ritualized mourning.) But the critics who recognize the importance of this scene have not remarked the strangeness of its circumstances. Bayard has just been in a near-fatal accident. Several of his ribs are broken, and he is about to spend several months confined to bed rest. Yet it is at this moment, when every breath is like "hot needles," that he manages to go through his brother's effects, gather them, take them outside, and kindle a fire (213–14). The way Faulkner tells it, Bayard's own wounds bring him closer to being able to mourn his brother's loss. Pain allows him to recall in a bit more detail and to specify, through the analogy provided by his own wounded body, the damage that Johnny's plane and body sustained. Bayard thinks to himself, "This wasn't anything: just a few caved slats. Patch up his fuselage with a little piano wire in ten minutes. Not like Johnny. They were all going right into his thighs. Damn butcher wouldn't even raise his sights a little" (214). This is not mystified "violence and speed and death": this is actual detail about what he saw happen to his brother. Being damaged allows Bayard to think back to the scene of his brother's crash in detail, though even here his awareness of wounds filters through a distancing metaphor that compares his own body to the inert parts of an airplane (his ribs are "slats," his torso a "fuselage").

Bayard, in putting his body at risk, seems to bring his story into a more conscious form. Paradoxically, the wound acts as a therapy by bringing him back to the accident but giving him something tangible to feel; as Freud observed, "a wound or injury inflicted simultaneously works as a rule *against* the development of a neurosis."[57] But Bayard's mourning ritual is insufficient. He continues to be haunted by his brother. Indeed, when he is gathering Johnny's belongings together, he has a sensation that seems to border on hallucination. He picks up his brother's coat and smells it, then whispers his name, then "with the coat half raised he look[s] swiftly over his shoulder," then "recover[s] himself" and kneels with the garment for several moments (214–15). His backward glance betrays his fantasy that Johnny is there in the room. As Orpheus's look back for Eurydice does, it symbolizes the fact that Bayard has not emerged back into the world of daylight and presence. He still lingers in a twilight shadow land of neither life nor death. He prefers to hang on to a diminished vision of what he once had instead of turning his back, once and for all, on his lost love object. This scene hints at what Faulkner reveals in detail, finally, in Bayard's third attempt to tell his story—Johnny's disappearance. Bayard imagines Johnny is still alive because he never saw him die.

A Nurse for His Wounds: Narcissa Benbow

If Bayard has been unable to tell his story to his grandfather or to Rafe MacCallum, his physical wounds bring him in contact with a new audience. His accident places him at home and in the care of women. Faulkner suggests that the domestic sphere may offer a more supple environment in which to remember, because it is here that he stages the fullest telling of Bayard's story. However, if women provide Bayard's best audience, they also become most culpable for the failure to listen.

Bayard's move into the sphere of feminine nurture is an anxious one. Faulkner portrays this anxiety through the presence of Narcissa Benbow, a character whose perspective borders on the psychotic. Throughout *Sartoris*, the narrator moves in and out of different characters' perspectives and also provides a range of third-person commentary. Among the various perspectives we have access to, Narcissa's is by far the most symbolic and unstable. If Bayard's perspective seems intermittently dreamlike and condensed, Narcissa's is even more florid. Faulkner presents what she thinks and feels in a densely symbolic language largely bereft of referents. Her perspective is like a window into childhood, where fantasy and reality have not yet been distinguished.

When Bayard hurts himself in the car accident, Narcissa obliges his Aunt Jenny by visiting his bedside and reading to him. The situation evokes the tension between the wounded soldier and the pretty but threatening nurse that is familiar from other narratives such as *One of Ours*. As usual, gender relations seem uncomfortably reversed: he is wounded and flat on his back, she is mobile and comparatively powerful. Despite the oddity of Narcissa's point of view, Faulkner devises circumstances that place her in a position of relative superiority over Bayard. He, the man, is the hysterical patient whose body's inarticulate symptoms call out for interpretation. For despite his physical wounds and his recent mourning rite, he continues to be plagued by nightmares. In a disruption of cultural assumptions, Faulkner depicts Bayard's male body as a symptom-ridden text in need of interpretation. It makes an "indescribable sound," and his breath "hiss[es] between his teeth" (251). He screams "a wordless sound that merg[es] into a rush of profanity" (251). Bayard's sickbed doubles as a neurotic's couch. While he drifts in and out of troubled sleep, Narcissa provides the wakeful, and therefore more conscious, perspective. She observes Bayard as he alternates between rational and possessed states of mind. The particular process Faulkner depicts is not wholly dissimilar from the celebrated case of Miss Beauchamp, in which Doctor Prince used hypnosis to elicit and observe his patient's multiple personalities.[58] Only here, instead of hypnosis, Bayard's repressed psychological material surfaces in dreams, and his "doctor" is a woman. As a doctor does for a patient, Narcissa, by her presence, forms a bridge between the Bayards of different mental states. She witnesses his dream, and her act of witnessing allows Bayard to remember it himself.

Finally, then, after a long wait, Faulkner gives us the story we have been waiting for:

"Soon as I saw him sideslip I knew it was all over. Then I saw the fire streaking out along his wing, and he was looking back. He wasn't looking at the Hun at all; he was looking at me. The Hun stopped shooting then, and all of us sort of just sat there for a while. I couldn't tell what John was up to until I saw him swing his feet out. Then he thumbed his nose at me like he was always doing and flipped his hand at the Hun and kicked his machine out of the way and jumped. He jumped feet first. You can't fall far feet first, you know, and pretty soon he sprawled out flat. There was a bunch of cloud right under us and he smacked on it right on his belly, like what we used to call gut-busters in swimming. But I never could pick him up below the cloud. . . . I went down fast, until I knew I was below him, and looked again. But I couldn't find him and then I thought that maybe I hadn't gone far enough, so I dived again. I saw the machine crash about three miles away, but I never could pick John up again. And then they started shooting at me from the ground—"

He talked on and her hand came . . . and tugged at his fingers.

"Please," she whispered, "Please!" He ceased then. (251–52)

Bayard has been haunted not because he witnessed his brother's death but because he did not. *Not* finding his brother's body seems to have left Bayard suspended in midair, still looking, still wondering what happened to Johnny. At a rational level, he knows that no one could have survived the fall. But in the absence of physical evidence, the desire to believe otherwise cannot be completely relinquished.

The war in the air, though less muddy that that fought in the trenches, has its own horrors. Johnny's disappearance constitutes an unprecedented way to die in battle. Despite its lack of gore, it haunts Bayard as a "natural" death would not. Bayard can talk about the wounds Johnny received and the shooting the other pilot did. Those belong within the realm of received war stories. But Johnny's utter disappearance is fantastic. Bayard reproaches himself for not finding Johnny or his body, rather than admitting the strange fact that it just could not be found. The modernity of flying machines has brought Bayard into a new era, the violence of which exceeds the existing repository of stories, idioms, and imagery. Johnny's disappearance is Faulkner's singular example of what was so abundant during World War I: death that defies traditional representation.

Some critics have read Johnny's disappearance as a failure of imagination, insisting that "the manner of Johnny's death does not so much remake its subject—the violence of war—or reveal its hidden truth, as simply ignore it."[59] I want to argue something else: not that Faulkner could not imagine the violence of the war but that he imagined it and its effects accurately. In soldiers' letters and diaries, Joanna Bourke finds repeated articulation of the horror evoked by New Death—by death that seemed uncanny, death that outstripped what men were prepared to see. To them, "what was wretched about the death of war" was not only or even primarily "the fact that men had been killed, but that war-time corpses" were so "mean-looking," "vile," and "filthy." For, she continues, "death was obscene: . . . it was like black magic: bodies continued walking after decapitation; shells burst and bodies simply vanished. . . . In death, white soldiers turned blackish and black Senegalese soldiers turned whitish. Bodies lay forever unburied, eaten by the dogs, birds, and rats."[60] The litany could continue. But the point is made: there is more to dying than its end result. For the living, taking care of the corpse offers one final chance to have contact with the deceased. Traditional mourning rituals work to ease the suddenness of death. The corpse is cleaned, dressed, and kept in state. Friends and relatives visit and often view the corpse. All this is impossible in the cases Bourke describes. One can hardly imagine that these dead are merely going to a "peaceful rest." Johnny's disappearance exhibits the same problem: it, too, seems like black magic. Indeed, Johnny's disappearance in *Sartoris* is far more disturbing than his mere death was when Faulkner first wrote about it in "All the Dead Pilots."[61]

Johnny's disappearance has, in fact, cast a kind of spell over Bayard. It engenders the fantasy that Johnny might still be alive. Not telling anyone what happened has enabled Bayard to cherish this fantasy. Telling the story, however, has the potential of breaking the delusional spell. As long as no one knows, anything is possible. The things one may not want to know can be kept at bay through omission. In contrast, narration introduces a privately held and inarticulate vision into the verbal processes of corroboration, refutation, and interpretation.

At last, then, we arrive at a moment of full disclosure. Or do we? Faulkner again draws our attention to the situation of narrative, to the relationship not just between the teller and the tale but between the teller and his audience. Narcissa brings an end to Bayard's story with her "Please, please." Her response to Bayard's story echoes what he has encountered so many times already from others—"Hush." It is both a command and a request, and it reestablishes a more traditionally gendered relationship in which men do not speak about their feelings and do not reveal weakness. Faulkner floods this scene with references to power, manipulation, and the difficult negotiation involved in the acts of telling and listening. While Bayard speaks, he grips Narcissa's hand in his own, bruising her. But although he seems to have physical power over her, it is actually an expression of need—he needs her to listen. While he grips one of her hands, she uses the other to cover her mouth, in a displaced sign of her refusal to hear the words he is speaking. "Please, please" is Narcissa's request to be set free from his grip and from the responsibility of hearing his story and perceiving his need.

Narcissa's response seems to foreclose the possibility of change. Despite the fact that Bayard has finally narrated his story and described the particular horror of losing his brother's body in the air, he continues to be haunted by the crash and to reenact it. Once again, the failure to mourn through the telling of the story is shared. This time, it is not that Bayard cannot find the words but that Narcissa stops him from saying them. Faulkner shifts our curiosity away from Bayard and his memories and draws our attention to Narcissa and her strange and inarticulate gestures. She too becomes a welter of mysterious affects, and thus the question comes to rest on her (in)-adequacy as a listener rather than on Bayard's as a storyteller.

Faulkner signals that the attempt to mourn through narration has failed by catching Bayard up in a scene that repeats aspects of his trauma. Narcissa's inarticulate pantomime repeats Johnny's inscrutable gesture. Like Johnny did, she stares at Bayard. As Johnny had, she makes a silent but seemingly significant gesture. In both scenes, body signals function in the place of language, and in both scenes, what those gestures mean remains unclear to Bayard. What Narcissa feels is unclear. Once again, Faulkner withholds what we most want to know and provides an excess of textual implications, a surfeit of possible interpretations. Perhaps Narcissa loved Johnny and cannot bear to hear about his death. Perhaps she is feeling sexual desire that she cannot admit. Perhaps, as is suggested later, Bayard frightens her. But what is certain is that her request, "Please, please," brings the story to an end and reinstates the roles of lady and gentleman. She issues a plea for decorum, silence, return to normalcy. If his story had broken the bounds of idiomatic intelligibility (the narrator describes it as being "without preamble," as well as "profane and gross"), Narcissa calls for a return to conventional expression. In Faulkner's novel, the potentially powerful figure of the nurse becomes the advocate and enforcer of traditional gender distinctions.

With the telling of this story, it becomes Narcissa's fault that Bayard's "cure" fails. Although the bonds forged between them at this moment hold Bayard for a while, he ultimately resumes his pattern of self-destruction and traumatic repetition. It is difficult to say whether Narcissa fails to save Bayard because she is too weak (and cannot bear to hear about Bayard's experience) or because she is too strong (and does not need him enough to hold him). She seems to fall short on both counts. She is not strong enough to give Bayard back what he lost. She fails to be an adequate replacement for Johnny. She cannot endure Bayard's loneliness and his reckless driving. So, when Bayard takes her hunting, he spends the trip missing his brother. She merely reflects a vision of what he has lost. But on the other hand, Narcissa's fault seems to be that she does not need Bayard enough.

As in other postwar fiction discussed here, an unsympathetic female figure serves to distract the reader away from the discomforting spectacle of male inadequacy and vulnerability. Narcissa is another unsympathetic nurse figure who can be held to blame for a soldier's/veteran's death. When Bayard dies, it is in part because Narcissa failed. But her failure is vague and unsatisfying—she is no scapegoat. Her fault is simply her loyalty to the cult of masculinity that, paradoxically, counts men cheap by holding them to a code of "brave" exploit. In *Sartoris*, women—namely, Jenny and Narcissa—are portrayed as enforcers of gender and class distinctions, including the aristocratic masculinity according to which men are expected to act as heroes and to die in war. Jenny upbraids Bayard for not being enough of a gentleman:

> "Helling around the country in that car just because you think there may be somebody who cares a whoop whether or not you break your neck, and then coming in to the supper-table smelling like a stable hand! Just because you went to a war. Do you think you're the only person in the world that ever went to a war? Do you reckon that when my Bayard came back from The War that he made a nuisance of himself to everybody that had to live with him? But he was a gentleman: he raised the devil like a gentleman, not like you Mississippi country people. Clod-hoppers. Look what he did with just a horse," she added. "He didn't need any flying machine."
>
> "Look at the little two-bit war he went to," young Bayard rejoined. . . . "Little two-bit war," young Bayard repeated, "and on a horse. Anybody can go to war on a horse. No chance for him to do much of anything."

"At least he got himself decently killed," Miss Jenny snapped. "He did more with a horse than you could do with that aeroplane." (230)

Narcissa and Jenny hold Bayard accountable to an idealized role that values gestures—even meaningless gestures—over life. And here I disagree with John Limon's opinion that Narcissa acts "with Faulkner's approval" and that he uses her to praise "the endurance of a woman" as superior to the "castration" of men in war.[62] For me, the novel seems far less sympathetic toward Jenny's and Narcissa's refusal to reconsider this code in light of the new levels of casualties and damage enabled by modernity and technological change. Rather than adjusting their expectations based on new circumstances of warfare, they want men to observe the decencies of a defunct world. According to Jenny, it is better to die as a "gentleman" than to live on in a way that challenges the rigid code of southern identity or any of its racialized, classed, and gendered rules. Jenny and Narcissa are depicted by Faulkner as enforcers of the codes of masculinity that send men to war and then expect them either to die or to remain silent.

In this way, I would argue, Faulkner insists that the female-gendered home front shares the responsibility for death in the war and for postwar suffering. Jenny's response to Bayard's making a "nuisance" of himself—her desire for him either to get himself "decently killed" or to pretend that the war did not affect him—is callous and inadequate. But on the other hand, Jenny's and Narcissa's nostalgia for an older code of masculine stoicism is held generally. Men—Old Bayard, the MacCallums, even Simon—share their belief in and insistence on tradition. Thus, women are most obviously, but not singularly, at fault for the violence men suffer in the name of manliness.

Conclusion: Questioning the Logic of Attrition

Narcissa, Jenny, Old Bayard, the MacCallums, Simon, and most of the inhabitants of Yoknapatawpha County seem to share a nostalgia for chivalric masculinity epitomized by soldiers on horseback. In the face of their collective adherence to that ideal, Bayard's attempts to tell them about its failure in World War I fail. His stories, repetitive as they are, fall on deaf ears. Faulkner portrays a collective inability to mourn and to take account of the full implications of Johnny Sartoris's loss. Characters prefer to hang on to their old view of Johnny and their old ideas about the heroic possibilities of war. The inadequacy that haunts Bayard in the wake of his brother's death and disappearance is compounded by the lack of empathy his story receives.

Bayard's plot comes to a close with a final, and uncanny, reenactment of his brother's death in the war. He agrees to fly an experimental plane, knowing, and seeking, the obvious risk. Before he flies, a fellow pilot warns him and the reader of what will come: "Look here, Sartoris . . . let that crate alone. These birds show up here every week with something that will revolutionize flying, some new kind of mantrap that flies fine—on paper. If the C.O. won't give him a pilot (and you know we try anything with a prop on it) you can gamble it's a washout" (364–65). In other words, this plane is "a goddam little popgun." The pilot's warning repeats Bayard's own warning to Johnny, and with the same futile result. Once in the air, Bayard finds "himself in the wildest skid he had seen since his Hun days" (366)—his war experience comes back to him. This time, he does not survive.

The structure of Faulkner's plot denies the separation between "over here" and "over there." Bayard's death is essentially a war death. He kills himself in order to prove himself as a man and to redeem his bond to Johnny. The only way Bayard can bring his brother's body back and to give it meaning is to sacrifice his own in exactly the same manner. Faulkner demonstrates the logic of attrition by portraying it on an individual level. As World War I became a war of attrition, the body count was portrayed as calling for its own increase. According to chivalric codes, the only way to honor the sacrifices of the dead is to send more men into battle. The more men you lose, the more committed you become to winning rather than negotiating. The more men you lose, the more you have to be willing to lose more men. There is a terrible circularity to this new "strategy" and its justifications. Faulkner uses that circularity to organize the plot of *Sartoris*.

But if Bayard's actions seem to be an uncanny repetition of Johnny's death, the narrator describes this crash differently. Bayard's flight and mechanical failure are described in terrific detail. He notes the machine's problems, its faulty response, even his own dispassionate awareness of his imminent death. His intense awareness in this scene is distinctly different from the first accident. The event that haunts everyone in the novel and the novel itself, Johnny's fatal fall, is relived and told in detail. But this time, it is not heroic. Bayard performs no mysterious gesture. There is no doubt that Bayard dies. Indeed, his body is returned to his family. Perhaps more important, there is no Miltonic imagery. What is "missing" this time—and its omission is striking—is the fantasy of heroism.

Faulkner, then, both in his plot and in his manipulation of the narrator's voice, doubles back to Johnny's death in order to represent it with a difference. François Pitavy has characterized this difference as "degradation":

> John's twin brother Bayard (the compulsion to repeat the game seems written into his first name), obsessed by the death of his brother whom he failed to pick up and to save with his own plane, plays with death in his turn, riding a wild stallion and a no less wild automobile (but he also plays with the death of others, as he indirectly brings about that of his grandfather in an automobile accident), and ends mimicking the death of John, getting himself killed testing a new plane which he knew to be unsafe. Only in death can he coincide with his ideal being, that twin part of himself. But unlike his great-granduncle, he cannot claim the alibi of a war: the reenacting of the game is also a degradation.[63]

"Degradation" is right. But it is not Bayard's death that is degraded so much as the code of masculinity that demands it. The novel's anticlimactic climax degrades a once-meaningful masculine code. Bayard's crash demands a critique, rather than a mystification, of what the war was about. Crashing in a plane no longer seems glorious—it no longer seems like "meteoric doom." On the contrary, it is the logical end to Bayard's story of modern war—the story no one wanted to hear. Finishing Bayard's story in this way is Faulkner's way of issuing a "silent scream" in protest of the costs of the war.

Conclusion: New Death, Blood Simple

Play with murder enough and it gets you one of two ways. It makes you sick, or you get to like it.

—DASHIELL HAMMETT, *RED HARVEST*

In Dashiell Hammett's novel *Red Harvest* (1929), the detective who tells the story plays with murder and, as he puts it, "get[s] to like it."[1] He arrives in Personville (alias "Poisonville") on a routine assignment but finds himself in the middle of a gang war. After being threatened by a corrupt police chief, the detective himself, Hammett's "Continental Op," becomes a killer. He also uses his powers of detection and deduction not to fight crime but to pit the criminals against each other so that they will kill each other off. In other words, he joins the war. About two-thirds through the novel, the narrator takes a moment to count up the dead and concludes, "If I don't get away [from here] soon I'll be going blood-simple like the natives. There's been what? A dozen and a half murders since I've been here. . . . I've arranged a killing or two in my time, when they were necessary. But this is the first time I've ever got the fever" (154). Just pages after this speech, he wakes up next to a murdered woman, his hand tight around the ice pick that killed her. He has no memory of the night before, and neither he nor the reader knows for sure that he did not kill her himself.

World War I has a strange status in *Red Harvest*. No characters are explicitly identified as veterans. And yet the novel both alludes to the war and textualizes the problems of New Death enumerated in the previous chapters. Hammett's characters live in constant proximity to death: one shoots a man dead and then will not "let them take the body away" because he "want[s] it there to look at, to keep panic away" (43); a woman "heave[s] the corpse" in her living room at another man to knock him down (106); liquor "tastes a little bit like it had been drained off a corpse" (134); men fire machine guns and throw bombs; dying men tell their last words; newspapers report the daily deaths. In *Red Harvest*, killing is ubiquitous, bodies bleed, pile up, and are reckoned by the dozen, and yet, as in other narratives of New Death, the central murder is mysterious and then imagined as an "accident." Though it is virtually an all-male world, that most spectacular corpse is a woman's. Taken together, these elements suggest that *Red Harvest*, like other texts of its era, responds to the world of New Death brought into being by the war. Though usually located within the genre of crime fiction, *Red Harvest* belongs alongside *Gatsby* and other modernist novels in a canon of post-World War I American Literature.

Red Harvest epitomizes one of the things that, according to Greg Forter and others, makes hardboiled fiction in general distinct from previous detective fiction: it offers its reader "an opportunity to let the mind play over death as one's ownmost destiny" through its insistent presentation of "the hardboiled corpse," which "fixates us on a brute physicality."[2] Corpses in hardboiled fiction are not reducible to puzzles that must be solved or crimes that must be paid for but instead resist easy explanation and delay, sometimes exceed, narrative resolution.

The premise of the foregoing chapters has been that four particular texts by canonical American writers center around a problem that came out of the cultural experience of World War I: how could the horror of young men's death on a mass scale be represented in narratives? This representational problem leads Cather to split the war's heroism from its modernity and, thus, contain some of its threat. Fitzgerald evokes the war in its ethos. *Gatsby*'s plot enacts the violence that machines do to bodies in modern war. Despite that violence, its narrative grows out of a desire to preserve a vision of male death as sacrifice, as a means to making things "tur[n] out all right at the end."[3] Hemingway revisits the scene of his own wounding and portrays the damage men suffer in modern war but manages to relocate the most abject aspects of death and suffering. All three authors manage these contradictory portrayals of New Death by relocating aspects of modernity and violence to either female actors (Enid in *One of Ours*) or female victims (Myrtle Wilson in *Gatsby*; Catherine Barkley in *A Farewell to Arms*). Faulkner represents the horror of bodily disappearance in modern war and the traumatic symptoms and repetitions that open around the *absence* of witnessing death. He portrays the suffering of male veterans who return to the home front wounded by New Death and the inability or unwillingness of civilians—particularly women—to witness their pain.

I put all these narratives in the particular historical context of post-war American culture—a culture in which World War I was still very much on people's minds and in which the war's New Death still haunted survivors. If many had tired of talking about the war, if publishers could not count on it as a consistently popular subject with readers, its ghost nevertheless stalks the pages of these narratives. New Death, which in Winifred Kirkland's vision and on most battlefields involved men killing other men, is reimagined in these fictions as happening to and/or because of women. Reconfiguring the settings and gendered meanings of New Death allowed writers and the public to consider the war's violence but to consider it according to a series of inexact analogies. As a result of reading these narratives in relation to the war's New Death, in other words, we emerge with a new understanding of the historical wounds that various modernist aesthetics both evoke and resist naming directly.

Reading these texts this way has implications for how we read other works by the same authors. As other scholars have recently shown, World War I was more central to Willa Cather's writing than was long thought. In *Memorial Fictions*, Steven Trout, in particular, traces the sad experiences that Cather's family had with New Death when her cousin's body was shipped home for burial. His recovery of that context helps explain what he and other critics have described as a long-running, but subtle, thread in Cather's work, particularly in her novels of the 1920s. My own argument here works in the same vein and, in addition, draws connections between Cather's aesthetic representation of war and that—supposedly quite different—exhibited in the works of other modernist writers such as Hemingway and D. H. Lawrence. Cather's gender identifications and her place in the modernist pantheon pivot in surprising ways around her attitude toward the war.

The present study also has implications for reading Fitzgerald's oeuvre as a whole. The recurrence of car crashes in his fiction and his work in Hollywood signify, as we have seen, his own attempt to represent—perhaps even to repeat and work through—the traumatic aspects of the war and of modernity, more generally. I trace his preoccupation not just with loss—a familiar topic, as we have seen—but with traumatic damage. His work, in fact, challenges us to develop better theoretical understanding of the overlapping, but perhaps not exactly continuous, existence of "loss" and "trauma." I have argued that *Gatsby* works to transform the latter into the former. As a result, trauma becomes more narratable but also fixed. How idiosyncratic this strategy may be and what the implications this interpretation of *Gatsby* might be for others who engage the problem of mourning remain to be seen.

My reading of gender and war in Hemingway coincides with work by other scholars, notably Alex Vernon, who likewise insist on the interconnection of those two categories across his writing. *Hemingway's Second War: Bearing Witness to the Spanish Civil War* takes up questions that both differ from and run parallel to the concerns I raise here, and it relates them to what has long been an understudied part of Hemingway's career. The present reading attempts to raise new questions about the realistic, journalistic aesthetic Hemingway supposedly used when writing about war. The question I ask in regard to Hemingway's writing is the same one Judith Butler has asked of more recent war journalism: whose lives, in these accounts, are grievable? "The public sphere," she insists, "is constituted in part by what cannot be said and what cannot be shown."[4] My argument takes Hemingway's novel as a case study in the topic of showing and not-showing, saying and not-saying. Then as now, gender marks a—if not *the*—dividing line. As blurred as gendered lines become in war, they continue to offer means to representational sleights of hand. Hemingway's modernist strategies illustrate how gender has been used to sanitize war and its violence.

Perhaps by observing this parallel, the present work will invite others to develop an account of how these modernists and their representations of war in their own time compare to our own. Such a comparison would surely reveal both continuities and differences. Instead of attempting to trace them here, however, I want to illustrate briefly and by way of conclusion merely the possibility of broadening the consideration of texts that respond to World War I's New Death. Recent contributions to the fields of cultural history (generally and specifically of World War I), memory and violence studies have collectively given us new ways of measuring the ways in which Americans experienced, thought about, and represented that war. We stand to gain new access into far more texts than the few I have considered here. The insights gained here augur well for further study of these and other writers with our new and developing understanding of war and its pain.

As the epigraph to this conclusion suggests, two related genres that deserve new attention in this vein are crime fiction and gangster films, which often reflect a particular anxiety born out of war experience—specifically, what happens when a nation mobilizes millions of men, trains them as killers, and then sends them home? The perceived social problem of demobilizing "killers" is both ubiquitous in the 1920s and 1930s and also often indirect or underplayed. As we have already seen, *The Great Gatsby* tells a version of this story. Gatsby returns from the war a decorated hero who cannot, apparently, find legal work. He takes a job with Meyer Wolfsheim and becomes something vague but illicit—a "gangster," a "bootlegger," someone "who has killed a man" and sometimes looks capable of doing it again. Gatsby's potential as a killer is something the novel downplays in order to emphasize, instead, his vulnerability. But elsewhere in Fitzgerald's work, as Sean McCann points out, the "menacing" figure of the "displaced American veteran" returns when, in *Tender Is the Night*, a seedy-looking veteran approaches Dick Diver and tries to sell him a newspaper.[5] But particularly in his early work "May Day" (1920) Fitzgerald depicts the dangerous and self-destructive potential lurking in the bodies of demobilized soldiers. In that story, unemployment is both the cause and effect of violent male "restlessness." Left without enough to do, the undisciplined body of the demobilized soldier is both threatening and vulnerable. Two veterans in the story join a mob that roves the streets of New York looking for "Bolsheviks" and "Reds" to attack. When they assault and maim a journalist, one of the veterans accidentally falls out of a window to a grotesque death ("He had fallen thirty-five feet and split his skull like a cracked coconut" [892]). Fitzgerald's story makes it hard to reckon whether the veteran is a perpetrator or a victim. Were soldiers dangerous killers? Or victims of a brutal war and the unemployment that followed?

Mark Hellinger's portrayal of New York gangsters, produced in 1939 as *The Roaring Twenties*, explores the same problem through its depiction of doughboy Eddie Bartlett (James Cagney). Like Gatsby, Bartlett returns and "finds that times are different—that the town ha[s] forgotten its soldier heroes, that prohibition ha[s] come, that his garage job [i]s already filled and that he [ca]n't get a job anywhere else. So he turns bootlegger."[6] As this reviewer's summary suggests, it is hard not to feel sympathetic for Bartlett, who turns to crime not out of a love of killing but out of a need to work. But his is only one story. His partner and fellow veteran (played by Humphrey Bogart) "want[s] to go on having fun shooting people."[7] In this and other ways, the film "neatly plants the blame for both [gangs and the bootlegging business] back in the trenches."[8] The historical experience of the war, in other words, negates the difference between ostensibly good men and killers. "Forgotten heroes" become "heroes for sale," who become violent criminals. And, some films suggest, perhaps they were all along. When Mike Powers, the returned war hero in Warner Bros.'s hit *The Public Enemy* (1931), confronts his brother Tom for bootlegging, it sounds like this:

MIKE   You murderers! There's not only beer in that keg—there's beer and blood—blood of men!

TOM   You ain't changed a bit. Besides your hands ain't so clean—you killed and liked it. You didn't get those medals holding hands with those Germans.[9]

The Powers brothers are alike and different: they are both killers, but Tom's acts of killings are criminal, Mike's heroic. This precode Hollywood film raises troubling questions that its ending tries—but barely manages—to contain. The film concludes with a visual insistence that Tom—the criminal, the "public enemy"—gets what he deserves: a rival gang delivers his brutalized corpse to the family's doorstep (see figure 12). Ostensibly, the message is clear: crime doesn't pay. But the public's fascination with criminals was fueled by such images, and the genre became a reliable big-box-office formula. Death—the more gruesome, the better—was attractive.

Though these genres and the "murderers" they portray are routinely linked to the historical context of the 1920s, and specifically to Prohibition, many texts hint at the importance of recent international history. They point to the 1910s, not just '20s. For instance, in *Red Harvest*, chapter 19, "The Peace Conference," brings the various Poisonville "delegates" around "Wilsson's table" so that they can negotiate a peace (146). None of the men around the table trust each other. "The old man," Wilsson, does not have the leverage he needs to force a compromise. Worst of all, they are all motivated more by grudges and ambition than by a desire for peace. So the conference, as the loose and playful allusions suggest it will, fails. Future violence is a foregone conclusion, as if because of the very nature of the men gathered around the table. But Poisonville's war will continue, I would suggest, not only because of these men's natures but their histories. Keith Gandal cautions us not to "characterize our decades" too neatly and specifically not to imagine the 1920s as a decade that opens with "a clean slate on which to think freshly" and that concludes on the other end with the Depression.[10] Though Prohibition is certainly central to the historical rise of organized crime at the center of these popular genres, *Red Harvest* for one makes a point of tracing its gang war back into the 1910s. The violence in Poisonville starts because of the war. In order to deal with labor shortages and strikes exacerbated by mass mobilization, Poisonville mine owner Wilsson brings in "hired

FIGURE 12. Frame from Warner Bros.'s *The Public Enemy* (1931). (Stills, Posters and Paper Collections, Motion Picture Department, George Eastman House [Rochester, New York])

thugs"—"gunmen, strike-breakers, national guardsmen and even parts of the regular army" (9). Those men refuse to leave when the job is done and keep the city itself as "their spoils" (9). The war, in other words, plants the crop of men who yield the novel's "harvest" of violence and bloodshed.

The 1920s, in other words, may have roared in pain from a brutal war that had killed too many, damaged too many others, and had left a trail of unburied bodies. These bodies, like the body of Tommy Powers in figure 12, still hovered on the threshold of consciousness, still seemed weirdly alive and unburied. What to do with male corpses was an unfinished problem that "We, the Public, Must Solve," admonished Warner Bros., in the film's final frame. The film actually works to make tolerable what had been, during the early 1920s, a horrible and not unique experience. In the government's complicated attempt to bring home the bodies of American dead, coffins sometimes failed to get to the right address or arrived unexpectedly. In one such instance, "a New Jersey father returned home and unexpectedly found his son's coffin sitting on his front porch. 'Four soldiers just backed the truck to the curb and carried the coffin to the porch,' neighbors reported."[11] Owen Wister—the same Wister to whom Max Perkins complained about *A Farewell to Arms*—wrote a withering critique of the repatriation process. "Unclaimed bodies were piled up at the Hoboken Pier," he inveighed, and "many went to Potter's Field."[12] In other words, the spectacle of a beloved son arriving dead on the doorstep *was* a "public" problem in ways we can only appreciate when we resituate this film in its broader postwar context. Despite the film's admonition to the viewer, male violence and death remained as a matter of public concern, at least in theaters, well into the 1930s, as the gangster film genre played repetitively to popular audiences.

The New Death has hopefully established a new interpretive context within which to consider canonical American modernist texts alongside and in comparison with less celebrated texts like *Red Harvest* and others in the fictional and cinematic genres that focus on crime and gangsters. This recontextualization goes, to some extent, against the grain of current criticism of the American 1920s and '30s, which treats genre fiction as a thing apart. That criticism has, on the one hand, been more interested in abstract philosophical questions than in historical ones. On the other hand, when interested in questions of genealogy, criticism routinely links the crime novel and its rise to domestic class politics and to a literary tradition of the American detective story.[13] Without disputing the relevance of those concerns and contexts, however, I suggest that looking at these texts as postwar texts might allow us to expand our sense of the cultural work these popular genres did in post–World War I America. The corpses they portray recall, in both inexact and gruesome ways, the unfinished business of New Death.

Notes

Introduction

1. Winifred Kirkland, *The New Death* (Boston: Houghton Mifflin, 1918), 28, 48.

2. Paul Fussell, *The Great War and Modern Memory* (New York: Oxford University Press, 1975), 109.

3. For more on the popular literature of the World War I period, see Patrick J. Quinn, *The Conning of America: The Great War and American Popular Literature* (Amsterdam: Rodopi, 2001).

4. Two other examples of this popular genre include *Kitchener's Mob: The Adventures of an American in the British Army*, by James Normal Hall (Boston: Houghton Mifflin, 1916), and *A Yankee in the Trenches*, by R. Derby Holmes, "Corporal of the 22nd London Battalion of the Queen's Royal West Surrey Regiment," published in Boston by Little, Brown in 1918 and whose popularity was such that it was reprinted five times in its first two months. Though precise sales data is unavailable, book trade magazines identify these and others like them as highly popular with readers.

5. Alexander McClintock, *Best O' Luck: How a Fighting Kentuckian Won the Thanks of Britain's King* (New York: Grosset and Dunlap, 1917), 12. Subsequent references are to this edition and are given parenthetically in the text.

6. The genre of the World War I combat narrative, which McClintock's narrative exemplifies, took shape quickly. Its narrative arc was used to codify men's (and some women's) experiences of modern war from very early on until long after the war ended. Indeed, its essential shape remains intact in combat narratives even from the present day. McClintock's plot, with some variations, undergirds World War I narratives across the political spectrum and across media, from the British propaganda "documentary" film *The Battle of the Somme* (1916) to Charlie Chaplin's parodic comedy *Shoulder Arms* (1918) and through King Vidor's epic and purportedly antiwar film *The Big Parade* (1925); from unvarnished autobiographical accounts such as McClintock's own and others like it to fictional novels such as *Through the Wheat* (1923) by the likes of more literary veterans such as Thomas Boyd, Robert Graves's British memoir

208 / NOTES TO INTRODUCTION

Good-Bye to All That (1929) or Erich Maria Remarque's controversial German novel *All Quiet on the Western Front* (1929). Despite the presupposed male gender of this journey's protagonist, this plot is repeatedly, perhaps surprisingly, adapted to structure women's accounts of the war, from the early autobiographical accounts of nurses such as the anonymous *"Mademoiselle Miss"* (1916) to the revisionary, postwar novels such as Helen Zenna Smith's *Not So Quiet . . .* (1930) and Mary Lee's *It's a Great War* (1929). As the range of these comparisons suggests, I use McClintock here to illustrate what occurs over a much wider body of material.

7. Paul K. Saint-Amour, "Bombing and the Symptom: Traumatic Earliness and the Nuclear Uncanny," *diacritics* 30, no. 4 (Winter 2000): 65, 64.

8. Samuel Hynes, *The Soldiers' Tale: Bearing Witness to Modern War* (New York: Penguin, 1997), 26.

9. Evelyn Cobley, *Representing War* (Toronto: University of Toronto Press, 1993). She argues that war experience prompted several writers to innovate nonrealistic, modernist strategies because they sought to disrupt the empiricist philosophical values that contributed to the methods used to wage the war.

10. For a more philosophical consideration of the relationship between war and language, see James Dawes, *The Language of War: Literature and Culture in the U.S. from the Civil War through World War II* (Cambridge, MA: Harvard University Press, 2002).

11. Sandra M. Gilbert and Susan Gubar, *No Man's Land: The Place of the Woman Writer in the Twentieth Century*, 3 vols. (New Haven, CT: Yale University Press, 1988).

12. John Keegan, *The First World War* (New York: Vintage, 2000), 421–22.

13. Pauline Boss, *Ambiguous Loss: Learning to Live with Unresolved Grief* (Cambridge, MA: Harvard University Press, 1999), 6.

14. Ibid., 8.

15. Drew Gilpin Faust, *This Republic of Suffering: Death and the American Civil War* (New York: Vintage Books, 2008), xv.

16. Seth Moglen, *Mourning Modernity: Literary Modernism and the Injuries of American Capitalism* (Stanford, CA: Stanford University Press, 2007), 3.

17. For instance, in *America's Great War: World War I and the American Experience* (Lanham, MD: Rowman and Littlefield, 2000), Robert H. Zeiger shows that "neutrality did not mean noninvolvement" (vii); on the contrary, America was soon "at the center" of the war's economy and politics (7). Jennifer Keene has described World War I as a "pivotal experience" that "shaped the contours of the modern American military and [that] was responsible for the most sweeping piece of social welfare legislation in American history, the G.I. Bill" (*Doughboys, the Great War, and the Remaking of America* [Baltimore: Johns Hopkins University Press, 2001], x). Nancy Gentile Ford's research underscores the way that World War I revolutionized the U.S. military (*The Great War and America: Civil-Military Relations during World War I* [Westport, CT: Praeger, 2008]). Others have measured the impact of returning black World War I veterans on the ensuing struggle for civil rights: see Mark R. Schneider, *We Return Fighting: The Civil Rights Movement in the Jazz Age* (Boston: Northeastern University Press, 2002); Chad L. Williams, *Torchbearers of Democracy: African American Soldiers in World War I Era* (Chapel Hill: University of North Carolina Press, 2010); and Mark Whalan, *The Great War and the Culture of the New Negro* (Gainesville: University Press of Florida, 2008). In *On the Battlefield of Memory*, Steven Trout recovers the

gendered and politicized disagreements between Americans about how to remember and memorialize the war during the 1920s and '30s. Trout argues that this "lost consensus over the meaning of the war" persists and has "decentered," if not wholly obscured, the war's place in national memory ([Tuscaloosa: University of Alabama Press, 2010], 4, 22).

18. Recent critics who have begun to embed the texts of American writers in this newly understood cultural experience of World War I challenge Stanley Cooperman's *World War I and the American Novel* (Baltimore: Johns Hopkins University Press, 1967), reflecting the intervening decades' changes in both historical understanding of the impact of total war and feminist interventions into literary studies. The stark gender categories that organize Cooperman's account no longer hold. Jennifer Haytock's *At Home, at War* (Columbus: Ohio State University Press, 2003) charts the blurred line between domestic and war literature of the period, showing just how much writing about the war informed writing about the home and vice versa. Haytock describes a "system of literary interdependence" between male and female American writers who were similarly concerned about the war and wrote about it across gendered lines and genres (xviii). Steven Trout puts the war at the center of discussions of Willa Cather, both in an issue of *Cather Studies* devoted to war (introduction to *Cather Studies*, vol. 6, *History, Memory and War*, ed. Steven Trout, xi–xxv [Lincoln: University of Nebraska Press, 2006]) and in his monograph, *Memorial Fictions: Willa Cather and the First World War* (Lincoln: University of Nebraska Press, 2002), where he argues that her "analysis of the First World War in [*One of Ours* and *The Professor's House*] emerges as a major achievement" that deserves as much consideration as her other works (12). In *Literature of the Great War Reconsidered*, coeditors Patrick Quinn and Steven Trout include essays that analyze canonical, popular, and forgotten American texts about the war. As studies seek to go "beyond the geographical boundaries that so often circumscribe English and American study of the Great War," they have shown that the war was economically, institutionally, and socially definitive. Quinn and Trout, introduction to *The Literature of the Great War Reconsidered: Beyond Modern Memory* (New York: Palgrave, 2001), 2.

19. Alfred Kazin, *On Native Grounds: An Interpretation of Modern American Prose Literature* (New York: Harcourt, Brace, 1942), 313.

20. Instead, Lynn argues, the important battle in Hemingway's life and work is the one he carried on with his mother. See Kenneth S. Lynn, *Hemingway* (New York: Simon and Schuster, 1987), especially 106–7.

21. Keith Gandal, *The Gun and the Pen: Hemingway, Fitzgerald, Faulkner, and the Fiction of Mobilization* (New York: Oxford University Press, 2008), 14.

22. Lewis Mumford, *The Culture of Cities* (New York: Harcourt Brace, 1938), 275, qtd. by Paul K. Saint-Amour in "Air War Prophecy and Interwar Modernism," *Comparative Literary Studies* 42, no. 2 (2005): 131.

23. See Pearl James, ed., *Picture This: World War I Posters and Visual Culture* (Lincoln: University of Nebraska Press, 2009); and Celia Malone Kingsbury, *For Home and Country: World War I Propaganda on the Home Front* (Lincoln: University of Nebraska Press, 2010).

24. Walton Rawls, *Wake Up, America! World War I and the American Poster* (New York: Abbeville, 1988), 12.

25. Joseph Pennell, *Joseph Pennell's Liberty-Loan Poster: A Text-Book for Artists*

and Amateurs, Governments and Teachers and Printers, with Notes, an Introduction and Essay on the Poster by the Artist, Associate Chairman of the Committee on Public Information, Division of Pictorial Publicity (Philadelphia: J. B. Lippincott, 1918).

26. Meirion and Susan Harries describe this and other acts of terrorism committed in the United States by German-paid agents. Black Tom Island was a man-made peninsula in upper New York Bay behind the Statue of Liberty that was used as the primary loading point for American-manufactured munitions being sent to Europe. The Harrieses report that on Sunday, July 30, 1916, two "gigantic explosions shook the entire area of greater New York as 2,132,000 pounds of shells, nitrocellulose, high explosives, fuses, and TNT went up." Black Tom completely disintegrated, craters pocked the bed of the Hudson River, and a "hail of molten metal fell onto Ellis Island and tore holes in the Statue." *The Last Days of Innocence: America at War, 1917–1918* (New York: Random House, 1997), 31.

27. Carol R. Byerly, *Fever of War: The Influenza Epidemic in the U.S. Army during World War I* (New York: NYU Press, 2005).

28. Katherine Anne Porter, *Pale Horse, Pale Rider*, in *Pale Horse, Pale Rider: Three Short Novels* (1939; repr., New York: Harcourt Brace Jovanovich, 1963), 158.

29. Byerly cites the findings of evolutionary biologist Paul Ewald to support this argument. Byerly, *Fever of War*, 93.

30. Ibid., 131–2. Byerly also argues that our morbidity rates are inaccurate and that more died of the flu than was probably reported. But even if underreported, flu deaths outnumbered combat deaths: 57,460 deaths by disease to 50,280 battle deaths, according to the War Department's accounting in 1919 (see ibid., 186–87).

31. Trout, *On the Battlefield of Memory*, 33.

32. Ibid., 31.

33. Fussell, *The Great War*; Modris Eksteins, *Rites of Spring: The Great War and the Birth of the Modern Age* (New York: Doubleday, 1989); Jay Winter, *Sites of Memory, Sites of Mourning: The Great War in European Cultural History* (Cambridge: Cambridge University Press, 1995).

34. This premise motivates chapters within Margot Norris's *Writing War in the Twentieth Century* (Charlottesville: University of Virginia Press, 2000) and the whole of Vincent Sherry's *The Great War and the Language of Modernism* (New York: Oxford University Press, 2003).

35. See Alan Sinfield, *The Wilde Century: Effeminacy, Oscar Wilde, and the Queer Moment* (London: Cassell, 1994).

36. An instance of this occurs in *The Great Gatsby* when Nick Carraway's evening with Mr. McKee disappears in various ellipses and gaps in time. F. Scott Fitzgerald, *The Great Gatsby* (1925; repr., New York: Scribner, 2004), 37–38.

37. Bertrand Russell, *Has Man a Future?* (New York: Simon and Schuster, 1962), 78, qtd. in Elaine Scarry, *The Body in Pain: The Making and Unmaking of the World* (New York: Oxford University Press, 1985), 80–81.

38. Scarry, *The Body in Pain*, 80–81.

39. Joanna Bourke, *An Intimate History of Killing: Face-to-Face Killing in 20th Century Warfare* (London: Granta Books, 1999), 1–2.

40. Stéphane Audoin-Rouzeau and Annette Becker, *14–18: Understanding the Great War*, trans. Catherine Temerson (New York: Hill and Wang, 2002), 14.

41. Ibid., 3.

42. Ibid., 14.

43. Hynes, *The Soldiers' Tale*, 19.

44. Joanna Bourke, *Dismembering the Male: Men's Bodies, Britain, and the Great War* (Chicago: University of Chicago Press, 1996), 213–14.

45. Audoin-Rouzeau and Becker, *14–18*, 9.

46. See G. Kurt Piehler, *Remembering War the American Way* (Washington, DC: Smithsonian Books, 1995); and Adrian Gregory, *The Silence of Memory: Armistice Day, 1919–1946* (Oxford, UK: Berg, 1994).

47. See Allyson Booth, *Postcards from the Trenches: Negotiating the Space between Modernism and the First World War* (New York: Oxford University Press, 1996).

48. See Boss, *Ambiguous Loss*.

49. James J. Farrell, *Inventing the American Way of Death, 1830–1920* (Philadelphia: Temple University Press, 1980), 120–21. The misspelling is original to his source: Bayley Smith, "An Outdoor Room on a Cemetery Lot," *Country Life in America* 17 (March 1910): 539.

50. Ibid., 121–22.

51. Ibid., 144.

52. Hynes, *The Soldiers' Tale*, 19.

53. Lisa M. Budreau, *Bodies of War: World War I and the Politics of Commemoration in America, 1919–1933* (New York: NYU Press, 2010), 6.

54. Faust, *This Republic of Suffering*, xv.

55. Ibid., xiv.

56. Ibid., xii.

57. Ernest Hemingway, *A Farewell to Arms* (1929; repr., New York: Scribner, 1995), 332, 214.

58. Budreau, *Bodies of War*, 15.

59. Ibid., 45.

60. Ibid.

61. Ibid., 15.

62. Ibid.

63. Trout, *On the Battlefield of Memory*, 39, 37.

64. Elizabeth A. Grosz, *Volatile Bodies: Toward a Corporeal Feminism* (Bloomington: Indiana University Press, 1994), 200–201.

65. Bourke, *Dismembering the Male*, 211.

66. Greg Forter, *Gender, Race, and Mourning in American Modernism* (New York: Cambridge University Press, 2011), 4.

67. Moglen, *Mourning Modernity*, 29.

68. Ernest Hemingway, *Death in the Afternoon* (1932; repr., New York: Touchstone, 1996), 192.

69. See "Interview with Ernest Hemingway," in *Writers at Work: The Paris Review Interviews*, ed. George Plimpton, second series, 215–40 (New York: Penguin, 1963).

70. Willa Cather, "The Novel Démeublé," in *Willa Cather on Writing: Critical Studies in Writing as an Art*, 33–44. (Lincoln: University of Nebraska Press, 1988).

71. Cathy Caruth, *Unclaimed Experience: Trauma, Narrative, and History* (Baltimore: Johns Hopkins University Press, 1996).

72. In Judith Fetterly's essay "Hemingway's 'Resentful Cryptogram'" (in *Critical Essays on Ernest Hemingway's "A Farewell to Arms,"* ed. George Monteiro [New York:

G. K. Hall, 1994], 117–29), she demonstrates the misogyny in Hemingway's depiction of Catherine's death. Fetterly points out that while soldiers die without shame, Catherine keeps apologizing for dying, suggesting that she feels guilty for leaving Frederick alone.

1 / "Clean" Wounds and Modern Women

1. On the figure of the "New Woman," see especially Carroll Smith-Rosenberg, "Discourses of Sexuality and Subjectivity: The New Woman, 1870–1936," in *Hidden from History: Reclaiming the Gay and Lesbian Past*, ed. Martin Bauml Duberman, Martha Vicinus, and George Chauncey, Jr., 264–80 (New York: Penguin, 1989).

2. Gilbert and Gubar, *No Man's Land*.

3. Marilee Lindemann, *Willa Cather: Queering America* (New York: Columbia University Press, 1999), 85.

4. The question of Cather's misogyny has been addressed elsewhere. Sharon O'Brien argues that Cather overcomes her misogyny by outgrowing her identification with a male literary tradition and creating an image of the female artist (*Willa Cather: The Emerging Voice* [Oxford: Oxford University Press, 1987]). Sandra M. Gilbert and Susan Gubar make essentially the same argument, connecting Cather's "distrust of New Women" to her "ambivalence toward her female literary inheritance" but asserting that she eventually found a way of "reject[ing]" "masculinist ideology" through her creation of a heroic and feminine pastoral (*No Man's Land*, vol. 2, chap. 5, quotations from 175 and 183). But as I argue here, Cather's misogynist constructions return after the positive versions of femininity she created in texts of the 1910s. For discussions of Cather's misogyny in relation to her lesbianism, see Eve Kosofsky Sedgwick, "Willa Cather and Others," in *Tendencies*, 167–76 (Durham, NC: Duke University Press, 1993); and Judith Butler, *Bodies That Matter: On the Discursive Limits of "Sex"* (New York: Routledge, 1993), especially chap. 5.

5. Willa Cather, *One of Ours* (New York: Vintage, 1991), 367. Subsequent references are to this edition and are given parenthetically in the text.

6. McClintock, *Best O' Luck*, 153.

7. Fussell, *The Great War*, 75, 77.

8. Henri Barbusse, *Under Fire* (*Le Feu: Journal d'une escouade*), trans. W. Fitzwater Wray (New York: Dutton, 1926), 300–301. Italics and capitalization in the original.

9. See Rawls, *Wake Up, America!*, frontispiece.

10. Scarry, *The Body in Pain*, 64.

11. H. L. Mencken, "Portrait of an American Citizen," review of *One of Ours*, by Willa Cather, in *Willa Cather: The Contemporary Reviews*, ed. Margaret Anne O'Connor (New York: Cambridge University Press, 2001), 142.

12. Hemingway's words appeared in print in 1952 when Edmund Wilson published *Shores of Light: A Literary Chronicle of the Twenties and Thirties* (New York: Farrar, Straus, and Young, 1952). Since then, they have been repeatedly invoked by critics and scholars. For an insightful discussion of Hemingway's response to Cather's novel as a manifestation of both professional jealousy and homosexual panic, see D. A. Boxwell, "In Formation: Male Homosocial Desire in Willa Cather's *One of Ours*," in *Eroticism and Containment: Notes from the Flood Plain*, ed. Carol Siegel and Ann Kibbey, 285–310 (New York: NYU Press, 1994). Hemingway's words appear on 289.

13. Cooperman, *World War I and the American Novel*, 129–37.

14. Ibid., 136.

15. Trout's *Memorial Fictions* offers both an authoritative account of this debate and a convincing argument for Cather's skepticism toward the war. See also Lindemann, *Willa Cather*, 69–78; Patricia Lee Yongue, "For Better and for Worse: At Home and at War in *One of Ours*," in *Willa Cather: Family, Community, and History*, ed. John J. Murphy, 141–54 (Provo, UT: Brigham Young University Humanities Publishing Center, 1990), 141; Boxwell, "In Formation," 285–310; Janis P. Stout, "The Making of Willa Cather's *One of Ours*: The Role of Dorothy Canfield Fisher," *War, Literature and the Arts* 11, no. 2 (1999): 48–59; Jean Schwind, "The 'Beautiful' War in *One of Ours*," *Modern Fiction Studies* 30, no. 1 (1984): 53–72; Marilyn Arnold, "*One of Ours*: Willa Cather's Losing Battle," *Western American Literature* 13, no. 3 (1978): 259–66; Raymond J. Wilson III, "Willa Cather's *One of Ours*: A Novel of the Great Plains and the Great War," *Midamerica* 11 (1984): 20–33; and Maureen Ryan, "No Woman's Land: Gender in Willa Cather's *One of Ours*," *Studies in American Fiction* 18, no. 1 (1990): 65–76.

16. Trout, *Memorial Fictions*, 10, 14–15, emphasis in the original.

17. Ibid., 18.

18. Lindemann, *Willa Cather*, 74.

19. Sinclair Lewis, "A Hamlet of the Plains," review of *One of Ours*, by Willa Cather, in O'Connor, *Willa Cather: The Contemporary Reviews*, 128.

20. Ibid., 129.

21. Cather, "The Novel Démeublé."

22. See Timothy R. Cramer, "Claude's Case: A Study of Homosexual Temperament in Willa Cather's *One of Ours*," *South Dakota Review* 31, no. 3 (1993): 147–60.

23. See E. Anthony Rotundo, *American Manhood: Transformations in Masculinity from the Revolution to the Modern Era* (New York: Basic Books, 1993); Michael Kimmel, *Manhood in America* (New York: Free Press, 1996); Gail Bederman, *Manliness and Civilization: A Cultural History of Gender and Race in the United States, 1880–1917* (Chicago: University of Chicago Press, 1995); and Forter, *Gender, Race, and Mourning*.

24. Blanche H. Gelfant makes this point but then cannot resist filling in what it is that Claude is searching for: the happiness of family life. See "'What Was It . . . ?' The Secret of Family Accord in *One of Ours*," *Modern Fiction Studies* 36, no. 1 (1990): 61–78.

25. Cramer, "Claude's Case," 151. As mentioned earlier, the phrase "the thing not named" comes from Cather's account of her own style in the essay "The Novel Démeublé."

26. Cramer argues that "the experience of war itself . . . makes it possible for Claude and David to experience their intense relationship. . . . Far from the constraints of society, Claude is finally able to confront and accept his homosexuality, and, by doing so, he can love David without reservations" (ibid., 158).

27. Frederick E. Pierce, "Nervous New England," *North American Review* 210, no. 764 (1919): 81.

28. Susan Rosowski glosses Claude's problem as his resistance to traditional gender codes: "[Claude's] best moments are those in which he assumes conventionally female roles. . . . Conversely, he is most miserable—and violent—when doing what is expected of him as a man" (*The Voyage Perilous: Willa Cather's Romanticism* [Lincoln: University of Nebraska Press, 1986], 111).

29. Lindemann, *Willa Cather*, 12.

30. Anthony Giddens, *Modernity and Self-Identity: Self and Society in the Later Modern Age* (Stanford, CA: Stanford University Press, 1991), chap. 1.

31. Cather's first book-length biographer, E. K. Brown, makes this point in his analysis of the "cult of machinery" in the novel, which he compares to Cather's descriptions of the automobile elsewhere. In her story "Coming, Aphrodite!" (1920), she describes the sight of "an automobile, misshapen and sullen, like an ugly threat in a stream of things that were bright and beautiful and alive" (in *Youth and the Bright Medusa* [1920; repr., Boston: Houghton Mifflin, 1937], 8). Similarly, in her essay "Nebraska" (published in the *Nation* in 1923), she writes, "The generation now in the driver's seat hates to make anything, wants to live and die in an automobile, scudding past those acres where the old men used to follow the long corn-rows up and down. They want to buy everything ready-made: clothes, food, education, music, pleasure." See E. K. Brown, *Willa Cather: A Critical Biography* (New York: Knopf, 1953), 219–21.

32. See Wilfred Owen, "The Parable of the Old Man and the Young," in *The Poems of Wilfred Owen*, ed. Jon Stallworthy (New York: Norton, 1986), 151.

33. Rosowski, *The Voyage Perilous*, 97.

34. Rosowski explains that although Willa Cather described her usual writing method as "scene" making—"When a writer has a strong or revelatory experience with his characters, he unconsciously creates a scene; gets a depth of picture, and writes, as it were, in three dimensions instead of two"—in the case of *One of Ours*, she claimed that she "cut out all picture making because that boy [Claude] does not see pictures" (ibid., 96–97). This scene is a crucial exception.

35. See Trout, *Memorial Fictions*.

36. Some other war posters exhibit the same problem, in which one model's face is repeated over and over again in the same image. It is particularly disturbing in depictions of men marching in a row, where all the men have the same face. By showing the same individual, the illustrators unwittingly acknowledge the meaninglessness of the individual's life. While portraying many men in the same uniform can convey a sense of solidarity and strength, portraying many men with the same face conveys the logic of expendability.

37. Rawls, *Wake Up, America!*, 12.

38. See my "Images of Femininity in American World War I Posters," in *Picture This: World War I Posters and Visual Culture*, ed. Pearl James, 273–311 (Lincoln: University of Nebraska Press, 2009). See also Anne Classen Knutson, "Breasts, Brawn and Selling a War: American World War I Propaganda Posters 1917–1918" (Ph.D. diss., University of Pittsburgh, 1997).

39. Apparently an admirer of Benda's war posters, Cather had him do the illustrations for *My Ántonia* in 1918, which included a strikingly similar image of the same model, knitting again, though on the prairie. See Willa Cather, *My Ántonia* (Boston: Houghton Mifflin, 1918), 188.

40. Lettie Gavin, *American Women in World War I: They Also Served* (Niwot: University Press of Colorado, 1997), chap. 1.

41. Susan Zeiger, *In Uncle Sam's Service: Women Workers with the American Expeditionary Force, 1917–1919* (Ithaca, NY: Cornell University Press, 1999), 3–4.

42. Ibid., 56.

43. Ibid., 57.

44. Kimberly Chuppa-Cornell, "The U.S. Women's Motor Corps in France," *Historian* 56, no. 3 (1994): 469.

45. Rosowski, *The Voyage Perilous*, 111.

46. Edith Cavell was a nurse in the British Red Cross. While in charge of a hospital in occupied Belgium, she was arrested by the German army and accused of helping wounded Allied soldiers escape to the Dutch border. Despite international protest, she was executed by firing squad in October 1915 and became a martyr of German "atrocity." Her image was a centerpiece in anti-German propaganda campaigns throughout the war. Klaus Theweleit offers a provocative psychoanalytic account of why nurses aroused so much anxiety (particularly in Germany) during World War I: the nurse is a woman who wields a knife, and she is also "a castrated doctor"—male fantasies of castration, therefore, become cathected to the figure of the nurse (*Male Fantasies Volume 1: Women, Floods, Bodies, History*, trans. Erica Carter, Stephen Conway, and Chris Turner [Minneapolis: University of Minnesota Press, 1987], 132).

47. For a history of images of the woman driver, see Virginia Scharf, *Taking the Wheel: Women and the Coming of the Motor Age* (New York: Free Press, 1991).

48. "The typical driver was a woman of culture and means who was familiar with both the French language and the intricacies of auto mechanics. Drivers usually performed their own maintenance work, including oil changes, small repairs, and cleaning. Since the essence of the unit's work was its deliveries, maintaining a reliable vehicle was a top priority" (Chuppa-Cornell, "The U.S. Women's Motor Corps in France," 468). For more on the realities of women drivers for the war, see also Zeiger, *In Uncle Sam's Service*, chap. 6 ("Serving Uncle Sam"), Gavin, *American Women in World War I*, chap. 9, and Scharf, *Taking the Wheel*, 94.

49. I thank Richard Harris and Steven Trout for bringing this to my attention.

50. Enid is an atypical illustration of the New Woman, primarily because the New Woman was more often associated with liberal sexuality. Carol Smith-Rosenberg argues ("Discourses of Sexuality and Subjectivity") that the New Woman's sexuality seemed a betrayal of the previous generations of feminists and that to young women, older feminists seemed to have betrayed them. She suggests that members of the older generation—that is, Cather's—were not discursively equipped to think of themselves as "sexual subjects," and sexuality was simply avoided (as it is in Enid's case). But the younger generation, coming of age when sexuality was discussed (by sexologists, by doctors, and in the popular media), were able to think of themselves as sexual subjects but, at the same time, had difficulty forming alliances with older feminists. The generation gap between women formed a more forbidding obstacle than the political gap between men and women seemed to. Cather's illustration of the New Woman runs counter to these general patterns: Enid is both politically active for Prohibition (a descendant of the classic nineteenth-century feminist cause, Temperance) and avoids all sexuality.

51. This quote comes from Cather's story "Coming, Aphrodite!" (1920) and is cited by E. K. Brown as an example of Cather's negative depictions of modernity (*Willa Cather*, 219–20). See note 50.

52. See O'Brien. *Willa Cather*, 4–5.

53. See Forter, *Gender, Race, and Mourning*, chap. 4.

54. Mencken, "Portrait of an American Citizen," 142, my emphasis.

2 / The Story Nick Can't Tell

1. Richard D. Lehan, *F. Scott Fitzgerald and the Craft of Fiction* (Carbondale: Southern Illinois University Press, 1966); and Lehan, *The Great Gatsby: The Limits of Wonder* (Boston: Twayne, 1990).

2. F. Scott Fitzgerald, *The Great Gatsby: A Facsimile of the Manuscript*, ed. Matthew J. Bruccoli (Washington, DC: Microcard Editions Books, 1973), 212.

3. F. Scott Fitzgerald, *The Great Gatsby* (1925; repr., New York: Scribner, 2004), 59. Subsequent references are to this edition and are given parenthetically in the text.

4. H. L. Mencken, "As H. L. M. Sees It," in *F. Scott Fitzgerald: Critical Assessments*, vol. 2, ed. Henry Claridge, 156–59 (The Banks, East Sussex, UK: Helm Information, 1991).

5. Ronald Berman, *The Great Gatsby and Fitzgerald's World of Ideas* (Tuscaloosa: University of Alabama Press, 1997), 18.

6. See, for instance, John F. Callahan, *The Illusions of a Nation: Myth and History in the Novels of F. Scott Fitzgerald* (Urbana: University of Illinois Press, 1972); David Minter, *A Cultural History of the American Novel: Henry James to William Faulkner* (Cambridge: Cambridge University Press, 1994); Walter Benn Michaels, *Our America: Nativism, Modernism, and Pluralism* (Durham, NC: Duke University Press, 1995). John Limon's analysis comes closest to the one I advance here: he briefly identifies that the action of the novel functions as an analogy for war. See his *Writing after War: American War Fiction from Realism to Postmodernism* (New York: Oxford University Press, 1994), chap. 4.

7. Moglen, *Mourning Modernity*, xiii, 5, 4.

8. Forter, *Gender, Race, and Mourning*, 28.

9. Moglen, *Mourning Modernity*, 4.

10. Fussell, *The Great War*, 23.

11. Edmund Wilson, "F. Scott Fitzgerald," in *Modern Critical Views: F. Scott Fitzgerald*, ed. Harold Bloom (New York: Chelsea House, 1985), 12.

12. Gandal, *The Gun and the Pen*, 108. This paragraph draws freely from his chapter, 78–121.

13. Ibid., 81.

14. Ibid., 117.

15. Ibid., 109.

16. Ibid., 107.

17. Ibid., 79.

18. Ibid., 13.

19. John R. Gillis, "Memory and Identity: The History of a Relationship," in *Commemorations: The Politics of National Identity*, ed. John R. Gillis, 3–26 (Princeton, NJ: Princeton University Press, 1994), 5.

20. Caruth, *Unclaimed Experience*, introduction.

21. David Lynn's argument is typical: Nick "has already lost something of his innocence in the Great War. . . . Yet this characteristic detachment is qualitatively different from his later one of general irony. . . . The story Nick tells" shows that a "transformation has occurred; with the naive, complacent assumptions of youth shaken from him, Nick has had to fashion a new moral identity for himself" (David H. Lynn, *The Hero's Tale: Narrators in the Early Modern Novel* [London: Macmillan, 1989], 73–74).

22. Peter Brooks, "Illicit Stories," in *Trauma and Self*, ed. Charles B. Strozier and Michael Flynn, 231–44 (Lanham, MD: Rowman and Littlefield, 1996), 242.

23. Sigmund Freud, "Negation," in *The Standard Edition of the Complete Psychological Works of Sigmund Freud*, vol. 19, ed. James Strachey, 234–39 (London: Hogarth, 1961), 235, emphasis in the original.

24. Fussell, *The Great War*, 30.

25. In postwar writing generally, irony becomes so conventional, so stereotyped, that many writers self-reflexively disparage its usefulness even in the absence of alternatives. So Bill Gorton in Hemingway's *The Sun Also Rises* (1926) banters, "Irony and Pity. . . . Don't you know about Irony and Pity? . . . They're mad about it in New York" (Ernest Hemingway, *The Sun Also Rises* [New York: Scribner, 1926], 118–19). Likewise, in Nathanael West's satirical first novel, he spoofs the clichés of the aspiring writer of the 1920s: "At present I am writing a biography. . . . Stark, clever, disillusioned stuff, with a tenderness devoid of sentiment, yet touched by pity and laughter and irony" (Nathanael West, "The Dream Life of Balso Snell" (1931), in *Nathanael West: Novels and Other Writings*, ed. Sacvan Bercovitch, 1–54 [New York: Library of America, 1997], 30). In these and other instances, postwar writers themselves express a frustrated awareness with the limits of irony. Paradoxically, as the privileged idiom of postwar exhaustion, irony's own ability to signify became, in turn, clichéd and exhausted.

26. For more on the novel's relationship to Stoddard and his writings, see Walter Benn Michaels, *Our America*.

27. Michael Holquist identifies oxymoron as the novel's central trope in his essay "The Inevitability of Stereotype: Colonialism in *The Great Gatsby*," in *The Rhetoric of Interpretation and the Interpretation of Rhetoric*, ed. Paul Hernadi, 201–20 (Durham, NC: Duke University Press, 1989), 212.

28. "The thing not named" is Willa Cather's phrase from her essay "The Novel Démeublé," discussed in the previous chapter.

29. Sigmund Freud, "The Uncanny" (1919), in *The Standard Edition*, vol. 17, 235, 236. Referring to his evolving ideas about compulsive repetition, Freud concludes, "whatever reminds us of this inner 'compulsion to repeat' is perceived as uncanny."

30. The problem of Nick's (un)reliability has been a longstanding critical crux. Early critics described Nick as reliable, even as morally wise. Henry Dan Piper, for instance, compares Nick Carraway's "moral sense" to the priest in Fitzgerald's story "Absolution" (originally intended as a part of *Gatsby*) but argues that Nick is superior for several reasons: "Nick . . . although, like the priest, . . . both sympathizes with and judges the hero, he is capable of a much wider sympathy as well as a more universal and less dogmatic kind of judgment" (Henry Dan Piper, "The Untrimmed Christmas Tree: The Religious Background of *The Great Gatsby*," in *The Great Gatsby: A Study*, ed. Frederick J. Hoffman, 321–34 [New York: Scribner, 1962], 328). This line of argument has come under various kinds of modification and scrutiny in subsequent decades. David Parker and others find Nick reliable within the normal bounds of human fallibility (he may be "slow thinking" and may come to know the "complexity of human beings" only "eventually," but he nonetheless gives an accurate estimation of both his own honesty and the novel's events) (David Parker, "*The Great Gatsby*: Two Versions of the Hero," in *Modern Critical Views: F. Scott Fitzgerald*, ed. Harold Bloom, 141–56 [New York: Chelsea House, 1985], 147–48); see also Gary Scrimgeour, "Against *The Great Gatsby*," in Claridge, *F. Scott Fitzgerald: Critical Assessments*, vol. 2, 489–99. At

a certain point, the critical question shifted to how to interpret Nick's *limits* as a narrator—his inconsistencies, his aporia, his omissions. Ron Neuhaus argues that Fitzgerald never made basic decisions about Nick's limitations. He complains that the novel's "point of view makes some blatant shifts late in the novel," that Fitzgerald cheats by "attempt[ing] to maintain, however thinly, the moral perspective of the first person narration, while at the same time trying to bring in third person credibility." He calls this the novel's "genitive fault" and chalks it up to Fitzgerald's limitations as a writer (Ron Neuhaus, "*Gatsby* and the Failure of the Omniscient 'I,'" in Claridge, *F. Scott Fitzgerald: Critical Assessments*, vol. 2, 359–68). Ernest Lockridge describes Nick as a murderer in "F. Scott Fitzgerald's *Trompe l'Oeil* and *The Great Gatsby*'s Buried Plot," *Journal of Narrative Technique* 17 (1987): 163–83. To date, James Phelan has offered the most sustained analysis of the evidence in "Reexamining Reliability: The Multiple Functions of Nick Carraway," in *Narrative as Rhetoric: Technique, Audiences, Ethics, Ideology*, 105–18 (Columbus: Ohio State University Press, 1996).

31. The arguments relevant here are those that identify Nick's relationship to Gatsby as the source of his unreliability. Keath Fraser broke this ground in "Another Reading of *The Great Gatsby*" (*English Studies in Canada* 5, no. 3 [1979]: 330–43), in which he traces a line of homoerotic desire between Nick and Gatsby. Edward Wasiolek furthers this line of interpretation in "The Sexual Drama of Nick and Gatsby," *International Fiction Review* 19, no. 1 (1992): 14–22. Most relevant is Mitchell Breitwieser's interpretation of Nick's story as a melancholic remembrance of Gatsby's death (and thus an instance of failed mourning) in "*The Great Gatsby*: Grief, Jazz, and the Eye-Witness," *Arizona Quarterly* 47 (Autumn 1991): 17–70.

32. Wasiolek, "The Sexual Drama," 15.

33. Though I ultimately agree with Breitwieser's contention that any account of Nick's investment in Gatsby that serves to "localize or concretize the novel's panic—to decode anxiety, to dissolve it" seems inconsistent with "the experience of reading" the novel, the text itself invites its reader to trace its panic back to the war (Breitwieser, "*The Great Gatsby*," 33).

34. A. J. P. Taylor, *Illustrated History of the First World War* (London: George Rainbird, 1963), 139.

35. Tom's declaration, "I've heard of making a garage out of a stable, . . . but I'm the first man who ever made a stable out of a garage" (92), reverses E. M. Forster's novel *Howards End* (1910), in which the Wilcox family changes their pony-paddock into a garage. This instance illustrates how the war's violence compounded already-complicated codes of masculinity and violence. In *Howards End*, building the garage means doing violence to old country ways and foreshadows Charles Wilcox's manslaughter of Leonard Bast. But the intervening experience of World War I has shown the sinister underbelly of the nostalgia Forster's text honors. Tom's renovation of the garage does not mark him as more versed in country things than Charles Wilcox. Instead, Tom's fetishization of polo ponies is just as dangerous in *Gatsby*'s world as the Wilcox men's fetishization of automobiles is in Forster's. Tom and Charles are similar characters, both violent sons of privilege: wealthy, athletic, anti-intellectual manslaughterers.

36. Fitzgerald, *The Great Gatsby; A Facsimile of the Manuscript*, 3.

37. Ibid., 8.

38. Athletes, including both baseball and football players, were the targets of specific recruiting efforts. An anonymous recruiting poster, for instance, draws the eye

to an illustration of a baseball pitcher and then makes reference to the war: "That Arm—Your Country Needs It!" (color lithograph, 25 × 37 inches, Sterling Memorial Library Manuscripts and Archive Collection, Yale University, War Poster Collection, MS 671, AUS 277).

39. Hynes, *The Soldiers' Tale*, 34. Such images were not just the stuff of propaganda. British officers and infantrymen used boys' athletics as sources of motivation for soldiers in the line. During the Battle of the Somme, for instance, Captain W. P. Nevill distributed footballs to kick off the offensive. As Fussell comments, "his little sporting contest did have the effect of persuading his men that the attack was going to be ... a walkover" (*The Great War*, 27).

40. Lehan, *F. Scott Fitzgerald and the Craft of Fiction*, 4–5. For a recent military history of the American Expeditionary Force in World War I, see John S. D. Eisenhower, *Yanks: The Epic Story of the American Army in World War I* (New York: Free Press, 2001). See also David M. Kennedy, *Over Here: The First World War and American Society* (New York: Oxford University Press, 1980).

41. Fitzgerald himself would have been aware of this history, especially living in Europe while writing *Gatsby*. In addition to newspapers, histories, and other accounts, it seems likely that Fitzgerald may have visited former battlefields (as Dick Diver does in *Tender Is the Night*). He probably would have used the popular *Illustrated Michelin Guides to the Battle-Fields (1914–1918)* (1919; repr., Easingwold, UK: G. H. Smith and Son, 1970), especially those devoted to "The Americans in the Great War," which outline this history.

42. Holquist, "The Inevitability of Stereotype," 209.

43. Dominick LaCapra argues in his essay "Trauma, Absence, Loss" (*Critical Inquiry* 25 [Summer 1999]: 696–727) that absence is often mistakenly conflated with loss. While absence is transhistorical, loss is the result of specific historical situations and events. To conflate one with the other is to initiate a melancholic cycle in analysis: instead of mourning for particular losses, and working through those losses, we tend to conflate them with absence, which is not particular and therefore cannot be mourned. "When loss is converted into (or encrypted in an indiscriminately generalized rhetoric of) absence, one faces the interminable aporia in which any process of working through the past and its historical losses is foreclosed or prematurely aborted" (698).

44. Shell-shock has received a great deal of attention from historians and cultural critics. In *The Female Malady* (New York: Random House, 1985), Elaine Showalter analyzes the slippery and politically expedient use of the shell-shock diagnosis in the career of Siegfried Sassoon. His public protest of the war, ostensibly a political utterance, was sanitized and reinterpreted as the voice of a suffering, traumatized soldier. Ironically, Showalter argues, it is only once he is "cured" of his "shell-shock"—meaning his political protest—that Sassoon actually began to experience symptoms. For an account of shell-shock in Britain, see Bourke, *Dismembering the Male*. For a collection of essays comparing the discourse surrounding male war trauma and posttraumatic symptoms in the various combatant nations, see "Shell-Shock," special issue, ed. Jay Winter, *Journal of Contemporary History* 35, no. 1 (2000). See also Ben Shephard, *War of Nerves: Soldiers and Psychiatrists in the Twentieth Century* (Cambridge, MA: Harvard University Press, 2000).

45. This anxiety is at the center of Roger Burlingame's *Peace Veterans: The Story of*

a Racket and a Plea for Economy (New York: Minton, Balch, 1932). Showalter makes this point as well (*The Female Malady*, 190).

46. The authoritative history of the term and the condition is Ben Shephard's *A War of Nerves*. He reports that the use of "shell-shock" in military psychiatry came to an official end in September 1918 (55).

47. "An American Soldier," "Shell-Shocked—and After," *Atlantic Monthly* 128 (December 1921): 738–49.

48. F. Scott Fitzgerald, *Tender Is the Night* (New York: Scribner, 1933), 179.

49. Showalter gives this statistic (*The Female Malady*, 168), citing Martin Stone's "Shellshock and the Psychologists," in *The Anatomy of Madness*, ed. Roy Porter, W. F. Bynum, and Michael Shepherd (London: Tavistock, 1985).

50. A few examples: Virginia Woolf's *Mrs. Dalloway* (1925), Rebecca West's *The Return of the Soldier* (1918), Eugene O'Neill's one-act play "Shell-Shock" (1918), Gordon Sterrett and Amory Blaine in Fitzgerald's own "May Day" (1920) and his *This Side of Paradise* (1921), William Faulkner's Bayard Sartoris in *Sartoris* (1929).

51. Shephard, *A War of Nerves*, 76, 150.

52. Showalter, *The Female Malady*, 190; Shephard, *A War of Nerves*, 197.

53. Sigmund Freud, "Beyond the Pleasure Principle" (1920), *The Standard Edition*, vol. 18, 11–12. In this passage, Freud quotes a phrase from his earlier essay "On the Psychical Mechanism of Hysterical Phenomena" (1893).

54. Freud, "Beyond the Pleasure Principle," 12–13, emphasis in the original. The American edition of Freud's text appeared in 1924, and although there is no evidence that Fitzgerald read the text, he was undoubtedly familiar with some of its premises.

55. Judith Lewis Herman, "Crime and Memory," in Strozier and Flynn, *Trauma and Self*, 5.

56. Sigmund Freud, "Moses and Monotheism" (1939), in *The Standard Edition*, vol. 23, 67.

57. Grace McDougal reports in her memoir, *A Nurse at the War: Nursing Adventures in Belgium and France* (New York: Robert M. McBride, 1917), that a patient offered her "a little souvenir—a German ear!" (96).

58. Keene, *Doughboys*, 59–60.

59. Fitzgerald's depiction of Wolfsheim also owes something to popular justifications of anti-Semitism, in particular, that Jews were cannibals.

60. Sigmund Freud, "On Fetishism" (1927), in *The Standard Edition*, vol. 21, 154.

61. Joseph Conrad, preface to *The Nigger of the Narcissus* (1897; repr., New York: Doubleday, Doran, 1914), xiv, emphasis in the original.

62. F. Scott Fitzgerald, *The Great Gatsby* (New York: Cambridge University Press, 1991), 211–14.

63. Leo Marx, *The Machine in the Garden: Technology and the Pastoral Ideal in America* (New York: Oxford University Press, 1964), chap. 6.

64. Hynes, *The Soldiers' Tale*, 53.

65. By emphasizing this visuality, Fitzgerald intuits what contemporary researchers have confirmed as a fundamental aspect of traumatic memory: "circumstances of overwhelming terror" mobilize a "highly visual and enactive form of memory" (Herman, "Crime and Memory," 8). Cognitive psychologists have attributed this "highly visual" form of memory to the way that the brain processes traumatic information (bypassing the cortical layer and going directly to the amygdala, a more primitive part of the brain).

66. Fitzgerald, *The Great Gatsby: A Facsimile*, 33.

67. Ibid., 212.

68. Just to give one example of this, consider this account of the advent of the war of attrition as a result of technology: "In fact it was not some inherited Gallic pusillanimity but the cruel realities of modern military technology that had forced all sides, not just the French, into the stalemated trench warfare of 1914–17. Long-range artillery and especially the deadly concentrated fire of the machine gun had given tremendous advantage to the defensive position, locking the opposing armies in an iron checkmate" (Kennedy, *Over Here*, 174). I do not question this account of military technology and how it changed conditions of warfare. Instead, I draw attention to the fact that the author ascribes agency to technology rather than to humans.

69. Audoin-Rouzeau and Becker, *14–18*, 3.

70. Moglen, *Mourning Modernity*, 27.

71. For an account of "Good Death" and how the American Civil War compromised people's ability to practice and find solace in its attendant rituals, see Faust, *This Republic of Suffering*.

72. Pearl James, "History and Masculinity in F. Scott Fitzgerald's *This Side of Paradise*," *Modern Fiction Studies* 51, no. 1 (2005): 1–33.

73. Freud, "Moses and Monotheism," 67–68.

74. In *Unclaimed Experience*, Cathy Caruth argues, following Freud, that "the experience of trauma . . . [seems] to consist, not in the forgetting of a reality that can hence never fully be known, but in an inherent latency within the experience itself. The historical power of the trauma is not just that the experience is repeated after its forgetting, but that it is only in and through its inherent forgetting that it is first experienced at all. . . . For history to be a history of trauma means that it is referential precisely to the extent that it is not fully perceived as it occurs; or to put it somewhat differently, that a history can be grasped only in the very inaccessibility of its occurrence" (18). On the question of representing history that is traumatic, see Dominick LaCapra, *Writing History, Writing Trauma* (Baltimore: Johns Hopkins University Press, 2001); LaCapra, *Representing the Holocaust: History, Theory, Trauma* (Ithaca, NY: Cornell University Press, 1994); Saul Friedlander, "Trauma, Transference, and Working Through," *History and Memory* 4, no. 1 (1992): 39–59; Hayden White, "The Politics of Historical Interpretation: Discipline and Desublimation," in *The Content of Form: Narrative Discourse and Historical Representation*, 58–82 (Baltimore: Johns Hopkins University Press, 1987); Eric Santner, "History beyond the Pleasure Principle: Some Short Thoughts on the Representation of Trauma," in *Probing the Limits of Representation: Nazism and the "Final Solution,"* ed. Saul Friedlander, 143–54 (Cambridge, MA: Harvard University Press, 1992); and Ruth Leys, *Trauma: A Genealogy* (Chicago: University of Chicago Press, 2000). This debate is beyond the scope of my project. My interest is primarily in asserting a similarity between Freud's theoretical understanding of traumatic history and the idea of traumatic history implied by the patterns of forgetting and repetition in *Gatsby*'s plot.

75. Joanna Bourke reports that "the First World War led to amputations on a scale never seen before, or since. One-quarter of battle casualties arriving in military hospitals were orthopaedic cases." She cites the statistics for the British forces: "Over 41,000 men had their limbs amputated during the war" (Bourke, *Dismembering the Male*, 33). Living in France in the years after the war, Fitzgerald would have seen amputees,

who were a visible part of postwar society in all combatant nations, but more so in Europe than in the United States. Exact statistics on the number of Americans who had limbs amputated during the war are not available, to my knowledge. According to Byron Farwell, American wounded numbered 237,135 (*Over There: The United States in the Great War, 1917–1918* [New York: Norton, 1999], 265). The fact of amputation was dramatized in 1925 in King Vidor's extremely popular war film *The Big Parade*, in which the protagonist returns from France with his leg removed below the knee. The likeliness of amputation was something Fitzgerald had referred to in his short story "May Day," in a scene in which a socialist appeals to returned veterans: "'—What have you got outa the war?' he was crying fiercely. 'Look aroundja, look aroundja! Are you rich? Have you got a lot of money offered you?—no; you're lucky if you're alive and got both your legs; you're lucky if you came back an' find your wife ain't gone off with some other fella that had the money to buy himself out of the war! That's when you're lucky! Who got anything out of it except J. P. Morgan an' John D. Rockefeller?'" (F. Scott Fitzgerald, "May Day" [1920], in *Novels and Stories, 1920–1922*, ed. Jackson R. Bryer [New York: Library of America, 2000], 862–63).

76. See Caruth, *Unclaimed Experience*.

77. Peter Brooks, *Reading for the Plot: Design and Intention in Narrative* (Cambridge, MA: Harvard University Press, 1984), 99–100.

78. Ibid., 101.

79. Irving S. Saposnik argues for the importance of cars in the novel in "The Passion and the Life: Technology as Pattern in *The Great Gatsby*," *Fitzgerald/Hemingway Annual* 11 (1979): 181–88. More recently, Lauraleigh O'Meara makes an argument for the importance of cars as commodities and exchange nexuses in *Gatsby*. See her essay "Medium of Exchange: The Blue Coupé Dialogue in *The Great Gatsby*," *Papers on Language and Literature* 30 (Winter 1994): 73–87.

80. According to Walter Benn Michaels, Gatsby's desire for Daisy should be understood as a desire for class, for something like a pedigree. He reads Daisy's whiteness as a reference to race, suggesting that she provides Gatsby with proof of a racially pure American identity: "Gatsby . . . [has] all the nice shirts [he needs]—what [he wants] is something that seems . . . more plausibly married than bought" (Michaels, *Our America*, 8–9). Crudely, Gatsby wants "breeding," and the only way he can get it is to find a "'nice' girl" to breed with (ibid., 117).

81. David Kennedy describes the various shifts in the labor market that occurred as workers moved in time with wartime demand. He persuasively argues that after the war, "the old order . . . settled heavily back into place" and "crush[ed] many of the aspirations that the war had giddily lifted" particularly among African Americans and women. But the reestablishment of the older order occurred through violent means, including raids and lynchings by vigilante groups, government-led raids against radical unions such as the IWW (International Workers of the World, or the "Wobblies"), the sometimes violent suppression of organized labor strikes, and so on. See Kennedy, *Over Here*, chap. 5.

82. Gandal, *The Gun and the Pen*, 119.

83. Fitzgerald, *The Great Gatsby: A Facsimile*, 29.

84. Ronald Berman argues that Myrtle's class position connects *Gatsby* to a genre of works involving the figure of the "working girl" who desires financial uplift and becomes a sexual victim in hopes of securing it. His analysis of that connection allows

another, more sympathetic, reading of Myrtle Wilson, as a character who, like Gatsby, has and loses a version of the "American dream." Berman's analysis, then, seems consistent with my point here: that various experiences of loss—including ones incurred during the war—get attached to and remembered through borrowed and mirrored stories. Ronald Berman, *The Great Gatsby and Modern Times* (Urbana: University of Illinois Press, 1994), 10.

85. Neuhaus, "*Gatsby* and the Failure of the Omniscient 'I,'" 359.

86. Russell, *Why Men Fight*, 7–8.

87. Kennedy, *Over Here*, 90–92.

88. W. Russell Gray, "Corinthian Crooks Are Not Like You and Me: Mystery, Detection and Crime in *The Great Gatsby*," *Clues* 16, no. 1 (1995): 37.

89. Barbara Ehrenreich, *Blood Rites: Origins and History of the Passions of War* (New York: Metropolitan Books, 1997), 47; Scarry, *The Body in Pain*.

90. F. Scott Fitzgerald to Maxwell Perkins, January 24, 1925, in *The Letters of F. Scott Fitzgerald*, ed. Andrew Turnbull (New York: Scribner, 1963), 175, emphasis in the original.

91. Fitzgerald's imagery, Forter explains, grants Gatsby "a kind of creatively maternal self-suckling in which he is at once the source and recipient of the breast's bounty" (*Gender, Race, and Mourning*, 30).

92. James, "Images of Femininity," 284–85.

93. In this quote, I have replaced the Scribner edition's "transit" with the Cambridge edition's word, "compass." It is clearer.

94. Matthew Bruccoli, "Explanatory Notes," in Fitzgerald, *The Great Gatsby* (Cambridge University Press), 203.

95. F. Scott Fitzgerald, *This Side of Paradise*, in *Novels and Stories, 1920–1922*, ed. Jackson R. Bryer, 1–248 (New York: Library of America, 2000), 232.

96. Ibid., 86, 246.

97. Farrell, *Inventing the American Way of Death*, 172–74.

98. Ibid., 180–81.

99. Kirkland, *The New Death*, 67.

100. Ibid., 62–63.

101. Moglen, *Mourning Modernity*, xvi.

102. Kirkland, *The New Death*, 23–24.

103. Audoin-Rouzeau and Becker, *14–18*, 9.

104. Moglen, *Mourning Modernity*, 33.

105. World War I was the first time that cars were used extensively as weapons both as tanks (*la voiture armée*) and as a crucial part of the infrastructure of total war. For instance, the "taxicabs of the Marne" provide a perfect and much-publicized example of total war. During the Battle of the Marne in 1914, the French army commandeered taxicabs to move soldiers up to the Marne River to meet the advancing Germans and to protect the capital. *Gatsby* illustrates a larger idiom in which the car came to be part of the iconography of the war while retaining its other connotations (freedom, sexuality, desire, modernity, fashion, violence, and so on) as well.

106. Kenneth Burke, *A Grammar of Motives* (1945; repr., Berkeley: University of California Press, 1969), 328–29.

107. Kennedy describes the various acts of violent suppression of African Americans and workers in the aftermath of the war. See *Over Here*, especially chaps. 1 and 5.

3 / Regendering War Trauma and Relocating the Abject

1. Ernest Hemingway, *A Farewell to Arms* (1929; repr., New York: Scribner, 1995), 184–85. Subsequent references are to this edition and are cited parenthetically in the text.

2. Gandal describes the novel's stance as "not particularly antiwar" but instead "antimilitary" (*The Gun and the Pen*, 31).

3. Fussell, *The Great War*; Norris, *Writing War*; Kennedy, *Over Here*; Peter Buitenhuis, *The Great War of Words: Literature as Propaganda, 1914–18 and After* (Vancouver: University of British Columbia Press, 1987); David Traxel, *Crusader Nation: The United States in Peace and the Great War, 1898–1920* (New York: Knopf, 2006); Leo Braudy, *From Chivalry to Terrorism: War and the Changing Nature of Masculinity* (New York: Knopf, 2003); Hugh Kenner, *A Homemade World: The American Modernist Writers* (Baltimore: Johns Hopkins University Press, 1975); Gandal, *The Gun and the Pen*.

4. Qtd. by George Montiero in his introduction to *Critical Essays on Ernest Hemingway's "A Farewell to Arms"* (New York: G. K. Hall, 1994), 12.

5. Norris, *Writing War*, 63.

6. Ibid., 67.

7. Others have noted the parallelism between Frederic Henry's wounds and Catherine Barkley's pregnancy. For instance, in *Hemingway's Quarrel with Androgyny* (Lincoln: University of Nebraska Press, 1990), Mark Spilka realizes that "Catherine has been caught in that 'biological trap' which, in its absurdity and futility, is the female equivalent for death on the modern battlefield; and certainly her death has been carefully foreshadowed in just those cosmic terms" (215). Margot Norris also explores "mirrored and echo-like structures of the love story" and the war story (*Writing War*, 69). But until now no one has spelled out this comparison's ramifications, particularly insofar as it serves to sanitize male wounds in wartime.

8. Linda Wagner-Martin, *Ernest Hemingway's "A Farewell to Arms": A Reference Guide* (Westport, CT: Greenwood, 2003), 6.

9. Alan Price, "'I'm Not an Old Fogey and You're Not a Young Ass': Owen Wister and Ernest Hemingway," *Hemingway Review* 9, no. 1 (1989): 88. Original letter: Perkins to Wister, 17 May 1929, held by Princeton University in its collection of Scribner's papers.

10. Philip Young, *Hemingway: A Reconsideration* (University Park: Pennsylvania State University Press, 1966).

11. See Nancy R. Comley and Robert Scholes, *Hemingway's Genders: Rereading the Hemingway Text* (New Haven, CT: Yale University Press, 1996); Carl P. Eby, *Hemingway's Fetishism: Psychoanalysis and the Mirror of Manhood* (Albany: State University of New York Press, 1999); Debra Moddelmog, *Reading Desire: In Pursuit of Ernest Hemingway* (Ithaca, NY: Cornell University Press, 1999); and especially Thomas Strychacz, *Hemingway's Theaters of Masculinity* (Baton Rouge: Louisiana State University Press, 2003.

12. James Nagel, "Hemingway and the Italian Legacy," in *Hemingway in Love and War: The Lost Diary of Agnes von Kurowsky, Her Letters, and Correspondence of Ernest Hemingway*, by Agnes Von Kurowsky, ed. Henry Serrano Villard and James Nagel, 197–269 (Boston: Northeastern University Press, 1989).

13. K. Lynn, *Hemingway*, especially 104–8, quote from 106.

14. See Matthew C. Stewart, "Ernest Hemingway and World War I: Combatting Recent Psychobiographical Reassessments, Restoring the War," *Papers on Language and Literature* 36, no. 2 (2000): 198–217; and Alex Vernon, "War, Gender, and Ernest Hemingway," *Hemingway Review* 22, no. 1 (2002): 36–57, quote from 48.

15. Hemingway, *Death in the Afternoon*, 135. Although Hemingway introduces the anecdote as if he had already become quite accustomed to the sight of dead male bodies, saying that "the sight of a dead woman is quite shocking" precisely because "one becomes so accustomed to the sight of all the dead being men," his biographers establish the fact that the duty of burying the female factory workers near Milan came to him upon his arrival in Italy and before he had been to the front.

16. See Rena Sanderson, "Hemingway's Italy: Paradise Lost," in *Hemingway's Italy: New Perspectives*, ed. Rena Sanderson, 1–37 (Baton Rouge: Louisiana State University Press, 2006). Margot Norris interprets the fact that "A Natural History of the Dead" seems out of place in both *Death in the Afternoon* and *Winner Take Nothing* as symptomatic of its banishment to "moral exile as an unwanted and transgressive text that should have found its proper place and function in Hemingway's World War I novel" (*Writing War*, 61).

17. Hemingway, "Interview with Ernest Hemingway," 235.

18. McClintock, *Best O' Luck*, 115.

19. Scarry, *The Body in Pain*, 63–64.

20. See Fussell, *The Great War*, 86–90.

21. Booth, *Postcards from the Trenches*, 21.

22. Bourke, *Dismembering the Male*, 211.

23. In *Official British Film Propaganda during the First World War* (London: Croom Helm, 1986), Nicholas Reeves explains that for the American release, *Battle of the Somme* was reedited, and footage of American ambulances at the front was added. "By the end of 1917, *Battle of the Somme* had been screened in 16,000 cinemas, and was seen by an audience of 65 million. British propaganda makers worked had to compete for attention in the intensely competitive, but all-important, American market" (232).

24. *The Battle of Somme*, intertitle number 37.

25. Ibid., intertitle number 37A.

26. David Williams, *Media, Memory, and the First World War* (Montreal: McGill-Queen's University Press, 2009), 30.

27. Bourke, *Dismembering the Male*, 216.

28. Booth, *Postcards from the Trenches*, 22.

29. Samuel Hynes, *A War Imagined: The First World War and English Culture* (New York: Atheneum, 1991), 122–25.

30. The film itself is now commercially available through the United Kingdom's Imperial War Museum.

31. Sherry, *The Great War*, 9, 19.

32. Malcolm Cowley with Glenway Wescott, "American Writers and the First World War," *Proceedings of the American Academy of Arts and Letters and the National Institute of Arts and Letters*, second series, 18 (1968): 42.

33. Fussell, *The Great War*, 21.

34. A Farewell to Arms MS, box 6, folder 10, Hemingway Papers, John F. Kennedy Presidential Library. See also Michael S. Reynolds, *Hemingway's First War: The Making of "A Farewell to Arms"* (New York: Blackwood, 1987), 60–61.

35. See Preston Lockwood, "Henry James's First Interview," *New York Times*, 21 March 1915.

36. Hemingway's *Sun Also Rises* includes a comparison between Jake Barnes's war injury and "Henry's bicycle" injury, both of which, the implication goes, caused impotence. Scribner convinced Hemingway to drop the last name "James" from the reference (*Sun Also Rises*, 180).

37. Hemingway's actual experience has been much debated. He initially exaggerated his war experience and for years allowed readers to assume that Frederic's experience was based on his own. Reynolds separated fact from fiction in *Hemingway's First War*.

38. Bernard Oldsey, *Hemingway's Hidden Craft: The Writing of "A Farewell to Arms"* (University Park: Pennsylvania State University Press, 1979), 30.

39. Cowley with Westcott, "American Writers and the First World War," 45.

40. Reynolds, *Hemingway's First War*, 5, 15.

41. Thomas W. Laqueur, "Memory and Naming in the Great War," in *Commemorations: The Politics of National Identity*, ed. John R. Gillis, 150–67 (Princeton, NJ: Princeton University Press, 1994), 160.

42. William March, *Company K* (Tuscaloosa: University of Alabama Press, 1989). In John Atherton's essay "The Itinerary and the Postcard: Minimal Strategies in *The Sun Also Rises*" (*ELH* 53, no. 1 [1986]: 199–218), he describes Hemingway's use of proper names to establish his narrator's authority as a traveler and a guide and "to define the (implied) reader as the sort of person who would know Paris—or perhaps, for other (equally implied) readers, provide assurance that, were they to come to Paris, it would be possible to trace the route" (202). The names of roads are facts that both allow "access" and also constitute a "form of denial" (205) because they give the reader the "artific[ial]" impression that the narrator is seeing and relating everything that there is to see and relate (206).

43. Norris, *Writing War*, 75.

44. Scarry, *The Body in Pain*, 80.

45. Reynolds, *Hemingway's First War*, 87, 116–17.

46. Atherton, "The Itinerary and the Postcard," 205.

47. Norris, *Writing War*, 74.

48. Trevor Dodman, "'Going All to Pieces': *A Farewell to Arms* as Trauma Narrative," *Twentieth-Century Literature* 52, no. 3 (2006): 249.

49. Hynes, *The Soldiers' Tale*, 40–41.

50. Here, I am going against the grain of most extant criticism, which, according to Linda Wagner-Martin, does not "view Frederic Henry as emotionally stymied" and which "wants to find him changed—for the better—because of his involvement with Catherine. The very fact that he can narrate his mournful story (his narration becoming *A Farewell to Arms*) bespeaks his comparative health" (*Ernest Hemingway's "A Farewell to Arms*," 99). "Laconic and nostalgic, he tells the story of World War I and his escape from that horror through his love for Catherine in suitably terse language" (117).

51. Reynolds, *Hemingway's First War*, 15.

52. Norris identifies this emotional unreliability as a deliberate effect of Hemingway's narrative structure, which he uses to "thematiz[e]" and "dramatiz[e]" the desire to lie about war's violence. Hemingway, she insists, "conjoins two narrative

strategies—a detailed and virtually unambiguous description of the action with an utterly impersonal, objective narrative that betrays no emotion." Actions of violence related "without affect places the reader in a position of judgment without a clear moral compass, and with the necessity of judging both an action and an act of narration" (*Writing War*, 72).

53. Reynolds, *Hemingway's First War*, 91.

54. For instance, Kenneth Lynn declares that the image of soldiers "'six months gone with child' compose[s] a forecast of Catherine Barkley's fatal pregnancy" (*Hemingway*, 384); likewise, Mark Spilka argues that "Catherine has been caught in that 'biological trap' which, in its absurdity and futility, is the female equivalent for death on the modern battlefield; and certainly her death has been carefully foreshadowed in just those cosmic terms" (*Hemingway's Quarrel*, 215). Though both authors note the connection, neither of them considers its ramifications.

55. Vernon, "War, Gender, and Ernest Hemingway," 48.

56. Hemingway, *Death in the Afternoon*, 140.

57. Spilka, *Hemingway's Quarrel*, 215. I refer also to Sandra Whipple Spanier, "Catherine Barkley and the Hemingway Code: Ritual and Survival in *A Farewell to Arms*," in *Ernest Hemingway's "A Farewell to Arms*," ed. Harold Bloom, 131–48 (New York: Chelsea House, 1987).

58. Fetterly, "Hemingway's 'Resentful Cryptogram,'" 119.

59. Ibid.

60. Julia Kristeva, *Powers of Horror: An Essay on Abjection*, trans. Leon S. Roudiez (New York: Columbia University Press, 1982), 3. Her account of the abject draws on anthropologist Mary Douglas's *Purity and Danger* (New York: Routledge and Kegan Paul, 1966).

61. Kristeva, *Powers of Horror*, 4.

62. Ibid., 3.

63. Grosz, *Volatile Bodies*, 198. She notes that "the borderline literatures of homosexuality and voyeurism" are the exception. Hemingway's text does not belong to those.

64. Ibid., 200–201.

65. Wilfred Owen, "Dulce et Decorum Est," in *The Poems of Wilfred Owen*, 117–18.

66. Qtd. in Oldsey, *Hemingway's Hidden Craft*, 93.

67. Ibid., 97–98.

68. Ernest Hemingway, "Soldier's Home," in *In Our Time* (1925; repr., New York: Scribner, 1996), 69.

69. A Farewell to Arms MS, 124. It is handwritten; this is my transcription.

70. Ibid., 143, 145.

71. Ibid., 174–75. See also Reynolds, *Hemingway's First War*, 32–33.

72. Reynolds, *Hemingway's First War*, 33.

73. Ibid., 24.

74. Wagner-Martin, *Ernest Hemingway's "A Farewell to Arms*," 29, emphasis in the original.

75. Ibid., 30. Wagner-Martin offers one tantalizing sentence that gestures in the direction my argument here takes. She writes, "Catherine's death almost takes the fall for the fact that Hemingway writes very little unpleasant description of the battles of war per se," adding, "One of the problems with marketing war novels was that

readers did not want to know what trench warfare ... [was] like" (ibid., 79). Similarly, Mark Spilka speculates that "it may be that [Catherine] is sacrificed to male survival" (*Hemingway's Quarrel*, 215). However, neither critic develops this insight as I do here.

76. Norris, *Writing War*, 63.

77. Ellen Andrews Knodt, "'Suddenly and Unreasonably': Shooting the Sergeant in *A Farewell to Arms*," in Sanderson, *Hemingway's Italy*, 153. She provides a generous account of how various critics—including Scott Donaldson, James Phelan, and Charles Nolan—have interpreted this passage.

78. Ibid., 150.

79. Robert A. Martin, "Hemingway and the Ambulance Drivers in *A Farewell to Arms*," in *Ernest Hemingway: Six Decades of Criticism*, ed. Linda W. Wagner, 195–204 (East Lansing: Michigan State University Press, 1987), 201.

80. Reynolds, *Hemingway's First War*, 245.

81. Moddelmog, *Reading Desire*, 122–23.

82. My sense that Catherine's behavior in this chapter should be read as a camp male impersonation is corroborated by Debra Moddelmog's claims that elsewhere in Hemingway's fiction it is men of color or homosexual men who "react to [the wound] in despicable ways" such as "a weak or cowardly way" (ibid., 123).

83. Spilka, *Hemingway's Quarrel*, 217.

84. See Cathy Caruth, *Unclaimed Experience*.

85. Ernest Hemingway, "The Original Conclusion to *A Farewell to Arms*," in *Ernest Hemingway: Critiques of Four Major Novels*, ed. Carlos Baker (New York: Scribner, 1962), 75.

86. Wagner-Martin, *Ernest Hemingway's "A Farewell to Arms*," 135.

4 / The Missing of *Sartoris*

1. Winter, *Sites of Memory*, 103–5. Winter qualifies Vincent Scully's reading of the Thiepval monument as a "silent scream," which appears in "The Terrible Art of Designing a War Memorial," *New York Times*, 14 July 1991, Arts and Leisure, 28.

2. Booth, *Postcards from the Trenches*, 36.

3. Keegan, *The First World War*, 298 and 299. He gives exact figures on 299.

4. Despite the list of names' pretension to permanence on a surface such as the monument's, its authenticity may stem from its resemblance to a more ephemeral medium, the newspaper, which during World War I was filled up with lists. People left behind often encountered news that someone they knew was wounded, missing, or dead by reading their name in the paper. Visiting a monument inscribed with names allowed people to repeat their first discovery of death in familiar terms—that of searching for the name they know in a tragically long list.

5. Keegan, *The First World War*, 421–22.

6. Kirkland, *The New Death*, 23.

7. In addition to Jay Winter's *Sites of Memory*, see Gregory, *The Silence of Memory*. For a comparison of postwar mourning rituals with those of the Victorian period, see David Cannadine, "War and Death, Grief and Mourning in Modern Britain," in *Mirrors of Mortality: Studies in the Social History of Death*, ed. Joachim Whaley, 187–242 (London: Europa, 1981). Another manifestation of postwar desires to mourn the dead and to understand the war was the unprecedented numbers of travelers to battlefields, explored by David W. Lloyd in *Battlefield Tourism: Pilgrimage and*

the Commemoration of the Great War in Britain, Australia and Canada, 1919–1939 (Oxford, UK: Berg, 1998). Americans, including William Faulkner, also made visits to the battlefields. For a brief account of Faulkner's visit, see David Minter, *William Faulkner: His Life and Work* (Baltimore: Johns Hopkins University Press, 1980), 55.

8. Booth, *Postcards from the Trenches*, 33.

9. G. Kurt Piehler analyses several ways in which Americans mourned in the wake of World War I. In addition to receiving official tribute, the Unknown Soldier was honored and mourned by the American public: "Thousands paid their respect to the Unknown Soldier as he lay in state in the Capitol rotunda. Hundreds of thousands lined the funeral route from the Capitol to Arlington Cemetery" ("The War Dead and the Gold Star: American Commemoration of the First World War," in *Commemorations: the Politics of National Identity*, ed. John R. Gillis, 168–85 [Princeton, NJ: Princeton University Press, 1994], 175).

10. Robert Brooke, "The Soldier," in *The Collected Poems of Rupert Brooke*, ed. Edward Marsh (London: Sidgwick and Jackson, 1918), 9.

11. Piehler, "The War Dead," 171–74.

12. Budreau, *Bodies of War*, 15.

13. Notable exceptions include Keith Gandal (*The Gun and the Pen*) and John Limon, who writes about World War I in Faulkner's work, particularly *As I Lay Dying*, first in his *Writing after War* and again in "Addie in No-Man's-Land," in *Faulkner and War*, ed. Noel Polk and Ann J. Abadie, 36–54 (Jackson: University Press of Mississippi, 2004), and other contributors to that volume.

14. Faulkner wrote a manuscript he titled *Flags in the Dust*, which was rejected by several publishers in turn. His friend Ben Wasson, under Faulkner's (indeterminate) supervision, edited and shortened it. The resulting novel was rechristened *Sartoris* and published by Harcourt Brace in 1929. In 1973, Douglas Day consulted various typescripts and reconstructed *Flags in the Dust*, which was published by Random House. Since then, many critics have preferred to use that reconstructed text, despite its problems, arguing (somewhat tenuously) that it is closer to Faulkner's intention. Because I am interested in representations of World War I in the 1920s and 1930s, I prefer to consider the version of the text that was deemed publishable and that was read at the time. For more on the textual history and differences between the texts, see Merle Wallace Keiser, "*Flags in the Dust* and *Sartoris*," in *Fifty Years of Yoknapatawpha: Faulkner and Yoknapatawpha 1979*, ed. Doreen Fowler and Ann J. Abadie, 44–70 (Jackson: University Press of Mississippi, 1980); Douglas Day, "Introduction to *Flags in the Dust*," in *Critical Essays on William Faulkner: The Sartoris Family*, ed. Arthur F. Kinney (Boston: G. K. Hall, 1985), 227–29; Thomas L. McHaney and Albert Erskine, "[The Text of *Flags in the Dust*: An Interchange]," in ibid., 230–32; George F. Hayhoe, "William Faulkner's *Flags in the Dust*," in ibid., 233–45; and Judith Bryant Wittenberg's essay in the same volume titled "Vision and Re-vision: Bayard Sartoris," 323–31. See also Philip Cohen, "*Flags in the Dust*, *Sartoris*, and the Unforeseen Consequences of Editorial Surgery," *Faulkner Journal* 5 (Fall 1989): 25–44; and Joseph Blotner, "William Faulkner's Essay on the Composition of *Sartoris*," *Yale University Library Gazette* 47, no. 3 (1973): 121–24.

15. Moglen, *Mourning Modernity*; Forter, *Gender, Race, and Mourning*, 108–36.

16. For discussions of Faulkner's other fictional treatments of war, see especially the essays in Polk and Abadie, *Faulkner and War*.

17. Limon, "Addie in No-Man's-Land," 45.

18. Minter, *William Faulkner*, 31.

19. In addition to Minter's biography, see Joseph Blotner, *Faulkner: A Biography*, rev. ed. (New York: Random House, 1984).

20. The theory that Faulkner posed as a wounded veteran in order to conduct research was offered in conversation by Charles Peek and reported to me by Steven Trout via personal communication.

21. Doreen Fowler makes this argument in *Faulkner: The Return of the Repressed* (Charlottesville: University of Virginia Press, 1997), 3–4. Applying the theory of Jacques Lacan, she offers an account of Faulkner's major works (among which she does not include *Sartoris*) that emphasizes his unconscious consideration of subjectivity as a product of primal loss, the awareness of which his texts alternately manifest and repress. As I mentioned in chapter 3, Dominick LaCapra calls for a distinction to be made between primal *lack* and historical, particular *loss* ("Trauma, Absence, Loss"). Making that distinction, Fowler's argument is concerned with lack rather than loss. In contrast, the latter—historical loss—is what I am arguing is at the center of *Sartoris*.

22. For instance, when Malcolm Cowley was bringing out *The Portable Faulkner* in 1946, Faulkner persuaded him to present his war experience in wording that would maintain the illusion, or at least its possibility, that he had seen combat. See Minter, *William Faulkner*, 209.

23. Philip Young, "The Lost Generation: War, Home, and Exile," in *Dancing Fools and Weary Blues: The Great Escape of the 1920s*, ed. Lawrence R. Broer and John D. Walther, 77–85 (Bowling Green, OH: Bowling Green State University Popular Press, 1990), 81.

24. Gandal, *The Gun and the Pen*, 14.

25. William Faulkner, *Sartoris* (New York: Harcourt Brace, 1929), 1–2. Subsequent references are to this edition and are given parenthetically in the text.

26. These remarks are some of the most famous Faulkner made about his fiction. In a 1956 interview with Jean Stein Vanden Heuval, he is quoted as saying, "Beginning with *Sartoris* I discovered that my own little postage stamp of native soil was worth writing about and that I would never live long enough to exhaust it, and that by subli-mating the actual into the apocryphal I would have complete liberty to use whatever talent I might have to its absolute top" (Faulkner, "Interview," *Writers at Work: The Paris Review Interviews*, first series, ed. Malcolm Cowley, 119–41 [New York: Viking, 1958], 141). The phrase "germ of my Apocrypha" comes from Session 36, May 23, 1958, in *Faulkner in the University: Class Conferences at the University of Virginia, 1957–1958*, ed. Frederick L. Gwynn and Joseph L. Blotner (Charlottesville: University of Virginia Press, 1959), 285. For more on *Sartoris*'s place in the development of Faulkner's style, see James Gray Watson, "'The Germ of My Apocrypha': *Sartoris* and the Search for Form," *Mosaic* 7, no. 1 (1973): 15–34.

27. See citations in note 26.

28. Wittenberg writes, "As the new title suggests, [the revision] is a novel much more tightly focused on Bayard and other members of his family, on Bayard's futile efforts, after World War I and the death of his twin, to find some pattern by which he can live, and on his series of self-destructive actions and ultimate death" ("Vision and Re-vision," 324).

29. Limon, *Writing after War*; Limon, "Addie in No-Man's-Land."

30. Much has been written about representations of African Americans in *Sartoris*. See Esther Alexander Terry, "For 'Blood and Kin and Home': Black Characterization in William Faulkner's Sartoris Saga," in Kinney, *Critical Essays on William Faulkner*, 303–17. I agree with those critics, including Terry, who read Faulkner's characterization as complicated but most often sentimentalizing and dehumanizing. Most important in this context is Faulkner's satirical portrait of Caspey, Simon's grandson, who returns from his service in World War I within a week or two of Bayard. He, too, tells his war story, which is presented satirically. Although Faulkner never makes it explicit, the threat of lynching hangs over Caspey, whose postwar restlessness takes the form of impatience with the racist status quo of Jim Crow Mississippi.

31. Olga Vickery, *The Novels of William Faulkner*, rev. ed. (Baton Rouge: Louisiana State University Press, 1964).

32. Susan V. Donaldson, "Keeping Quentin Compson Alive: *The Last Gentleman*, *The Second Coming*, and the Problems of Masculinity," in *Walker Percy's Feminine Characters*, ed. Lewis A. Lawson and Elzbieta H. Oleksy (Troy, NY: Whitston, 1995), 72.

33. Ibid., 64.

34. Jean-Paul Sartre, "William Faulkner's *Sartoris*," in Kinney, *Critical Essays on William Faulkner*, 142–43, emphasis in the original.

35. Gail L. Mortimer makes a strong argument for the importance of loss as a theme and as a key to the form and style of his works. See *Faulkner's Rhetoric of Loss: A Study in Perception and Meaning* (Austin: University of Texas Press, 1983). Mortimer observes that "[Faulkner's] protagonists, . . . Horace Benbow, Bayard Sartoris, and [others], enact rituals that end simply as repeated obsessive behaviour; even the 'transcendence' they sometimes achieve is a perverse one, for it is a moment found in final despair, death, or castration" (9). Agreeing with Mortimer, I want to focus in this chapter on the particular loss of John Sartoris *and his body* and the importance of that double loss in the narrative.

36. Freud, "Beyond the Pleasure Principle," 13, emphasis in the original.

37. Freud, "Mourning and Melancholia," 244.

38. Barry Atkins, "Yoknapatawpha, History and the Matter of Origins: Locating *Flags in the Dust* within Faulkner's Modernist Project," *Renaissance and Modern Studies* 41 (1998): 95.

39. Eric Santner, *Stranded Objects: Mourning, Memory, and Film in Postwar Germany* (Ithaca, NY: Cornell University Press, 1990), 28.

40. Bayard refers, as a contemporary audience would have known, to "the Red Baron," Manfred von Richthofen, a German pilot.

41. Wittenberg makes a similar point about Bayard's storytelling. She writes, "Both the opening and closing sentences of his account are the same—'I tried to keep him from going up there on that goddamn little popgun'—suggesting in their implication of circularity that he is somehow enclosed in and by the tale. . . . Bayard's experience with the circularity and reiterativeness of grief-stricken and guilty memory entraps him; it is a circle from which the only exit is death" ("Vision and Re-vision," 330–31). Her essay compares Bayard's inferior storytelling to the several other storytellers and artist figures in the novel.

42. Sartre, "William Faulkner's *Sartoris*," 142–43.

43. Donald M. Kartiganer, "Modernism as Gesture: Faulkner's Missing Facts," *Renaissance and Modern Studies* 41 (1998): 20.

44. Booth, *Postcards from the Trenches*, 30.

45. Sigmund Freud, "Remembering, Repeating, and Working-Through," in *The Standard Edition*, vol. 12, 150–51, emphasis in the original.

46. Randall Waldron speculates that *Gatsby* may have been an influence on Faulkner's representation of the automobile in a short story, "Country Mice," published a few months after Fitzgerald's novel, a representation that he presents in detail. He writes, "Faulkner viewed automobiles (as well as airplanes and other fast, powerful machines . . .) with a mixture of good-humored affection, aesthetic admiration, and emotional—even psycho-sexual—exhilaration on the one hand, and on the other, ridicule, abhorrence and dread—as symbols of social and moral decadence, disruptors of the natural order, and instruments of violence and death. Both dimensions of these complex attitude are inchoate in 'Country Mice'" ("Faulkner's First Fictional Car—Borrowed from Scott Fitzgerald?," *American Literature* 60, no. 2 [1988]: 284).

47. Herschel Brickell, "Romance Has Its Gall," in Kinney, *Critical Essays on William Faulkner*, 123–25. (Originally published in *New York Herald Tribune*, 24 February 1929, sec. ix, 5.)

48. Donald Davidson, "[An Early Recognition]," in Kinney, *Critical Essays on William Faulkner*, 141. (Originally published in *Nashville Tennessean*, 14 April 1929, Magazine section, 7.)

49. Many scholars have analyzed Bayard's death, its motivation, and its psychological underpinnings. My argument departs from this exchange in its comparison between Bayard's plot and trauma theory and in my attention to the role of Johnny's disappearance (rather than simply death) in Bayard's failure to mourn. See Vickery, *The Novels of William Faulkner*; Cleanth Brooks, *William Faulkner: The Yoknapatawpha Country* (New Haven, CT: Yale University Press, 1963); Ronald G. Walker, "Death in the Sound of Their Name: Character Motivation in Faulkner's *Sartoris*," in *Southern Humanities Review* 7, no. 3 (1973): 271–78; T. H. Adamowski, "Bayard Sartoris: Mourning and Melancholia," in *Literature and Psychology* 23, no. 4 (1973): 149–58; Arthur Blair, "Bayard Sartoris: Suicidal or Foolhardy?," *Southern Literary Journal* 15 (Fall 1982): 55–60; John William Corrington, "Escape into Myth: The Long Dying of Bayard Sartoris," in Kinney, *Critical Essays on William Faulkner*, 171–85; François L. Pitavy, "'Anything but Earth': The Disastrous and Necessary Sartoris Game," in ibid., 267–73; Janet St. Clair, "The Refuge of Death: Silencing the Struggles of a Hungry Heart," *Arizona Quarterly* 43, no. 2 (1987): 101–18; and John S. Williams, "Ambivalence, Rivalry, and Loss: Bayard Sartoris and the Ghosts of the Past," *Arizona Quarterly* 43, no. 2 (1987): 178–92.

50. Freud, "Remembering, Repeating, and Working-Through," 155.

51. See Dana Royce Baerger and Dan P. McAdams, "Life Story Coherence and Its Relation to Psychological Well-Being," *Narrative Inquiry* 9, no. 1 (1999): 69–96.

52. Bruce Kawin, "*War Birds* and the Politics of Refusal," in Kinney, *Critical Essays on William Faulkner*, 274–89.

53. Mitchell A. Yockelson, *Borrowed Soldiers: Americans under British Command, 1918* (Norman: University of Oklahoma Press, 2008).

54. Evidence that this term was so used colloquially by Americans during the World War I era can be found in Mildred Aldrich's *When Johnny Comes Marching Home* (Cambridge, MA: University Press, 1919), in which she compares American soldiers in France to "perfect Bayards of heroism—*sans peur et sans reproche*" (20).

55. Eksteins, *Rites of Spring*, 264–65.

56. Howard Hawks directed *Dawn Patrol*, based on a story by John Monk Saunders, in 1930. Although Faulkner did not have anything to do with the production of *Dawn Patrol*, he worked with Howard Hawks on "Turn About," his script for an aviation movie, in 1932. See Minter, *William Faulkner*, 140–41. For more on "Turn About," see also Kawin, "*War Birds*."

57. Freud, "Beyond the Pleasure Principle," 12–13.

58. Ruth Leys discusses this case and its popularity in *Trauma: A Genealogy*.

59. Donald M. Kartiganer, "'So I, Who Never Had a War . . .': William Faulkner, War, and the Modern Imagination," *Modern Fiction Studies* 44, no. 3 (1998): 635.

60. Bourke, *Dismembering the Male*, 213–14.

61. In Faulkner's short story "All the Dead Pilots," his narrator is not John Sartoris's brother but rather a friend and admirer, who is left to ponder his loss. But in that earlier story, John Sartoris's commanding officer writes a letter to the family that specifies that he "was buried by a minister" and that his "effects" will be sent home (in *Collected Stories of William Faulkner* [New York: Random House, 1950], 530).

62. Limon, "Addie in No-Man's-Land," 46.

63. Pitavy, "Anything but Earth," 270.

Conclusion

1. Dashiell Hammett, *Red Harvest* (New York: Vintage, 1992). All subsequent references are to this edition are given parenthetically in the text.

2. Greg Forter, *Murdering Masculinities: Fantasies of Gender and Violence in the American Crime Novel* (New York: NYU Press, 2000), 13. A full account of the differences between hardboiled detective fiction and detective fiction generally is beyond the scope of this conclusion. Forter summarizes the distinctions noticed by Tzvetan Todorov, Marty Roth, and Gertrude Stein and adds some of his own (ibid., 12–13).

3. Fitzgerald, *The Great Gatsby*, 2.

4. Judith Butler, *Precarious Life: The Powers of Mourning and Violence* (New York: Verso, 2004), xvii.

5. Sean McCann, "The Novel of Crime, Mystery, and Suspense," in *The Cambridge History of the American Novel*, ed. Leonard Cassuto, Clare Virginia Eby, and Benjamin Reiss, 798–812 (New York: Cambridge University Press, 2011), 798.

6. Rose Pelswick, "Jim Cagney Stars at Strand," *New York Journal-American*, 11 November 1939.

7. Bob Reel, "'Roaring 20's' Tale of Gin and Guns," *Chicago Herald American*, 29 October 1939, 4.

8. Ibid.

9. *The Public Enemy* (1931), dir. William Wellman, distributed by Warner Bros.

10. Gandal, *The Gun and the Pen*, 22–23.

11. Budreau, *Bodies of War*, 78.

12. Ibid.

13. See, for instance, McCann, "The Novel of Crime, Mystery, and Suspense."

Bibliography

Adamowski, T. H. "Bayard Sartoris: Mourning and Melancholia." *Literature and Psychology* 23, no. 4 (1973): 149–58.

Aldrich, Mildred. *When Johnny Comes Marching Home*. Cambridge, MA: University Press, 1919.

Allen, Hervey. *Toward the Flame*. New York: Doubleday, Page, 1925.

"An American Soldier." "Shell-Shocked—and After." *Atlantic Monthly* 128 (December 1921): 738–49.

Anonymous. *"Mademoiselle Miss": Letters from an American Girl Serving with the Rank of Lieutenant in a French Army Hospital at the Front*. Boston: W. A. Butterfield, 1916.

Arnold, Marilyn. "*One of Ours*: Willa Cather's Losing Battle." *Western American Literature* 13, no. 3 (1978): 259–66.

Atherton, John. "The Itinerary and the Postcard: Minimal Strategies in *The Sun Also Rises*." *ELH* 53, no. 1 (1986): 199–218.

Atkins, Barry. "Yoknapatawpha, History and the Matter of Origins: Locating *Flags in the Dust* within Faulkner's Modernist Project." *Renaissance and Modern Studies* 41 (1998): 86–100.

Audoin-Rouzeau, Stéphane, and Annette Becker. *14–18: Understanding the Great War*. Translated by Catherine Temerson. New York: Hill and Wang, 2002.

Ayres, Linda, and Jane Myers. *George Bellows: The Artist and His Lithographs, 1916–1924*. Ft. Worth, TX: Amon Carter Museum, 1988.

Baerger, Dana Royce, and Dan P. McAdams. "Life Story Coherence and Its Relation to Psychological Well-Being." *Narrative Inquiry* 9, no. 1 (1999): 69–96.

Baker, Carlos, ed. *Ernest Hemingway: Critiques of Four Major Novels*. New York: Scribner, 1962.

Barbusse, Henri. *Under Fire* (*Le Feu: Journal d'une escouade*). Translated by W. Fitzwater Wray. New York: Dutton, 1926.

The Battle of the Somme. Filmed by Geoffrey H. Malins and J. B. McDowell. London, 1916. Film.

Bederman, Gail. *Manliness and Civilization: A Cultural History of Gender and Race in the United States, 1880–1917.* Chicago: University of Chicago Press, 1995.

Berman, Ronald. *The Great Gatsby and Fitzgerald's World of Ideas.* Tuscaloosa: University of Alabama Press, 1997.

———. *The Great Gatsby and Modern Times.* Urbana: University of Illinois Press, 1994.

The Big Parade. Dir. King Vidor. 1925. Film.

Blair, Arthur H. "Bayard Sartoris: Suicidal or Foolhardy?" *Southern Literary Journal* 15 (Fall 1982): 55–60.

Blotner, Joseph L. *Faulkner: A Biography.* Rev. ed. New York: Random House, 1984.

———. "William Faulkner's Essay on the Composition of *Sartoris*." *Yale University Library Gazette* 47, no. 3 (1973): 121–24.

Booth, Allyson. *Postcards from the Trenches: Negotiating the Space between Modernism and the First World War.* New York: Oxford University Press, 1996.

Boss, Pauline. *Ambiguous Loss: Learning to Live with Unresolved Grief.* Cambridge, MA: Harvard University Press, 1999.

Bourke, Joanna. *Dismembering the Male: Men's Bodies, Britain, and the Great War.* Chicago: University of Chicago Press, 1996.

———. *An Intimate History of Killing: Face-to-Face Killing in 20th Century Warfare.* London: Granta Books, 1999.

Boxwell, D. A. "In Formation: Male Homosocial Desire in Willa Cather's *One of Ours*." In *Eroticism and Containment: Notes from the Flood Plain*, edited by Carol Siegel and Ann Kibbey, 285–310. New York: NYU Press, 1994.

Boyd, Thomas. *Through the Wheat.* New York: Scribner, 1923.

Braudy, Leo. *From Chivalry to Terrorism: War and the Changing Nature of Masculinity.* New York: Knopf, 2003.

Breitwieser, Mitchell. "*The Great Gatsby*: Grief, Jazz, and the Eye-Witness." *Arizona Quarterly* 47 (Autumn 1991): 17–70.

———. "Jazz Fractures: F. Scott Fitzgerald and Epochal Representation." *American Literary History* 12, no. 3 (2000): 359–81.

Brickell, Herschel. "Romance Has Its Gall." In *Critical Essays on William Faulkner: The Sartoris Family*, edited by Arthur F. Kinney, 123–25. Boston: G. K. Hall, 1985. Originally published in *New York Herald Tribune*, 24 February 1929, sec. ix, 5.

Brooke, Robert. *The Collected Poems of Rupert Brooke.* Edited by Edward Marsh. London: Sidgwick and Jackson, 1918.

Brooks, Cleanth. *William Faulkner: The Yoknapatawpha Country.* New Haven, CT: Yale University Press, 1963.

Brooks, Peter. "Illicit Stories." In *Trauma and Self,* edited by Charles B. Strozier and Michael Flynn, 231–44. Lanham, MD: Rowman and Littlefield, 1996.

———. *Reading for the Plot: Design and Intention in Narrative.* Cambridge, MA: Harvard University Press, 1984.

Brown, E. K. *Willa Cather: A Critical Biography.* New York: Knopf, 1953.

Budreau, Lisa M. *Bodies of War: World War I and the Politics of Commemoration in America, 1919–1933.* New York: NYU Press, 2010.

Buitenhuis, Peter. *The Great War of Words: Literature as Propaganda, 1914–18 and After.* Vancouver: University of British Columbia Press, 1987.

Burke, Kenneth. *A Grammar of Motives.* 1945. Reprint, Berkeley: University of California Press, 1969.

Burlingame, Roger. *Peace Veterans: The Story of a Racket and a Plea for Economy.* New York: Minton, Balch, 1932.

Butler, Judith. *Bodies That Matter: On the Discursive Limits of "Sex."* New York: Routledge, 1993.

———. *Precarious Life: The Powers of Mourning and Violence.* New York: Verso, 2004.

Byerly, Carol R. *Fever of War: The Influenza Epidemic in the U.S. Army during World War I.* New York: NYU Press, 2005.

Callahan, John F. *The Illusions of a Nation: Myth and History in the Novels of F. Scott Fitzgerald.* Urbana: University of Illinois Press, 1972.

Cannadine, David. "War and Death, Grief and Mourning in Modern Britain." In *Mirrors of Mortality: Studies in the Social History of Death,* edited by Joachim Whaley, 187–242. London: Europa, 1981.

Caruth, Cathy, ed. *Trauma: Explorations in Memory.* Baltimore: Johns Hopkins University Press, 1995.

———. *Unclaimed Experience: Trauma, Narrative, and History.* Baltimore: Johns Hopkins University Press, 1996.

Cather, Willa. "Coming, Aphrodite!" In *Youth and the Bright Medusa.* 1920. Reprint, Boston: Houghton Mifflin, 1937.

———. *My Ántonia.* Boston: Houghton Mifflin, 1918.

———. "Nebraska." *Nation,* 1923.

———. "The Novel Démeublé." In *Willa Cather on Writing: Critical Studies in Writing as an Art,* 33–44. Lincoln: University of Nebraska Press, 1988.

———. *One of Ours.* New York: Knopf, 1922. Reprint, New York: Vintage, 1991.

———. *O Pioneers!* Boston: Houghton Mifflin, 1913.

———. *The Professor's House.* New York: Knopf, 1925. Reprint, New York: Vintage, 1990.

Chuppa-Cornell, Kimberly. "The U.S. Women's Motor Corps in France, 1914–1921." *Historian* 56, no. 3 (1994): 465–76.

Claridge, Henry, ed. *F. Scott Fitzgerald: Critical Assessments*. 4 vols. The Banks, East Sussex, UK: Helm Information, 1991.

Cobley, Evelyn. *Representing War*. Toronto: University of Toronto Press, 1993.

Cohen, Philip. "*Flags in the Dust, Sartoris*, and the Unforeseen Consequences of Editorial Surgery." *Faulkner Journal* 5 (Fall 1989): 25–44.

Cole, Sarah. "Modernism, Male Intimacy, and the Great War." *ELH*, 2001, 469–500.

Comley, Nancy R., and Robert Scholes. *Hemingway's Genders: Rereading the Hemingway Text*. New Haven, CT: Yale University Press, 1996.

Conrad, Joseph. *The Nigger of the Narcissus*. 1897. Reprint, New York: Doubleday, Doran, 1914.

Cooperman, Stanley. *World War I and the American Novel*. Baltimore: Johns Hopkins University Press, 1967.

Corrington, John William. "Escape into Myth: The Long Dying of Bayard Sartoris." In *Critical Essays on William Faulkner: The Sartoris Family*, edited by Arthur F. Kinney, 171–85. Boston: G. K. Hall, 1985.

Cowley, Malcolm, with Glenway Wescott. "American Writers and the First World War." *Proceedings of the American Academy of Arts and Letters and the National Institute of Arts and Letters*, second series, 18 (1968): 25–46.

Cramer, Timothy R. "Claude's Case: A Study of Homosexual Temperament in Willa Cather's *One of Ours*." *South Dakota Review* 31, no. 3 (1993): 147–60.

Davidson, Donald. "[An Early Recognition]." In *Critical Essays on William Faulkner: The Sartoris Family*, edited by Arthur F. Kinney, 141. Boston: G. K. Hall, 1985. Originally published in *Nashville Tennessean*, 14 April 1929, Magazine section, 7.

Dawes, James. *The Language of War: Literature and Culture in the U.S. from the Civil War through World War II*. Cambridge, MA: Harvard University Press, 2002.

Dodman, Trevor. "'Going All to Pieces': *A Farewell to Arms* as Trauma Narrative." *Twentieth-Century Literature* 52, no. 3 (2006): 249–74.

Donaldson, Susan V. "Keeping Quentin Compson Alive: *The Last Gentleman, The Second Coming*, and the Problems of Masculinity." In *Walker Percy's Feminine Characters*, edited by Lewis A. Lawson and Elzbieta H. Oleksy, 62–77. Troy, NY: Whitston, 1995.

Dos Passos, John. *Three Soldiers*. New York: Doran, 1921.

Douglas, Mary. *Purity and Danger*. New York: Routledge and Kegan Paul, 1966.

Eby, Carl P. *Hemingway's Fetishism: Psychoanalysis and the Mirror of Manhood*. Albany: State University of New York Press, 1999.

Ehrenreich, Barbara. *Blood Rites: Origins and History of the Passions of War*. New York: Metropolitan Books, 1997.

Eisenhower, John S. D. *Yanks: The Epic Story of the American Army in World War I*. New York: Free Press, 2001.

Eksteins, Modris. *Rites of Spring: The Great War and the Birth of the Modern Age*. New York: Doubleday, 1989.

Eliot, T. S. "Hamlet." In *Selected Prose of T. S. Eliot*, edited by Frank Kermode, 45–49. New York: Harcourt Brace, 1975.

Farrell, James J. *Inventing the American Way of Death, 1830–1920*. Philadelphia: Temple University Press, 1980.

Farwell, Byron. *Over There: The United States in the Great War, 1917–1918*. New York: Norton, 1999.

Faulkner, William. "All the Dead Pilots." In *Collected Stories of William Faulkner*, 511–34. New York: Random House, 1950.

———. *A Fable*. New York: Random House, 1954.

———. *Flags in the Dust*. Edited by Douglas Day. New York: Random House, 1973.

———. "Interview." In *Writers at Work: The Paris Review Interviews*, edited by Malcolm Cowley, 119–41. New York: Viking, 1958.

———. *Sartoris*. New York: Harcourt Brace, 1929.

———. *Soldiers' Pay*. New York: Boni and Liveright, 1926.

Faust, Drew Gilpin. *This Republic of Suffering: Death and the American Civil War*. New York: Vintage Books, 2008.

Felman, Shoshana, and Dori Laub. *Testimony: Crises of Witnessing in Literature, Psychoanalysis, and History*. New York: Routledge, 1992.

Fetterly, Judith. "Hemingway's 'Resentful Cryptogram.'" In *Critical Essays on Ernest Hemingway's "A Farewell to Arms."* Edited by George Monteiro. New York: G. K. Hall, 1994.

Fitzgerald, F. Scott. *All the Sad Young Men*. New York: Scribner, 1926.

———. *The Beautiful and Damned* (1922). In *Novels and Stories, 1920–1922*, edited by Jackson R. Bryer, 435–795. New York: Library of America, 2000.

———. *The Great Gatsby*. 1925. Reprint, New York: Scribner, 2004.

———. *The Great Gatsby*. Edited by Matthew J. Bruccoli. Cambridge: Cambridge University Press, 1991.

———. *The Great Gatsby: A Facsimile of the Manuscript*. Edited by Matthew J. Bruccoli. Washington, DC: Microcard Editions Books, 1973.

———. *The Letters of F. Scott Fitzgerald*. Edited by Andrew Turnbull. New York: Scribner, 1963.

———. "May Day." In *Novels and Stories, 1920–1922*, edited by Jackson R. Bryer, 850–902. New York: American Library, 2000.

———. *Tender Is the Night*. New York: Scribner, 1933.

———. *This Side of Paradise*. In *Novels and Stories, 1920–1922*, edited by Jackson R. Bryer, 1–248. New York: Library of America, 2000.

Ford, Nancy Gentile. *The Great War and America: Civil-Military Relations during World War I*. Westport, CT: Praeger, 2008.

Forster, E. M. *Howards End*. London: Edward Arnold, 1910.

Forter, Greg. "Against Melancholia: Contemporary Mourning Theory, Fitzgerald's *The Great Gatsby*, and the Politics of Unfinished Grief." *differences* 14, no. 2 (2003): 134–70.

———. *Gender, Race, and Mourning in American Modernism*. New York: Cambridge University Press, 2011.

———. *Murdering Masculinities: Fantasies of Gender and Violence in the American Crime Novel*. New York: NYU Press, 2000.

Fowler, Doreen. *Faulkner: The Return of the Repressed*. Charlottesville: University of Virginia Press, 1997.

Fraser, Keath. "Another Reading of *The Great Gatsby*." *English Studies in Canada* 5, no. 3 (1979): 330–43.

Freud, Sigmund. "Beyond the Pleasure Principle." In *The Standard Edition of the Complete Psychological Works of Sigmund Freud*, vol. 18, translated and edited by James Strachey, 3–64. New York: Norton, 1961.

———. "Moses and Monotheism." In *The Standard Edition of the Complete Psychological Works of Sigmund Freud*, vol. 23, translated and edited by James Strachey, 3–137. New York: Norton, 1961.

———. "Mourning and Melancholia." In *The Standard Edition of the Complete Psychological Works of Sigmund Freud*, vol. 14, translated and edited by James Strachey, 243–58. New York: Norton, 1961.

———. "Negation." In *The Standard Edition of the Complete Psychological Works of Sigmund Freud*, vol. 19, translated and edited by James Strachey, 234–39. London: Hogarth, 1961.

———. "On Fetishism." In *The Standard Edition of the Complete Psychological Works of Sigmund Freud*, vol. 21, translated and edited by James Strachey, 149–57. London: Hogarth.

———. "Remembering, Repeating, and Working-Through." In *The Standard Edition of the Complete Psychological Works of Sigmund Freud*, vol. 12, translated and edited by James Strachey, 147–56. New York: Norton, 1961.

———. "The Uncanny." In *The Standard Edition of the Complete Psychological Works of Sigmund Freud*, translated and edited by James Strachey, vol. 17, 218–52. New York: Norton, 1961.

Friedlander, Saul. "Trauma, Transference, and Working Through." *History and Memory* 4, no. 1 (1992): 39–59.

Fussell, Paul. *The Great War and Modern Memory*. New York: Oxford University Press, 1975.

Gandal, Keith. *The Gun and the Pen: Hemingway, Fitzgerald, Faulkner, and the Fiction of Mobilization*. New York: Oxford University Press, 2008.

Gavin, Lettie. *American Women in World War I: They Also Served*. Niwot: University Press of Colorado, 1997.

Gelfant, Blanche H. "'What Was It . . . ?': The Secret of Family Accord in *One of Ours*." *Modern Fiction Studies* 36, no. 1 (1990): 61–78.

Giddens, Anthony. *Modernity and Self-Identity: Self and Society in the Later Modern Age*. Stanford, CA: Stanford University Press, 1991.

Gilbert, Sandra M., and Susan Gubar. *No Man's Land: The Place of the Woman Writer in the Twentieth Century*. 3 vols. New Haven, CT: Yale University Press, 1988.

Gillis, John R. "Memory and Identity: The History of a Relationship." In *Commemorations: The Politics of National Identity*, edited by John R. Gillis, 3–26. Princeton, NJ: Princeton University Press, 1994.

Graves, Robert. *Good-Bye to All That*. London: Jonathan Cape, 1929.

Gray, W. Russell. "Corinthian Crooks Are Not Like You and Me: Mystery, Detection and Crime in *The Great Gatsby*." *Clues* 16, no. 1 (1995): 35–43.

Gregory, Adrian. *The Silence of Memory: Armistice Day, 1919–1946*. Oxford, UK: Berg, 1994.

Grosz, Elizabeth A. *Volatile Bodies: Toward a Corporeal Feminism*. Bloomington: Indiana University Press, 1994.

Gwynn, Frederick L., and Joseph L. Blotner, eds. *Faulkner in the University*. Charlottesville: University of Virginia Press, 1959.

Hall, James Norman. *Kitchener's Mob: The Adventures of an American in the British Army*. Boston: Houghton Mifflin, 1916.

Hammett, Dashiell. *Red Harvest*. New York: Vintage, 1992.

Harries, Meirion, and Susan Harries. *The Last Days of Innocence: America at War, 1917–1918*. New York: Random House, 1997.

Haytock, Jennifer. *At Home, at War: Domesticity and World War I in American Literature*. Columbus: Ohio State University Press, 2003.

Hemingway, Ernest. *Death in the Afternoon*. 1932. Reprint, New York: Touchstone, 1996.

———. *A Farewell to Arms*. 1929. Reprint, New York: Scribner, 1995.

———. "Interview with Ernest Hemingway." In *Writers at Work: The Paris Review Interviews*, edited by George Plimpton, second series, 215–40. New York: Penguin, 1963.

———. "The Original Conclusion to *A Farewell to Arms*." In *Ernest Hemingway: Critiques of Four Major Novels*, edited by Carlos Baker, 75. New York: Scribner, 1962.

———. "Soldier's Home." In *In Our Time*, 67–77. 1925. Reprint, New York: Scribner, 1996.

———. *The Sun Also Rises*. New York: Scribner, 1926.

Herman, Judith Lewis. "Crime and Memory." In *Trauma and Self*, edited by Charles B. Strozier and Michael Flynn, 3–18. Lanham, MD: Rowman and Littlefield, 1996.

Holmes, R[obert]. Derby. *A Yankee in the Trenches*. Boston: Little, Brown, 1918.

Holquist, Michael. "The Inevitability of Stereotype: Colonialism in *The Great*

Gatsby." In *The Rhetoric of Interpretation and the Interpretation of Rhetoric*, edited by Paul Hernadi, 201–20. Durham, NC: Duke University Press, 1989.

Hynes, Samuel. *The Soldiers' Tale: Bearing Witness to Modern War*. New York: Penguin, 1997.

———. *A War Imagined: The First World War and English Culture*. New York: Atheneum, 1991.

Illustrated Michelin Guides to the Battlefields (1914–1918): The Americans in the Great War. 1919. Easingwold, UK: G. H. Smith and Son, 1970.

James, Pearl. "History and Masculinity in F. Scott Fitzgerald's *This Side of Paradise*." *Modern Fiction Studies* 51, no. 1 (2005): 1–33.

———. "Images of Femininity in American World War I Posters." In *Picture This: World War I Posters and Visual Culture*, edited by Pearl James, 273–311. Lincoln: University of Nebraska Press, 2009.

———, ed. *Picture This: World War I Posters and Visual Culture*. Lincoln: University of Nebraska Press, 2009.

Jarvis, Christina S. *The Male Body at War: American Masculinity during World War II*. DeKalb: Northern Illinois University Press, 2004.

Joseph, Tiffany. "'Non-combatant's Shell-Shock': Trauma and Gender in F. Scott Fitzgerald's *Tender Is the Night*." *NWSA Journal* 15, no. 3 (2003): 64–81.

Kartiganer, Donald M. "Modernism as Gesture: Faulkner's Missing Facts." *Renaissance and Modern Studies* 41 (1998): 13–28.

———. "'So I, Who Never Had a War . . .': William Faulkner, War, and the Modern Imagination." *Modern Fiction Studies* 44, no. 3 (1998): 619–45.

Kawin, Bruce. "*War Birds* and the Politics of Refusal." In *Critical Essays on William Faulkner: The Sartoris Family*, edited by Arthur F. Kinney, 274–89. Boston: G. K. Hall, 1985.

Kazin, Alfred. *On Native Grounds: An Interpretation of Modern American Prose Literature*. New York: Harcourt, Brace, 1942.

Keegan, John. *The First World War*. New York: Vintage, 2000.

Keene, Jennifer. *Doughboys, the Great War, and the Remaking of America*. Baltimore: Johns Hopkins University Press, 2001.

Keightley, Emily, and Michael Pickering. "Trauma, Discourse, and Communicative Limits." *Critical Discourse Studies* 6, no. 4 (2009): 237–49.

Keiser, Merle Wallace. "*Flags in the Dust* and *Sartoris*." In *Fifty Years of Yoknapatawpha: Faulkner and Yoknapatawpha 1979*, edited by Doreen Fowler and Ann J. Abadie, 44–70. Jackson: University Press of Mississippi, 1980.

Kennedy, David M. *Over Here: The First World War and American Society*. New York: Oxford University Press, 1980.

Kenner, Hugh. *A Homemade World: The American Modernist Writers*. Baltimore: Johns Hopkins University Press, 1975.

Kimmel, Michael. *Manhood in America*. New York: Free Press, 1996.

Kingsbury, Celia Malone. *For Home and Country: World War I Propaganda on the Home Front*. Lincoln: University of Nebraska Press, 2010.

Kinney, Arthur F., ed. *Critical Essays on William Faulkner: The Sartoris Family.* Boston: G. K. Hall, 1985.

Kirkland, Winifred. *The New Death.* Boston: Houghton Mifflin, 1918.

Knodt, Ellen Andrews. "'Suddenly and Unreasonably': Shooting the Sergeant in *A Farewell to Arms.*" In *Hemingway's Italy: New Perspectives,* edited by Rena Sanderson, 149–57. Baton Rouge: Louisiana State University Press, 2006.

Knutson, Anne Classen. "Breasts, Brawn and Selling a War: American World War I Propaganda Posters 1917–1918." Ph.D. diss., University of Pittsburgh, 1997.

Kristeva, Julia. *Powers of Horror: An Essay on Abjection.* Translated by Leon S. Roudiez. New York: Columbia University Press, 1982.

LaCapra, Dominick. *Representing the Holocaust: History, Theory, Trauma.* Ithaca, NY: Cornell University Press, 1994.

———. "Trauma, Absence, Loss." *Critical Inquiry* 25 (Summer 1999): 696–727.

———. *Writing History, Writing Trauma.* Baltimore: Johns Hopkins University Press, 2001.

Laqueur, Thomas W. "Memory and Naming in the Great War." In *Commemorations: The Politics of National Identity,* edited by John R. Gillis, 150–67. Princeton, NJ: Princeton University Press, 1994.

Lawrence, D. H. *Studies in Classic American Literature.* New York: T. Seltzer, 1923.

Lee, Mary. *It's a Great War.* Cambridge, MA: Riverside, 1929.

Lehan, Richard. *F. Scott Fitzgerald and the Craft of Fiction.* Carbondale: Southern Illinois University Press, 1966.

———. *The Great Gatsby: The Limits of Wonder.* Boston: Twayne, 1990.

Lewis, Robert W. *A Farewell to Arms: The War of the Words.* New York: Twayne, 1992.

Lewis, Sinclair. "A Hamlet of the Plains." Review of *One of Ours,* by Willa Cather. In *Willa Cather: The Contemporary Reviews,* edited by Margaret Anne O'Connor, 127–30. New York: Cambridge University Press, 2001.

Leys, Ruth. *Trauma: A Genealogy.* Chicago: Chicago University Press, 2000.

Limon, John. "Addie in No-Man's-Land." In *Faulkner and War,* edited by Noel Polk and Ann J. Abadie, 36–54. Jackson: University Press of Mississippi, 2004.

———. *Writing after War: American War Fiction from Realism to Postmodernism.* New York: Oxford University Press, 1994.

Lindemann, Marilee. *Willa Cather: Queering America.* New York: Columbia University Press, 1999.

Lloyd, David W. *Battlefield Tourism: Pilgrimage and the Commemoration of the Great War in Britain, Australia and Canada, 1919–1939.* Oxford, UK: Berg, 1998.

Lockridge, Ernest. "F. Scott Fitzgerald's *Trompe l'Oeil* and *The Great Gatsby*'s Buried Plot." *Journal of Narrative Technique* 17 (1987): 163–83.

Lockwood, Preston. "Henry James's First Interview." *New York Times*, 21 March 1915.

Lynn, David H. *The Hero's Tale: Narrators in the Early Modern Novel*. London: Macmillan, 1989.

Lynn, Kenneth S. *Hemingway*. New York: Simon and Schuster, 1987.

March, William. *Company K*. Tuscaloosa: University of Alabama Press, 1989.

Martin, Robert A. "Hemingway and the Ambulance Drivers in *A Farewell to Arms*." In *Ernest Hemingway: Six Decades of Criticism*, edited by Linda W. Wagner, 195–204. East Lansing: Michigan State University Press, 1987.

Marx, Leo. *The Machine in the Garden: Technology and the Pastoral Ideal in America*. New York: Oxford University Press, 1964.

McCann, Sean. "The Novel of Crime, Mystery, and Suspense." In *The Cambridge History of the American Novel*, edited by Leonard Cassuto, Clare Virginia Eby, and Benjamin Reiss, 798–812. New York: Cambridge University Press, 2011.

McClintock, Alexander. *Best O' Luck: How a Fighting Kentuckian Won the Thanks of Britain's King*. New York: Grosset and Dunlap, 1917.

McDougal, Grace. *A Nurse at the War: Nursing Adventures in Belgium and France*. New York: Robert M. McBride, 1917.

Mencken, H. L. "As H. L. M. Sees It." In *F. Scott Fitzgerald: Critical Assessments*, vol. 2, edited by Henry Claridge, 156–59. The Banks, East Sussex, UK: Helm Information, 1991.

———. "Portrait of an American Citizen." Review of *One of Ours*, by Willa Cather. In *Willa Cather: The Contemporary Reviews*, edited by Margaret Anne O'Connor, 141–43. New York: Cambridge University Press, 2001.

Michaels, Walter Benn. *Our America: Nativism, Modernism, and Pluralism*. Durham, NC: Duke University Press, 1995.

Minter, David. *A Cultural History of the American Novel: Henry James to William Faulkner*. Cambridge: Cambridge University Press, 1994.

———. *William Faulkner: His Life and Work*. Baltimore: Johns Hopkins University Press, 1980.

Moddelmog, Debra. *Reading Desire: In Pursuit of Ernest Hemingway*. Ithaca, NY: Cornell University Press, 1999.

Moglen, Seth. *Mourning Modernity: Literary Modernism and the Injuries of American Capitalism*. Stanford, CA: Stanford University Press, 2007.

Montiero, George, ed. *Critical Essays on Ernest Hemingway's "A Farewell to Arms."* New York: G. K. Hall, 1994.

Mortimer, Gail L. *Faulkner's Rhetoric of Loss: A Study in Perception and Meaning*. Austin: University of Texas Press, 1983.

Mumford, Lewis. *The Culture of Cities*. New York: Harcourt Brace, 1938.

Nagel, James. "Catherine Barkley and Retrospective Narration in *A Farewell to Arms*." In *Ernest Hemingway: Six Decades of Criticism*, edited by Linda W. Wagner, 171–86. East Lansing: Michigan State University Press, 1987.

————. "Hemingway and the Italian Legacy." In *Hemingway in Love and War: The Lost Diary of Agnes von Kurowsky, Her Letters, and Correspondence of Ernest Hemingway*, by Agnes Von Kurowsky, edited by Henry Serrano Villard and James Nagel, 197–269 (Boston: Northeastern University Press, 1989.

Neuhaus, Ron. "*Gatsby* and the Failure of the Omniscient 'I.'" In *F. Scott Fitzgerald: Critical Assessments*, vol. 2, edited by Henry Claridge, 359–68. The Banks, East Sussex, UK: Helm Information, 1991.

Norris, Margot. *Writing War in the Twentieth Century*. Charlottesville: University of Virginia Press, 2000.

O'Brien, Sharon. *Willa Cather: The Emerging Voice*. Oxford: Oxford University Press, 1987.

O'Connor, Margaret Anne, ed. *Willa Cather: The Contemporary Reviews*. New York: Cambridge University Press, 2001.

Oldsey, Bernard. *Hemingway's Hidden Craft: The Writing of "A Farewell to Arms."* University Park: Pennsylvania State University Press, 1979.

O'Meara, Lauraleigh. "Medium of Exchange: The Blue Coupé Dialogue in *The Great Gatsby*." *Papers on Language and Literature* 30 (Winter 1994): 73–87.

O'Neill, Eugene. *Complete Plays, 1913–1920*. Edited by Travis Bogard. New York: Literary Classics, 1988.

Owen, Wilfred. *The Poems of Wilfred Owen*. Edited by Jon Stallworthy. New York: Norton, 1986.

Parker, David. "*The Great Gatsby*: Two Versions of the Hero." In *Modern Critical Views: F. Scott Fitzgerald*, edited by Harold Bloom, 141–56. New York: Chelsea House, 1985.

Pennell, Joseph. *Joseph Pennell's Liberty-Loan Poster: A Text-Book for Artists and Amateurs, Governments and Teachers and Printers, with Notes, an Introduction and Essay on the Poster by the Artist, Associate Chairman of the Committee on Public Information, Division of Pictorial Publicity*. Philadelphia: J. B. Lippincott, 1918.

Phelan, James. "Reexamining Reliability: The Multiple Functions of Nick Carraway." In *Narrative as Rhetoric: Technique, Audiences, Ethics, Ideology*, 105–18. Columbus: Ohio State University Press, 1996.

Piehler, G. Kurt. *Remembering War the American Way*. Washington, DC: Smithsonian Books, 1995.

————. "The War Dead and the Gold Star: American Commemoration of the First World War." In *Commemorations: the Politics of National Identity*, edited by John R. Gillis, 168–85. Princeton, NJ: Princeton University Press, 1994.

Pierce, Frederick E. "Nervous New England." *North American Review* 210, no. 764 (1919): 81–85.

Piper, Henry Dan. "The Untrimmed Christmas Tree: The Religious Background of *The Great Gatsby*." In *The Great Gatsby: A Study*, edited by Frederick J. Hoffman, 321–34. New York: Scribner, 1962.

Pitavy, François L. "'Anything but Earth': The Disastrous and Necessary

Sartoris Game." In *Critical Essays on William Faulkner: The Sartoris Family*, edited by Arthur F. Kinney, 267–73. Boston: G. K. Hall, 1985.

Polk, Noel, and Ann J. Abadie, eds. *Faulkner and War*. Jackson: University Press of Mississippi, 2004.

Porter, Katherine Anne. *Pale Horse, Pale Rider: Three Short Novels*. 1939. Reprint, New York: Harcourt Brace Jovanovich, 1966.

Price, Alan. "'I'm Not an Old Fogey and You're Not a Young Ass': Owen Wister and Ernest Hemingway." *Hemingway Review* 9, no. 1 (1989): 82–90.

The Public Enemy. Dir. William Wellman. Warner Bros., 1931. Film.

Putzel, Max. "The Evolution of Two Characters in Faulkner's Early and Published Fiction." In *Critical Essays on William Faulkner: The Sartoris Family*, edited by Arthur F. Kinney, 186–89. Boston: G. K. Hall, 1985.

Quinn, Patrick J. *The Conning of America: The Great War and American Popular Literature*. Amsterdam: Rodopi, 2001.

Quinn, Patrick J., and Steven Trout, eds. *The Literature of the Great War Reconsidered: Beyond Modern Memory*. New York: Palgrave, 2001.

Rawls, Walton. *Wake Up, America! World War I and the American Poster*. New York: Abbeville, 1988.

Reeves, Nicholas. *Official British Film Propaganda during the First World War*. London: Croom Helm, 1986.

Remarque, Erich Maria. *All Quiet on the Western Front*. Translated by A. W. Wheen. Boston: Little, Brown, 1929.

Reynolds, Michael S. *Hemingway's First War: The Making of "A Farewell to Arms."* New York: Blackwell, 1987.

Richardson, John E., and Ruth Wodak. "On the Politics of Remembering (or Not)." *Critical Discourse Studies* 6, no. 4 (2009): 231–35.

Rosowski, Susan J. *The Voyage Perilous: Willa Cather's Romanticism*. Lincoln: University of Nebraska Press, 1986.

Rotundo, E. Anthony. *American Manhood: Transformations in Masculinity from the Revolution to the Modern Era*. New York: Basic Books, 1993.

Russell, Bertrand. *Has Man a Future?* New York: Simon and Schuster, 1962.

———. *Why Men Fight: A Method of Abolishing the International Duel*. 1916. Reprint, New York: Albert and Charles Boni, 1930.

Ryan, Maureen. "No Woman's Land: Gender in Willa Cather's *One of Ours*." *Studies in American Fiction* 18, no. 1 (1990): 65–76.

Saint-Amour, Paul K. "Air War Prophecy and Interwar Modernism." *Comparative Literary Studies* 42, no. 2 (2005): 130–61.

———. "Bombing and the Symptom: Traumatic Earliness and the Nuclear Uncanny." *diacritics* 30, no. 4 (Winter 2000): 59–82.

Sanderson, Rena. "Hemingway's Italy: Paradise Lost." In *Hemingway's Italy: New Perspectives*, edited by Rena Sanderson, 1–37. Baton Rouge: Louisiana State University Press, 2006.

Santner, Eric. "History beyond the Pleasure Principle: Some Short Thoughts on the Representation of Trauma." In *Probing the Limits of Representation: Nazism and the "Final Solution,"* edited by Saul Friedlander, 143–54. Cambridge, MA: Harvard University Press, 1992.

———. *Stranded Objects: Mourning, Memory, and Film in Postwar Germany.* Ithaca, NY: Cornell University Press, 1990.

Saposnik, Irving S. "The Passion and the Life: Technology as Pattern in *The Great Gatsby.*" *Fitzgerald/Hemingway Annual* 11 (1979): 181–88.

Sartre, Jean-Paul. "William Faulkner's *Sartoris.*" In *Critical Essays on William Faulkner: The Sartoris Family,* edited by Arthur F. Kinney, 142–46. Boston: G. K. Hall, 1985.

Scarry, Elaine. *The Body in Pain: The Making and Unmaking of the World.* New York: Oxford University Press, 1985.

Scharf, Virginia. *Taking the Wheel: Women and the Coming of the Motor Age.* New York: Free Press, 1991.

Schneider, Mark R. *We Return Fighting: The Civil Rights Movement in the Jazz Age.* Boston: Northeastern University Press, 2002.

Schwind, Jean. "The 'Beautiful' War in *One of Ours.*" *Modern Fiction Studies* 30, no. 1 (1984): 53–72.

Scrimgeour, Gary. "Against *The Great Gatsby.*" In *F. Scott Fitzgerald: Critical Assessments,* vol. 2, edited by Henry Claridge, 489–99. The Banks, East Sussex, UK: Helm Information, 1991.

Sedgwick, Eve Kosofsky. "Willa Cather and Others." In *Tendencies,* 167–76. Durham, NC: Duke University Press, 1993.

Shephard, Ben. *A War of Nerves: Soldiers and Psychiatrists in the Twentieth Century.* Cambridge, MA: Harvard University Press, 2000.

Sherry, Vincent. *The Great War and the Language of Modernism.* New York: Oxford University Press, 2003.

Shoulder Arms. Dir. Charles Chaplin. First National Pictures, 1918. Film.

Showalter, Elaine. *The Female Malady.* New York: Random House, 1985.

Sinfield, Alan. *The Wilde Century: Effeminacy, Oscar Wilde, and the Queer Moment.* London: Cassell, 1994.

Smith, Helen Zenna. *Not So Quiet . . . Stepdaughters of War.* London: Albert E. Marriott, 1930.

Smith-Rosenberg, Carroll. "Discourses of Sexuality and Subjectivity: The New Woman, 1870–1936." In *Hidden from History: Reclaiming the Gay and Lesbian Past,* edited by Martin Bauml Duberman, Martha Vicinus, and George Chauncey, Jr., 264–80. New York: Penguin, 1989.

Spanier, Sandra Whipple. "Catherine Barkley and the Hemingway Code: Ritual and Survival in *A Farewell to Arms.*" In *Ernest Hemingway's "A Farewell to Arms,"* edited by Harold Bloom, 131–48. New York: Chelsea House, 1987.

Spilka, Mark. *Hemingway's Quarrel with Androgyny.* Lincoln: University of Nebraska Press, 1990.

St. Clair, Janet. "The Refuge of Death: Silencing the Struggles of a Hungry Heart." *Arizona Quarterly* 43, no. 2 (1987): 101–18.

Stewart, Matthew C. "Ernest Hemingway and World War I: Combatting Recent Psychobiographical Reassessments, Restoring the War." *Papers on Language and Literature* 36, no. 2 (2000): 198–217.

Stone, Martin. "Shellshock and the Psychologists." In *The Anatomy of Madness*, edited by Roy Porter, W. F. Bynum, and Michael Shepherd. London: Tavistock, 1985.

Stout, Janis P. "The Making of Willa Cather's *One of Ours:* The Role of Dorothy Canfield Fisher." *War, Literature and the Arts: An International Journal of the Humanities* 11, no. 2 (1999): 48–59.

Strychacz, Thomas. *Hemingway's Theaters of Masculinity*. Baton Rouge: Louisiana State University Press, 2003.

Taylor, A. J. P. *Illustrated History of the First World War*. London: George Rainbird, 1963.

Terry, Esther Alexander. "For 'Blood and Kin and Home': Black Characterization in William Faulkner's Sartoris Saga." In *Critical Essays on William Faulkner: The Sartoris Family*, edited by Arthur F. Kinney, 303–17. Boston: G. K. Hall, 1985.

Theweleit, Klaus. *Male Fantasies, Volume 1: Women, Floods, Bodies, History*. Translated by Erica Carter, Stephen Conway, and Chris Turner. Minneapolis: University of Minnesota Press, 1987.

———. *Male Fantasies, Volume 2: Male Bodies: Psychoanalyzing the White Terror*. Translated by Erica Carter, Stephen Conway, and Chris Turner. Minneapolis: University of Minnesota Press, 1987.

Traxel, David. *Crusader Nation: The United States in Peace and the Great War, 1898–1920*. New York: Knopf, 2006.

Trout, Steven. Introduction to *Cather Studies*, vol. 6, *History, Memory, and War*, edited by Steven Trout, xi–xxv. Lincoln: University of Nebraska Press, 2006.

———. *Memorial Fictions: Willa Cather and the First World War*. Lincoln: University of Nebraska Press, 2002.

———. *On the Battlefield of Memory: The First World War and American Remembrance, 1919–1941*. Tuscaloosa: University of Alabama Press, 2010.

Vernon, Alex. *Hemingway's Second War: Bearing Witness to the Spanish Civil War*. Iowa City: University of Iowa Press, 2011.

———. "War, Gender, and Ernest Hemingway." *Hemingway Review* 22, no. 1 (2002): 36–57.

Vickery, Olga. *The Novels of William Faulkner*. Rev. ed. Baton Rouge: Louisiana State University Press, 1964.

Wagner-Martin, Linda. *Ernest Hemingway's "A Farewell to Arms": A Reference Guide*. Westport, CT: Greenwood, 2003.

Waldron, Randall. "Faulkner's First Fictional Car—Borrowed from Scott Fitzgerald?" *American Literature* 60, no. 2 (1988): 281–85.

Walker, Ronald G. "Death in the Sound of Their Name: Character Motivation in Faulkner's *Sartoris*." *Southern Humanities Review* 7, no. 3 (1973): 271–78.

Wasiolek, Edward. "The Sexual Drama of Nick and Gatsby." *International Fiction Review* 19, no. 1 (1992): 14–22.

Watson, James Gray. "'The Germ of My Apocrypha': *Sartoris* and the Search for Form." *Mosaic* 7, no. 1 (1973): 15–34.

West, Nathanael. "The Dream Life of Balso Snell" (1931). In *Nathanael West: Novels and Other Writings*, edited by Sacvan Bercovitch, 1–54. New York: Library of America, 1997.

West, Rebecca. *The Return of the Soldier*. New York: Doran, 1918.

Whalan, Mark. *The Great War and the Culture of the New Negro*. Gainesville: University Press of Florida, 2008.

White, Hayden. "The Politics of Historical Interpretation: Discipline and Desublimation." In *The Content of the Form: Narrative Discourse and Historical Representation*, 58–82. Baltimore: Johns Hopkins University Press, 1987.

Williams, Chad L. *Torchbearers of Democracy: African American Soldiers in the World War I Era*. Chapel Hill: University of North Carolina Press, 2010.

Williams, David. *Media, Memory, and the First World War*. Montreal: McGill-Queen's University Press, 2009.

Williams, John S. "Ambivalence, Rivalry, and Loss: Bayard Sartoris and the Ghosts of the Past." *Arizona Quarterly* 43, no. 2 (Summer 1987): 178–92.

Wilson, Edmund. "F. Scott Fitzgerald." In *Modern Critical Views: F. Scott Fitzgerald*, edited by Harold Bloom, 7–12. New York: Chelsea House, 1985.

———. *Shores of Light: A Literary Chronicle of the Twenties and Thirties*. New York: Farrar, Straus, and Young, 1952.

Wilson, Raymond J., III. "Willa Cather's *One of Ours*: A Novel of the Great Plains and the Great War." *Midamerica* 11 (1984): 20–33.

Winter, Jay. "Shell-Shock and the Cultural History of the Great War." In "Shell-Shock," special issue, *Journal of Contemporary History* 35, no. 1 (January 2000): 7–11.

———. *Sites of Memory, Sites of Mourning: The Great War in European Cultural History*. Cambridge: Cambridge University Press, 1995.

Wittenberg, Judith Bryant. "Vision and Re-vision: Bayard Sartoris." In *Critical Essays on William Faulkner: The Sartoris Family*, edited by Arthur F. Kinney, 323–31. Boston: G. K. Hall, 1985.

Woolf, Virginia. *Mrs. Dalloway*. New York: Harcourt Brace, 1925.

Yockelson, Mitchell A. *Borrowed Soldiers: Americans under British Command, 1918*. Norman: University of Oklahoma Press, 2008.

Yonce, Margaret. "'Shot Down Last Spring': The Wounded Aviators of Faulkner's Wasteland." In *Critical Essays on William Faulkner: The Sartoris Family*, edited by Arthur F. Kinney, 204–11. Boston: G. K. Hall, 1985.

Yongue, Patricia Lee. "For Better and for Worse: At Home and at War in *One of Ours.*" In *Willa Cather: Family, Community, and History,* edited by John J. Murphy, 141–54. Provo, UT: Brigham Young University Humanities Publishing Center, 1990.

Young, Philip. *Ernest Hemingway: A Reconsideration.* University Park: Pennsylvania State University Press, 1966.

———. "The Lost Generation: War, Home, and Exile." In *Dancing Fools and Weary Blues: The Great Escape of the 1920s,* edited by Lawrence R. Broer and John D. Walther, 77–85. Bowling Green, OH: Bowling Green State University Popular Press, 1990.

Zeiger, Robert H. *America's Great War: World War I and the American Experience.* Lanham, MD: Rowman and Littlefield, 2000.

Zeiger, Susan. *In Uncle Sam's Service: Women Workers with the American Expeditionary Force, 1917–1919.* Ithaca, NY: Cornell University Press, 1999.

Index